Italian Grammar

FOR DUMMIES
A Wiley Brand

by Beth Bartolini-Salimbeni

FOR DUMMIES
A Wiley Brand

Italian Grammar For Dummies®

Published by:
John Wiley & Sons, Inc.
111 River Street
Hoboken, NJ 07030-5774
www.wiley.com

For general information on our other products and services, please contact our Customer Care Department within the U.S. at 877-762-2974, outside the U.S. at 317-572-3993, or fax 317-572-4002. For technical support, please visit www.wiley.com/techsupport.

Wiley publishes in a variety of print and electronic formats and by print-on-demand. Some material included with standard print versions of this book may not be included in e-books or in print-on-demand. If this book refers to media such as a CD or DVD that is not included in the version you purchased, you may download this material at http://booksupport.wiley.com. For more information about Wiley products, visit www.wiley.com.

Library of Congress Control Number: 2013938103

ISBN 978-1-118-56600-8 (pbk); ISBN 978-1-118-565896-6 (ebk); ISBN 978-1-118-56602-2 (ebk); ISBN 978-1-118-56606-0 (ebk)

Manufactured in the United States of America

10 9 8 7 6 5 4 3 2 1

Contents at a Glance

Table of Contents

Introduction

*I*n your mother tongue, you need to know very little about grammar to communicate accurately and efficiently. You may not know a predicate adjective from a walrus, but you don't have to. To pick up a second language, like Italian, however, you definitely need to understand grammar. Grammar is the foundation on which you lay vocabulary — and vocabulary makes up the walls, roof, and furnishings that go on the foundation and that allow you to communicate. Grammar and vocabulary come together to produce something greater than the sum of its parts: communicative, living (*read:* useful) language.

Grammar doesn't mean diagramming sentences and labeling parts. It's more like building a house. The goal of this book is to enable you to construct solid Italian from the ground up and to have fun while doing so.

About This Book

Each chapter of *Italian Grammar For Dummies* introduces a particular piece of grammar, explaining what it is and showing you, through examples and practice, what it does. Each chapter ends with an answer key, which allows you to check your work as you go.

Italian Grammar For Dummies begins with the essentials — parts of speech, pronunciation, nouns, numbers, and descriptive words. These elements alone allow you to communicate, though at a rather basic level. So moving through the book, you discover how to add in verbs (in all their tenses and moods) and other critical parts of language, parts that let you elaborate and elucidate.

You probably don't want to read straight through this book, unless you're starting at the very beginning with Italian. (If you're a complete beginner to Italian, you may want to first check out *Italian For Dummies* by Teresa Picarazzi, Francesca Romana Onofri, and Karen Möller, published by Wiley.) If you're somewhat familiar with Italian, though, you can pick and choose chapters that clarify for you a particular grammar point.

I use the following conventions to make use of this book easy.

- Italian words, phrases, and sentences appear in **bold.**
- English equivalents, set in *italic,* follow the Italian.
- When putting Italian into English, I'm not always literal. For example, the Italian **prego** literally means *I pray,* but it's often used to mean *you're welcome, go ahead* (if you're holding a door for someone), or *May I take your order?* (when a waiter says it to you in a restaurant). In this book, I repeat the importance of context as a way to grasp meaning; **prego** is a good example of how important context is.

✔ At the end of each chapter is an answer key that provides the correct responses to all the practice exercises in that chapter.

✔ This book doesn't give you phonetic pronunciations after Italian texts. It focuses on grammar and written communication. The obvious source for pronunciation (besides Chapter 2) is the dictionary, though Italian movies, television, music, and radio can also be especially helpful.

Foolish Assumptions

As I was writing this book, I assumed the following things about you.

✔ You already know some Italian and may be interested in honing your communicative skills. (If you're truly a beginner, I recommend starting with *Italian For Dummies* [Wiley].)

✔ You want to practice skills as you review or learn them so you can cement and retain them.

✔ You love Italian — its sounds, its idiosyncrasies, its culture as expressed in language, and its grammar. Well, maybe not the last. Remember, though, that grammar makes the rest of language feasible for you.

Icons Used in This Book

To make certain kinds of information easier to reference, I use the following icons in this book.

This icon highlights information that's especially critical to your mastery of Italian. If you don't read anything else, read text marked with this icon.

This icon gives you tips for understanding Italian grammar.

This icon advises of something perhaps illogical, irregular, or just plain tricky about Italian grammar.

This icon leads you to practice exercises you can use to make sure you understand the concepts being discussed.

This icon gives more technical insights to Italian grammar.

Beyond the Book

In addition to the material in the book you're reading right now, this product also comes with some access-anywhere goodies on the web. Because verbs are critical to communication, you'll find more information on them on the free Cheat Sheet at www. dummies.com/cheatsheet/ItalianGrammar. Other useful information related to Italian Grammar can be found at www.dummies.com/extras/italiangrammar.

Where to Go from Here

You decide your next step. Do you need to review the basics? Go to Chapters 1 and 2 for pronunciation and general comments on the structure of Italian. Chapters 3 and 5 reinforce the idea that nouns have genders (masculine and feminine) and numbers (singular and plural) in Italian and that they need to agree with just about everything, including adjectives, articles, and verbs. Speaking of verbs, you can find all the nitty-gritty details — tenses and moods, reflexive or not, regular or irregular — in Parts II, IV, and V. You can also find chapters on particular verb forms here.

Each chapter in this book is self-contained; that is, you can pick and choose what you want to work on. The more chapters you read and work through, the better your Italian will be. **In bocca al lupo!** (*Good luck!*)

Part I
Getting Started with Italian Grammar

For Dummies can help you get started with lots of subjects. Visit www.dummies.com to learn more and do more with For Dummies.

In this part . . .

✔ Broaden and deepen your communication skills in Italian with the road map to Italian grammar. Get familiar with Italian grammar basics and prepare to master the language.

✔ Practice stressing the right syllable, adjusting your intonation, and pronouncing vowels, consonants, and diphthongs to help your Italian sound **bello** (*beautiful*).

✔ Expand your vocabulary by mastering not only the words for things but also how to recognize a noun's gender (yes, Italian nouns have gender!), how to make a noun plural, and how to use definite and indefinite articles.

✔ Add precision and context to your growing Italian by talking about when and where events occur, using numbers, dates, and times.

Chapter 1

Italian Grammar in a Nutshell

- -

In This Chapter

▶ Getting to know the parts of speech

▶ Figuring out how to conjugate verbs in the present tense

▶ Putting together simple sentences

▶ Looking at different verb tenses

- -

*I*talian grammar is both complex and logical, or as logical as any language's grammar may be. It has a lot of rules — and a lot of exceptions to those rules. So in this chapter, I provide an overview of all that's involved with Italian grammar before diving into the more specific aspects of grammar throughout the rest of this book.

Grammar consists of the parts of speech and their interrelationships and is the basis of the Italian (and any) language. Understanding grammar lets you expand your knowledge and control of the language.

Fortunately, Italian grammar is a lot like English grammar, and the two languages share the same parts of speech. Working from what you already know, you can use this chapter to begin building or to reinforce your command of Italian.

Recognizing the Parts of Speech

Learning another language involves starting with the basics — in this case, the parts of speech — and then putting those basics together. The parts of speech serve as a foundation for content to come and allow you to create and support content.

This section provides an overview of the parts of speech (which you probably haven't seen since elementary school) and shows their purpose and relation to each other.

Nouns

A noun (**sostantivo**) names a person, place, or thing. In Italian, a noun can be singular or plural, collective, concrete or abstract, common or proper, and even masculine or feminine. A noun functions as any of the following:

- **Subject:** the person, place, or thing performing an action or simply existing — that is, in a state of being, if that's not too existential

- **Direct object:** the person, place, or thing receiving the action transmitted by the verb from the subject

- **Indirect object:** to or for whom or what the action is directed

- **Object of a prepositional phrase:** the person, place, or thing that follows any of the prepositions

For example, in the sentence **Mario dà il regalo a Fausta** (*Mario is giving the gift to Fausta*), **Mario**, the subject, performs an action with the verb **dà** (*is giving*); **il regalo** (*the gift*) is the direct object, or what was given, so it receives the action; and **Fausta**, the indirect object, is the person to whom the action was directed. Technically, **a Fausta** is also a prepositional phrase serving as the indirect object, with **Fausta**, the person, following **a** (*to*), a preposition.

Just as nouns have different roles in a sentence, nouns also have different characteristics. A noun can be proper, common, abstract, or concrete. A name of a person, city, or country is a *proper noun* (in English, proper nouns are usually capitalized): Mario, Fausta, Roma, Italia. (In Italian, days of the week and months of the year aren't capitalized. For more on dates, see Chapter 4.)

Common nouns are objects, such as a cat, dog, car, or school. Common nouns aren't capitalized in Italian or in English. An *abstract noun* may be something intangible, like your thoughts or desires; a *concrete noun* is anything you can touch, see, or taste.

Collective nouns, like *family* or *people,* are singular in Italian. For example: **La famiglia è molto tradizionale.** (*The family is very traditional.*) **La gente è proprio simpatica.** (*The people are really nice.*) — note the plural verb in English. For more information on nouns and their number, gender, and functions, see Chapter 3.

Pronouns

Pronouns take the place of nouns and add variation to a sentence. They have the same jobs as nouns but are simply a little more vague. Table 1-1 lists the most commonly used pronouns in Italian.

Table 1-1	The Most Common Pronouns Used in Italian	
Pronoun as . . .	*Singular*	*Plural*
Personal subject	**io** (*I*)	**noi** (*we*)
	tu (*you*, familiar)	**voi** (*you*, familiar; *you guys, y'all*)
	lui, lei, Lei (*he, she, you* formal)	**loro, Loro** (*they, you* formal)
Direct object	**mi** (*me*)	**ci** (*us*)
	ti (*you*)	**vi** (*you*)
	lo (*him*)	**li** (*them*, masculine)
	la (*her*)	**le** (*them*, feminine)
	la (*you*, formal)	**le** (*you*, formal)
Indirect object	**mi** (*to/for me*)	**ci** (*to/for us*)
	ti (*to/for you*)	**vi** (*to/for you*)
	gli (*to/for him*)	**loro, gli** (*to/for them*)
	le (*to/for her*)	**loro, gli** (*to/for them*)
	le (*to/for you*, formal)	**loro, gli** (*to/for you*, formal)

In general, **loro**, which follows the verb, has been replaced by **gli**, which precedes it. For the full story on Italian pronouns, see Chapter 8.

Articles

Articles are the small words that precede nouns and can be specific, or definite, meaning *the,* such as *the* book*;* or they can be indefinite, or vague, meaning *a* or *an,* such as *a* book.

- ✔ Definite articles: **il, l', lo, la** (singlar); **i, le, gli** (plural)
- ✔ Indefinite articles: **un, un'** (singular); **una, uno** (plural)

Articles must agree in number and gender with the nouns they accompany. When using articles, you also need to consider the beginning letters of the words following the article. That's why so many articles exist: masculine singular, feminine singular, feminine plural, and masculine plural. Chapter 3 covers articles in much more detail.

Verbs

Verbs bring a language to life. You use verbs to show action and states of being, to comment and to question, to contemplate and to create. Language really doesn't exist without verbs, at least not sentient and sophisticated language.

For example: **Giovanni scrive canzoni ed è molto felice.** (*John writes songs and is very happy.*) **Scrive** (*he writes*) shows action; **è** (*is*) tells you how John is feeling.

Verbs change shape — must change shape — to show who's doing something or what's happening. Italian verbs characterize themselves by their *infinitives,* the unconjugated verb form that translates into the English *to* form (*to eat, to play,* and so on). After you understand the appropriate forms of conjugation for different verbs, you can use those same forms for hundreds of other verbs in the same category.

Besides the subject of the verb, you need to keep in mind verb tense (when an action is taking place), mood (the mood or point of view of the subject), and voice (active or passive). Verbs come in 14 tenses (past, present, and future, to name a few); they have four moods (indicative, subjunctive, conditional, and imperative); and they have two voices (active and passive). They follow a strict set of sequencing rules, as do English verbs.

Verbs are both complex and central to mastering the Italian language, but discovering verbs in all their forms will expand your vocabulary exponentially. For all the nitty-gritty details of Italian verbs, see Chapters 6, 7, 9, 10, and 16–22.

Adjectives

Adjectives add flavor, dimension, interest, and opinion. They let you describe in detail people, places, and things. They make self-expression possible.

Adjectives accompany nouns and pronouns. To say someone is happy or something is new, you use adjectives. Adjectives agree in number and gender with whatever they modify. For example, **rosso** (*red*) has masculine singular, masculine plural (**rossi**), feminine singular (**rossa**), and feminine plural (**rosse**) forms.

Here are a couple more facts about Italian adjectives:

- Some adjectives end in the letter **e** and have only two forms: singular, ending in **e,** and plural, ending in **i: importante** (*important*) in the feminine and masculine singular becomes **importanti** in the feminine and masculine plural, as in **una donna importante** (*an important lady*), **due donne importanti** (*two important ladies*); **un ragazzo importante** (*an important boy*), **due ragazzi importanti** (*two important boys*).

- Adjectives of nationality often end in **e: inglese** (*English*), **francese** (*French*), and **svedese** (*Swedish*).

For details on how to form and use adjectives, and to liven up your language, see Chapter 5.

Adverbs

Similar to adjectives, adverbs add detail and description but to actions rather than things. Adverbs can exaggerate, and they can understate. How much did you study? *A lot.* When? *Constantly.* Where? *Nearby.* For how long? *Endlessly.* How exactly did you go about studying? *Obsessively.* Really? *Absolutely.* Adverbs tell you the place, time, quantity, and quality of what's happening.

The good news about adverbs is that they're invariable. As the very name says, **a** (*to*) **verbi** (*verbs*), adverbs generally accompany verbs and, thus, don't have number and gender agreement issues. Even when they qualify adjectives, adverbs remain unchanged.

The most common adverb, in almost any language, is *very* (**molto**). For example: **La ragazza è molto bella.** (*The girl is very pretty.*); **I cani sono molto docili.** (*The dogs are very tame.*); **Le macchine sono molto eleganti.** (*The cars are very elegant.*) To delve more deeply into adverbs, see Chapter 15.

Prepositions

Prepositions are the unruly children of Italian. They are ever present, unpredictable, and idiosyncratic. They vary widely (and wildly) in meaning, depending on context.

The preposition **a**, for example, can mean *to, at,* or *in:* **Vado a Roma.** (*I'm going to Rome.*) **Sto a casa.** (*I'm at home.*) **Abito a Firenze.** (*I live in Florence.*) Likewise, **in** can mean *to, at,* or *in:* **Vado in Italia.** (*I'm going to Italy.*) **Sono in ufficio.** (*I'm at the office.*) **Lavoro in giardino.** (*I'm working in the garden.*)

Prepositions are small words with big impact. They connect nouns and pronouns to each other or to other phrases. They show the relationship among individual words, phrases, actions, places, and times.

Although prepositions are always first and foremost prepositions, they can function as adverbs, objects, or adjectives (usually as part of a phrase). They announce themselves by being prepositioned, or coming before a phrase: The girl *with* the pearl earring. The hordes are *at* the gates. For a complete rundown on prepositions, see Chapter 12.

Conjunctions

Conjunctions, as their name indicates, (con)join words, phrases, or sentence clauses. They make compound and complex sentences possible. The most common forms of conjunctions are **e** (*and*), **ma** (*but*), **perché** (*because*), and **come** (*as*). For example: **Il cane è grande perché mangia molto.** (*The dog is huge because he eats a lot.*)

In Chapter 14, I show you how to use conjunctions and transitional elements to move beyond simple sentences, such as "The dog is huge," to more complex ones, like "The dog is huge because he eats a lot."

Some conjunctions foreshadow the subjunctive mood, which I address in Chapter 20.

Interjections

Interjections are individual words or short phrases that express emotions. They're exclamatory, and Italian is peppered with them. You use interjections to say hello and goodbye (**ciao**), and you use them to be polite (**grazie**). Interjections can be mild or heated, sincere or sarcastic.

Interjections aren't only verbal. Hand gestures and whole body poses can be as expressive as words. I recommend leaving gestural language alone until you're completely comfortable speaking Italian, though. All too often foreign speakers of Italian misinterpret gestures they pick up from stereotypes in B-grade movies or television.

Hundreds of interjections exist, making up some of the most basic expressions. For example, did you know that **ciao** (*hi, bye*) is an interjection? These words often change, just as they do in English, to reflect current usages. Find out more about interjections in Chapter 14.

Conjugating Verbs in the Present Tense

When using and conjugating verbs, you not only have to know the meaning, and thus be able to choose which verbs to use, but you also have to keep in mind a bunch of other considerations, such as the following:

- The verb has to reflect and agree in number with the subject (be first-, second-, or third-person singular or plural).
- The verb has to tell when something is happening (present, past, future, and so on).
- The verb has to reveal the attitude or *mood* of the subject (indicative or factual, subjunctive or subjective, conditional or what if, imperative or commanding).
- The verb has a voice (active or passive).

All these elements allow you to conjugate a verb to make it useful and pertinent. To begin, you choose the infinitive and change endings that show tense, mood, and voice. I explain all these verb parts in the following sections, but I focus on the present tense. Rather than overwhelm you with fourteen different ways to conjugate verbs, I give individual space to the other tenses, all of them, in Chapters 9, 10, and 16 through 22.

Identifying infinitives

The infinitive form of a verb is raw — it shows no tense, mood, or voice. It has no subject. It reveals no action. An English infinitive uses *to* as an indicator that the verb hasn't been put into action; for example, *to eat, to sing, to sleep,* and *to travel* are infinitives. In Italian, most infinitives end in **-are, -ere,** or **-ire,** such as **parlare** (*to speak*), **scrivere** (*to write*), and **dormire** (*to sleep*).

To conjugate a verb, you drop the characteristic ending and add new endings that show the subject, tense, and mood.

Establishing subject-verb agreement

To conjugate a verb, you need to know who or what is doing the action of the sentence. The verb must agree with the subject in person (for example, *I, we, you, they, he, it*) and number (*I* is singular, and *we* is plural, for example). (Check out subject pronouns in Chapters 6 and 8.)

After you establish the subject, you choose the correct ending to the verb, which I explain in detail in Chapter 6.

In the present tense, you first remove the infinitive's ending (**-are, -ere,** or **-ire**), leaving the verb stem. **Parlare** (*to speak*), for example, drops the **-are** and leaves you with **parl**. You then add the infinitive's present tense endings. Present tense endings are letters that indicate who is doing the action of the verb.

The following table shows a simple conjugation of the **-are** verb **parlare** in the present tense. Notice that the subject pronoun and the verb endings both tell who's doing the action. Because the verb endings are so different, the conjugated verb alone often suffices to name the subject. So instead of saying **io parlo,** you can say simply **parlo** (*I speak*). However, because the third-person singular and plural forms have conjugations for multiple subjects, you may want to keep the specific subject named in those cases.

parlare (to speak)	
io parl**o**	noi parl**iamo**
tu parl**i**	voi parl**ate**
lui, lei, Lei parl**a**	loro, Loro parl**ano**

Check out Chapters 6 and 7 for more details and practice using verbs in the present tense.

Composing a Simple Sentence

In Italian, composing a sentence can be remarkably easy. You need a subject, a verb that agrees with that subject, and a tense, mood, and voice to tell you when and how something happened.

Taking a simple sentence like **io parlo** or **parlo** (*I speak*), you can embellish what you're saying by adding adjectives, adverbs, prepositions, or objects. And you can use conjunctions to make the sentence more complex. For example, here's a building process that makes a sentence more interesting:

Io parlo (*I speak*)

Io parlo italiano (*I speak Italian*)

Io parlo italiano bene (*I speak Italian well*)

Io parlo italiano bene perché lo parlo con degli amici italiani (*I speak Italian well because I speak it with some Italian friends*)

Chapters 6, 7, and 9 tell you how to put present tense verbs to use. Chapters 16–22 show you how to use endings to indicate tense, mood, and voice. You can find all you need to know about *special verbs* (those that express liking and missing, for example), which don't behave the same way as most verbs do, in Chapter 10.

Because you won't always make affirmative statements, Chapters 6, 7, and 9 also tell you how to make any statement negative. Italian can be emphatic in its use of negatives; sometimes it not only doubles but triples negative words in a single sentence! Chapter 11 shows you how.

To ask questions in Italian, you can invert subjects and verbs, or you can simply change your intonation. To invert a subject and verb, you can change **Carlo parla italiano** (*Carlo speaks Italian*) to something like **Parla italiano Carlo?** (*Does Carlo speak Italian?*)

Intonation makes the first sentence a statement by changing the high and low pitch of your sentence, much as you do when speaking English. The words *he speaks Italian* can be either a statement (He speaks Italian.) or a question (He speaks Italian?), depending on the tone and pitch of your voice.

To ask and respond to questions with more than a simple **sì** (*yes*) or **no** (*no*), you need interrogative words like **chi** (*who*), **che, che cosa** (*what*), **quanto** (*how much*), **dove** (*where*), and so on. Usually, these words come at the very beginning of a sentence: **Chi è?** (*Who is it?*)

For information about how to ask and understand answers to questions more complex than those requiring a simple yes or no answer, see Chapter 11.

Moving on to Other Verb Tenses

Italian has 14 verb tenses. Seven are compound, meaning they take a helping verb to form. In this book, I focus on the tenses you use most often: present, past, and future.

That sounds deceptively simple, but the present, past, and future tote up to the 14 tenses. For this reason, Chapters 6 and 7 open with the present tense; Chapters 9 and 10 also deal with present tense and include verbs that have their own idiosyncratic natures. The chapters in Parts IV and V introduce more tenses and show how tense and mood interact to make Italian both straightforward and nuanced.

Each tense has its own endings and peculiarities and combined with mood — conditional, what if; imperative, commanding; subjunctive, subjective; indicative, factual — makes speaking Italian both rewarding and challenging. Throughout this book, I show you how to combine tense and mood, and occasionally voice, to express yourself precisely and even elegantly.

Chapter 2

That's Italian! Sounding Out Italian Words the Right Way

Mastering a second language, Italian in this case, means figuring out how to read, listen, speak, and write in a new language — usually simultaneously. Ideally, you have a fluent speaker nearby who can demonstrate sounds and constructions for you. Short of that, you can watch Italian movies (a great many are available these days), listen to Italian singers (and read along with printed lyrics), and even watch Italian television.

Italian is almost completely phonetic. Unlike English, it doesn't use the same letters to produce several different sounds (consider the English en*ough*, b*ough*, th*ough*, and th*rough*). Italian is musical; it flows in patterns that make you feel as though you're singing.

In this chapter, I show you how to pronounce and accent your Italian and how to use intonation or cadence to give authenticity to your pronunciation. I explain how to adjust your intonation to make your Italian pronunciation more authentic and understandable. I suggest ways a really good dictionary can help you not only improve your vocabulary but also guide you in the correct way to say the words in Italian.

Starting with Basic Italian Sounds

Italian, like English, has five basic vowels (**a, e, i, o,** and **u**), with **j** occasionally substituting for **i.** The remaining letters of the 21-letter alphabet are consonants; not included are **j, k, w, y,** and **x,** though they appear in some foreign words imported into Italian.

Both vowel and consonant sounds are clipped, meaning you don't draw them out as you may in English, which allows you to speak clearly. Try holding your open hand about 2 inches in front of your mouth and saying the English word *popcorn*. Feel the air that you expel when saying *popcorn*. You don't breathe out, or aspirate, sounds in

Italian. You keep them crisp and clipped. As your vocabulary grows, you can occasionally try this hand exercise with Italian words; you shouldn't feel air coming from your mouth as you speak.

The vowels **e** and **o** vary their pronunciation slightly. The consonants work in concert with the vowels to produce specific sounds. I explain the details of these sounds in the following sections.

Sounding out the vowels

Italian has five vowels, which produce seven sounds. The vowel sounds are crisp, clear-cut, and never drawn out. The sounds of **a, i,** and **u** are always the same. Both **e** and **o**, however, have slightly different sounds, called *open* or *closed,* and their pronunciations vary depending on where you are in Italy.

These variations aren't consistent, but in general speech, the closed **e** (pronounced like the *e* in *they*) and the closed **o** (pronounced like *o* in *cold*) are predominant. I suggest following pronunciations as shown here and listening carefully to pick up regional variations.

- ✔ **a:** *ah,* like the *a* in *father*
- ✔ **e** (closed): *eh,* like the *e* in *they*
- ✔ **e** (open): *eh,* like the *e* in *hen*
- ✔ **i:** *ee,* like the second *i* in *cuisine*
- ✔ **o** (closed): *oh,* like the *o* in *cold*
- ✔ **o** (open): *oh,* like the *o* in *or*
- ✔ **u:** *ooh,* like the *u* in *duke*

Pronouncing the "e" and "o"

The open and closed **e** and **o** often appear in one word. For example, you pronounce **bene** as *beh-* (open) *-neh* (closed) (*well*). And you pronounce **modo** as *moh-* (open) *-doh* (closed) (*way, means*). Note that the open **e** and **o** are always in the stressed syllable of a word.

As you say the words **bene** and **modo,** you can feel that the vowel sounds come from different parts of the mouth. The open **o** and **e** come from the back of your tongue (while your mouth is slightly open) to the front of the mouth (with the mouth, and the sound, more closed).

Sometimes an acute accent indicates a closed **e,** as in **perché** (pehr-*keh*) (*why*). This accent shows that you use the closed sound of **e.** It also tells you to stress the syllable in which it appears.

The distinction between open and closed vowels varies from region to region. You may hear the closed **e** almost exclusively in words like **bene,** for example. The open and closed **o** can also be indistinguishable, though not as common as with the **e** sound.

Combining vowel sounds

When two vowels combine to produce one sound, you call them *diphthongs*. In Italian, the first of the two vowels in combination is usually **i** or **u.** They assume the sounds of English *y* and *w,* respectively.

Here are some examples in which the **i** sounds like the English *y:*

- **ieri** (*yeh*-ree) (*yesterday*)
- **invidia** (een-*veed*-yah) (*envy*)
- **più** (pyooh) (*more*)

In the following examples, the **u** sounds like the English *w:*

- **buono** (*bwoh*-noh) (*good*)
- **figliuolo** (fee-*wohl*-oh) (*son, good chap*)

Two diphthongs can appear in the same word, back to back, as these examples show:

- **muoio** (*mwoh*-yo) (*I'm dying*): The **uo** diphthong sounds like the English *woh;* the **io** sounds like the English *yo.*
- **acquaio** (ah-*kwah*-yo) (*sink*): The **ua** has the sound of the English *wa;* the **io** sounds like the English *yo.*

If three vowels combine to give a single sound, you call them *triphthongs,* but they're relatively rare in Italian.

- **suoi** (swoy) (*your, his, her, its*)
- **tuoi** (twoy) (*your*)

Note: The **u,** which sounds like the English *w,* combines with **oi** to produce the English sound *woy.*

Sounding out the consonants

Italian has 16 consonants. Of these, **b, d, f, l, m, n, p, t,** and **v** represent the same sounds as their English counterparts. The difference is that you pronounce the Italian consonants in staccato, or clipped, fashion and not by drawing them out. The remaining consonants — **c, g, h, q, r, s,** and **z** — are also crisply pronounced, but their sounds change, depending on which vowels or other consonants follow them. I explore these consonant sounds in the following sections:

Checking out the consonant "c"

Just as in English, you can pronounce the consonant **c** in Italian in a couple of different ways, depending on what letter(s) follows it. Here are some guidelines:

- **Hard c:** When **c** is followed by **a, o,** or **u,** it sounds like the English *k,* as in these examples: **caffè** (kah-*feh*) (*coffee*), **con** (kohn) (*with*), and **Cupido** (*kooh*-pee-doh) (*Cupid*).

To make the English *k* sound before **e** or **i**, you insert **h** between the **c** and the following vowel, for example, **chi** (kee) (*who*) and **che** (keh) (*what, that*).

✔ **Soft c:** When followed by **e** or **i**, **c** sounds like the English *ch,* like in the words **cello** (*chehl*-loh) (*cello*), **cinema** (*chee*-neh-mah) (*cinema*), and **cento** (*chehn*-toh) (*one hundred*).

To make the English *ch* sound before **a, o,** or **u,** you add the letter **i** between the **c** and the following vowel. You don't pronounce the **i**; it simply softens the hard *k* sound. Here are some examples: **ciao** (chou) (*hello; goodbye*), **Luciano** (Looh-*chah*-no) (*Luciano*), **arancia** (ah-*ahn*-chah) (*orange*), and **cacciatore** (kah-chah-*toh*-reh) (*hunter's style*).

Getting familiar with the sounds of "g"

Lucky for you, **g** makes things a little easier because it follows the same pattern as **c** — when it comes to the vowels that follow it, anyway.

✔ **Hard g:** When **g** is followed by **a, o,** and **u,** it uses the hard *g* sound, like the English *g* in *go.* Therefore, these words take the hard **g: gala** (*gah*-lah) (*gala*), **gondola** (*gohn*-doh-lah) (*gondola*), and **gusto** (*gooh*-stoh) (*gusto*).

To make the *g* sound before the letters **e** and **i,** you add an **h** after the **g,** like so: **ghetto** (*geht*-toh) (*ghetto*), **laghi** (*lah*-gee) (*lakes*).

Soft g: When followed by **e** and **i,** **g** sounds equivalent to the English *j,* like in the words **gelato** (jeh-*lah*-toh) (*gelato*) and **pagina** (*pah*-jih-nah) (*page*).

To make the *g* soft sound before **a, o,** and **u,** you insert an **i** between **g** and the following vowel. You don't pronounce the **i,** though; it's just there to soften the **g.** Here are some examples: **già** (jah) (*already*), **Giovanni** (joh-*vahn*-nee) (*John*), and **Giuseppe** (jooh-*zehp*-peh) (*Giuseppe*).

✔ Sometimes **g** combines with **li** to form **gli,** which sounds similar to the English double *l* in *billion:* **famiglia** (fah-*mee*-lyah) (*family*), **figlio** (*fee*-lyoh) (*son*), and **tagliatelle** (tah-lyah-*tehl*-leh) (*noodles*).

✔ When **g** is followed by **n,** it produces a sound like the English *ny* in *canyon,* for example: **lasagne** (lah-*sah*-nyah) (*lasagna*), **bagno** (*bah*-nyoh) (*bath*), **signore** (see-*nyoh*-reh) (*mister*), and **signorina** (see-nyoh-*ree*-nah) (*miss*).

Hearing (or not) the silent "h"

The consonant **h** often feels unnecessary because it doesn't have any sound; in fact an Italian saying goes **non vale un'acca** (*it's not worth an h*). Although **h** is silent, it's no less important than the consonants with a voice. By simply adding an **h,** you can change the sounds and meanings of many words, including the following:

ci (chee) (*there*) becomes **chi** (kee) (*who*)

c'è (cheh) (*there is*) becomes **che** (keh) (*what, that*)

getto (*jeht*-toh) (*I throw*) becomes **ghetto** (*geht*-toh) (*ghetto*)

Consider this: Without the **h,** you wouldn't have **spaghetti** (spah-*geht*-ti) (*spaghetti*).

Pairing "q" with "u"

As in English, the letter **q** in Italian is always accompanied by **u** and pronounced like *kw* as in the English word *quack*. It usually precedes a diphthong (see the earlier section "Combining vowel sounds"). Here are a few examples: **qui** (kwee) (*here*), **qua** (kwah) (*here*), and **quadro** (*kwah*-droh) (*picture*).

Rolling out the letter "r"

When you have a single **r** in a word, it has a sound comparable to the English *d*. For example, **Mari** sounds like *Madi*. You get this *d* sound by *trilling* the **r** — that is, by bouncing the tip of your tongue off the upper palate or right behind your front teeth. In English, when you say an *r*, you move the tongue toward the back of your mouth. Moving the tongue forward takes some practice. Try saying it in words like these: **prego** (*preh*-goh) (*you're welcome*), **arte** (*ar*-teh) (*art*), **grazie** (*grah*-tsee-eh) (*thanks*).

Sounding out "s" with success

The consonant **s** takes on different sounds in Italian, but there's no hard and fast rule about when **s** sounds like the English *s* and when it sounds like the English *z*. Where **s** appears in a word — at the beginning, between two vowels, or before a consonant — can influence the pronunciation, but it isn't always consistent. To pronounce the **s** correctly, you need to listen carefully to others' pronunciation. The following examples show general rules at work. Keep in mind that there are exceptions to these rules.

- ✔ When preceding a vowel or a consonant inside a word (that is, when the vowel or consonant doesn't start the word), **s** sounds like the English *s,* as in *mouse.* For example, **salame** (sah-*lah*-meh) (*salami*), **sabato** (*sah*-bah-toh) (*Saturday*), **testa** (*teh*-stah) (*head*), and **festa** (*feh*-stah) (*party*).

- ✔ When used between two vowels or before a consonant that starts a word, **s** can sound like the English *z,* as it does in English word *hose.* Here are a few examples: **rosa** (*roh*-zah) (*rose*), **sdegno** (*zdeh*-nyoh) (*disdain*), **tesoro** (teh-*zoh*-roh) (*treasure*), and **esercizio** (eh-zehr-*chee*-zee-oh) (*exercise*).

- ✔ When **s** is followed by **c** then **a, o,** or **u,** it has the English *k* sound, like so: **pesca** (*peh*-skah) (*peach*), **fresco** (*freh*-skoh) (*fresh, cool*), and **scuse** (*skoo*-seh) (*excuses*).

- ✔ When **sc** is followed by **e** or **i,** it sounds like the English *sh:* **pesce** (*peh*-sheh) (*fish*), **scena** (*sheh*-nah) (*scene*), and **sciagura** (shah-*goo*-rah) (*disgrace*).

- ✔ When you see **sch,** followed by **e** or **i** (it's never followed by **a, o,** or **u**), you pronounce it like the English *k,* like so: **pesche** (*peh*-skeh) (*peaches*) and **scheletro** (*skeh*-leh-troh) (*skeleton*).

The importance of spelling and pronunciation is never more clear than with words like **pesca, pesce,** and **pesche.** If you're in a restaurant and order **pesche,** you get *peaches;* if you order **pesce,** you get *fish.* Quite a difference.

Getting your z's in order

Last but not least in the sounds of single consonants, I give you **z.** It has two pronunciations:

- ✔ **z** sometimes sounds like the English *ts* in *gets* when it's doubled or when it has an **i** following it; for example, **pizza** (*pee*-tsah) (*pizza*), **grazie** (*grah*-tsee-eh) (*thanks*), and **Venezia** (Veh-*neh*-tsee-ah) (*Venice*).

➤ **z** sounds like the *ds* in *reds* when it's single, as in these words: **zero** (*dseh*-roh) (*zero*), **zanzara** (dsahn-*dsah*-rah) (*mosquito*), and **zingaro** (*dseen*-gah-roh) (*gypsy*).

Doubling up consonants

In Italian, you can double all consonants except for **h.** When you double consonants, you draw out the sound more than if the consonant was single. You have a sense of almost pausing between the two consonants. *Note:* When you have a double **r,** you roll it, like more of a sustained trill (see the earlier discussion on trilling *r*'s in "Rolling out the letter 'r'"). The double **s** takes on the sound of the English *s.*

Here are some examples of doubled consonants:

➤ **bello** (*behl*-lo) (*beautiful*)

➤ **ferro** (*fehr*-roh) (*iron*)

➤ **mamma** (*mahm*-mah) (*mom*)

➤ **Rossini** (rohs-*see*-nee) (*Rossini*)

➤ **soqquadro** (sohk-*kwah*-droh) (*mess, confusion*)

➤ **spaghetti** (spah-*geht*-tee) (*spaghetti*)

Give the Italian spelling that produces the same sounds as you see in the following English words. Keep in mind that you're not translating; you're simply giving the Italian spelling that produces an equivalent sound to the English word.

Q. *chow*

A. **ciao**

1. *get* _____

2. *jealous* _____

3. *shoe* _____

4. *concerto* _____

5. *herb* _____

6. *familial* _____

7. *Joe* _____

8. *Quito* _____

9. *Chile* _____

10. *judo* _____

Adding Stress with Accents

In Italian, you use accent marks (*grave,* as on **è,** and *acute,* as on **é**) for two reasons. If the accent falls on the last syllable of a word, it tells you to stress that syllable, as in these examples: **città** (chee-*tah*) (*city*), **cioè** (choh-*eh*) (*that is*), **però** (pehr-*oh*) (*however*), **virtù** (veer-*tooh*) (*virtue*), and **perché** (pehr-*keh*) (*why, because*). If the accent is acute, as in **perché** or **sé** (seh) (*themselves*), the **e** is closed.

Accents also show you the different meanings of two words with the same spelling, as in the following examples.

è (eh) (*is*)	**e** (eh) (*and*)
sì (see) (*yes*)	**si** (see) (*oneself*)
però (pehr-*oh*) (*however*)	**pero** (*pehr*-oh) (*pear tree*)
là (lah) (*there*)	**la** (lah) (*the, it, her*)
né (neh) (*neither, nor*)	**ne** (neh) (*some*)
dà (dah) (*gives*)	**da** (dah) (*from, by*)

Accents don't appear in the middle of words to show where you place stress. Knowing which syllable to stress is something you get from studying and practicing Italian. Placing stress on the appropriate syllable is important, because some words are spelled the same way but carry a different stress or pronunciation.

For example, in English, the words <u>conduct</u> (behavior) and <u>conduct</u> (lead, direct) are spelled the same, but you stress different syllables (underlined in this case) when you pronounce them to indicate which meaning you're using. Some Italian examples follow:

ancora (ahn-*coh*-rah) (*still*)	**ancora** (*ahn*-coh-rah) (*anchor*)
subito (sooh-*bee*-toh) (*suffered*)	**subito** (*sooh*-bee-toh) (*immediately*)
pagano (pah-*gah*-noh) (*pagan*)	**pagano** (*pah*-gah-noh) (*they pay*)

Polishing Your Italian Sound: Intonation

Intonation is the musical quality, the lilt and pitch of your voice, that you use in language to clarify meaning. Consider the difference in how you say *You're going* (a statement) and *You're going?* (a question). When making a statement, the pitch of your voice drops at the end of the phrase or sentence. When asking a question, you raise the pitch of your voice at the end.

In Italian, you do the same thing. For example, when you say **I bambini stanno mangiando** (*The kids are eating*), you lower your pitch on the last two syllables, **-giando.** To make this same sentence a question, **I bambini stanno mangiando?** (*Are the kids eating?*), you raise the pitch of your voice on **-gian** and drop it slightly on **-do.**

As in English, you can raise or lower the pitch of your voice to emphasize any part of a sentence.

Learning a language is like learning to play a musical instrument or to sing — it takes practice and patience. And Italian is especially musical.

Getting the Most Out of Dictionaries

Dictionaries are both a help and a hindrance. Using them to look up every word you're not sure of can be time-consuming and frustrating. It can also be misleading.

For example, trying to translate a recipe from English into Italian, a student once wanted to say, "First, you brush a chicken with oil." His searches in the dictionary led him to say, "First, you sweep a chicken with petroleum." Not quite the same thing, though it certainly is a compelling image. Another student kept using the word *prep.* I finally figured out that she was taking the first word of a dictionary definition, the word that indicates which part of speech is being defined, and using that.

Before giving you the meanings of words, dictionaries tend to give you their pronunciation, but usually only if the pronunciation deviates from the general rule that the stress in Italian words falls on the next-to-last syllable. They tend not to show the phonetics of words. They also show what part of speech words are. Here are two examples:

> **pizza**, n.f. *[noun feminine]* Neapolitan savory flatbread with toppings.

> **medico,** n.m. *[noun masculine]* (plural **medici)** mEdico *[shows that the stress falls on the third-to-last syllable]* Physician, doctor.

You can often decipher a word's meaning from its context. For this reason, I suggest putting the dictionary aside until you've tried reading an entire paragraph, for example. The surrounding text may provide clues to an unknown word's meaning.

If you do have to use the dictionary, I suggest making your own vocabulary list. Add words as you come across them for the first time, in a small notebook divided alphabetically, for example.

Navigating a monolingual Italian dictionary

There are many good monolingual Italian dictionaries, almost all of which include exemplary sentences that use words in context. Such dictionaries tend to be large and heavy, so I recommend using them online instead. And a bonus of using online dictionaries is that access is generally free.

Monolingual dictionaries give you two distinct advantages that bilingual dictionaries can't. First, they keep you from translating everything from English to Italian; that is, they keep you from filtering everything through extra layers and thus contribute to your ease of learning. Second, they allow you to build your Italian vocabulary dramatically. By reading a definition, you expose yourself to additional vocabulary and undergo what may be called passive learning.

A particularly useful type of monolingual Italian dictionary is a **dizionario ragionato dei sinonimi e dei contrari** (*dictionary of synonyms and antonyms*). I find it helpful when trying to teach adjectives, for example, to give pairs, such as **bello** (*beautiful*), **brutto** (*ugly*); **vecchio** (*old*), **giovane** (*young*); and **buono** (*good*), **cattivo** (*bad*). Often, if you can't remember one of the words in a pair, the opposite will trigger your memory.

Using a bilingual Italian-English/ English-Italian dictionary

Choosing one Italian-English/English-Italian dictionary from the multitudinous offerings can be baffling and overwhelming.

A thorough bilingual dictionary includes verb conjugations and gives stems for all verb tenses as well as usage and idiomatic expressions. It tells what part of speech a word is. It includes idiomatic expressions and alternate meanings for entries.

To evaluate a bilingual dictionary, I suggest looking up the word **mano** (*hand*). Apart from the basic translation of **mano,** any respectable dictionary will give six or eight other translations and point out that it can be used as a noun or a verb. The entry for **mano** should take up a good deal of ink on idiomatic expressions, everything from how to say *to make a clean sweep* (**far man bassa**) or *to shake hands* (**dare la mano**) to *to be heavy-handed* (**avere la mano pesante**) or *to play duets* (**suonare a quattro mani**).

Take a look at the entries immediately following **mano.** A good dictionary will have at least ten and usually more, everything from **manodopera** (*labor*), **manometro** (*pressure guage*), **manomorta** (*mortmain* [referring to property]), to **manopola** (*handlebar*).

Looking at visual dictionaries

Visual dictionaries range from glossy, four-color picture books to the more serious black-and-white, thin-papered kind with tiny, tiny typefaces. I recommend leafing through them at your local bookseller and seeing what works best for you. Do you want to know every single part of a bicycle? Or is a section on sports, which includes bicycles, enough for your purposes?

Investigate children's books. You can often find alphabet books as basic as having only one word for each letter in the alphabet. Other books aim to teach children between 500 and 1,000 words that are eminently useful in daily conversation. Some books are thematically arranged and have sections with titles like "At the Zoo," "On the Farm," and "In the Schoolroom."

Answer Key

1 ghet

2 gelos

3 sciù

4 concerto

5 erb

6 famiglial

7 Giò

8 Chito

9 Cile

10 giudo

Chapter 3

Talking about Things with Nouns and Articles

Nouns in Italian represent people, places, and things, just as nouns in English do. One key difference with nouns in Italian is that each noun is either feminine or masculine — that's right: Nouns have gender.

In Italian, the words *cars, cities, laws,* and *knees* are all feminine nouns. And *mistakes, winter, the Internet,* and *rice* are all masculine nouns. Why? Because. Don't look for a logic to the gender of nouns — there isn't any.

But don't despair: Clues abound for determining gender of nouns, not the least of which are the definite article (*the*) and indefinite articles (*a, an*). The articles tell you whether a noun is masculine or feminine, singular or plural.

In this chapter, I show you how to determine a noun's gender and number and which articles to put with that noun. You also figure out how to convert singular nouns to plural, which is important of course when you want to talk about all the operas you've seen in all your favorite Italian cities.

Not all nouns play by the rules, however, and I show you which ones deviate from the gender rules, which ones pair with the articles, how to expand your vocabulary by using prefixes and suffixes, and even when you can do away with definite and indefinite articles altogether.

Distinguishing between Masculine and Feminine Nouns

As I mention in the introduction to this chapter, every noun in Italian has a gender. It's either masculine or feminine. The endings on Italian nouns tell you their gender, which is also true for adjectives and pronouns, and even some verbs.

In the following sections, I show you how to determine and, more important, how to remember a noun's gender.

Recognizing common noun endings

Almost all Italian nouns, except for those imported, assimilated words from other languages (such as *film, computer, jeans,* and *stress*), end in vowels: **a, e, i, o,** and **u.**

If you think about Italian nouns that have come into English, this fact becomes clear. The names of foods top the list of linguistic immigrants — **pizza, spaghetti, minestrone, ravioli, zucchini, tiramisù, panino,** and **ricotta,** to name a few. The arts are equally well represented. For music, English picks up the Italian **aria, bravo, allegro, viola, piano,** and **opera.** From the visual arts and architecture, English has adopted (and in some cases adapted) **replica, graffiti, terracotta, veranda,** and **chiaroscuro.** General words that you use in daily life include **bimbo, stucco, bordello, confetti, motto, madonna, casinò,** and **credenza.**

Some Italian words have slightly modified meanings in their English incarnations, but the list goes on. And that's without even adding proper names — those of famous people in politics, the arts, business, or sports, for example. You can easily recognize a word of Italian origin, however, by the ending vowel.

Sorting nouns into three classes

Because almost all Italian nouns end in vowels, you sort them by gender, which the vowels indicate (usually). That is, you have nouns that are masculine and nouns that are feminine. There's no neutral gender in Italian.

Most *singular* nouns fall into one of three groups, having **-o, -a,** or **-e** endings. Generally, words ending in **-o** are masculine, such as **bimbo** (*baby boy*) and **libro** (*book*), and nouns ending in **-a** are feminine, such as **casa** (*house*) and **ragazza** (*girl*).

Nouns that end in **-e,** however, can be either masculine or feminine, and you have to rely on their inherent meanings or other clues to determine which they may be; for example, **madre** (*mother*) is obviously feminine, and **padre** (*father*) is obviously masculine. If an adjective accompanies the noun, its gender will be the same as that of the noun (**buona notte** [*good night*]). **Buona,** ending in **-a,** is feminine; it agrees in gender with **notte** and lets you know that *night* is a feminine noun.

Another clue to gender is the extended ending of a word. If a word ends in **-ione,** it's frequently feminine (like **nazione** [*nation*] and **opinione** [*opinion*]). Words that end in **-ore** are often masculine (such as **attore** [*actor*] and **professore** [*professor*]).

Approach nouns with singular endings other than **-o, -a,** or **-e** on a case-by-case basis. I deal with some of the more common forms in the section "Forming Plurals of Irregular Nouns and Other Exceptions," later in this chapter.

Categorize the following singular nouns as either masculine or feminine by writing "M" or "F" next to each word.

Q. **madre** (*mother*)

A. F

1. **bambina** (*baby girl*) _____

2. **macchina** (*car*) _____

3. **libro** (*book*) _____

4. **signore** (*man*) _____

5. **padre** (*father*) _____

6. **zio** (*uncle*) _____

7. **medico** (*doctor*) _____

8. **lezione** (*class*) _____

9. **zucchero** (*sugar*) _____

10. **casa** (*house*) _____

Moving from Singular to Plural with Regular Nouns

In addition to gender, every Italian noun has a plural and singular form. In English, forming plurals is pretty straightforward — all you have to do, usually, is add an *s* or *es: one car, two cars; one recess, two recesses.* Sometimes, if an English noun ends in *y,* you change the *y* to *i* before adding *es* (*hobby, hobbies*). English has a large number of irregular plurals that don't follow the *s, es, ies* rule (such as *ox, oxen; mouse, mice; goose, geese*).

In Italian, to make a singular noun plural, you change the vowel at the end of the word. (Keep in mind that nearly all Italian nouns end in a vowel.) Here are the basic rules:

✔ If a noun ends in **-o,** change it to **-i,** as in these examples:

panino (*sandwich*)	**panini** (*sandwiches*)
libro (*book*)	**libri** (*books*)
gatto (*tomcat*)	**gatti** (*tomcats*)

✔ If a noun ends in **-a,** change it to **-e,** like so:

casa (*house*)	**case** (*houses*)
scuola (*school*)	**scuole** (*schools*)

✔ If a noun ends in **-e,** change it to **-i,** as shown here:

madre (*mother*)	**madri** (*mothers*)
televisione (*television*)	**televisioni** (*televisions*)
professore (*professor*)	**professori** (*professors*)

Here are a few other gender-specific rules for making singular nouns plural:

✔ If a feminine singular noun ends in **-ca** or **-ga,** you change the ending to **-che** or **-ghe** to retain the hard sound of the singular form of the word; for example:

amica (*friend*)	**amiche** (*friends*)
lattuga (*lettuce*)	**lattughe** (*lettuces*)

✔ For feminine singular nouns ending in **-cia** or **-gia,** with a stressed **i,** simply replace the **-a** with an **-e,** as shown here:

farmacia (*pharmacy*)	**farmacie** (*pharmacies*)
bugia (*lie*)	**bugie** (*lies*)

If the **i** isn't stressed, you drop it before changing the **-a** to an **-e,** like so:

arancia (*orange*)	**arance** (*oranges*)
camicia (*blouse*)	**camice** (*blouses*)

✔ If a masculine singular noun ends in **-co** or **-go,** you generally keep the hard sound in the plural form by inserting an **h** before the new ending, as in these examples:

parco (*park*)	**parchi** (*parks*)
tedesco (*German*)	**tedeschi** (*Germans*)
fuoco (*fire*)	**fuochi** (*fires*)

If the singular **-co** and **-go** endings are preceded by an **e** or an **i,** however, you don't add an **h** but simply change the **-o** to **-i,** as shown here:

amico (*friend*)	**amici** (*friends*)
medico (*doctor*)	**medici** (*doctors*)

✔ For masculine nouns that end in **-cio, -gio,** or **-io,** with a stressed **i,** change the **-o** to another **-i,** like so:

zio (*uncle*)	**zii** (*uncles*)
leggio (*lectern*)	**leggii** (*lecterns*)

If the **i** isn't stressed, you simply drop the **-o** to get the plural form, as in these examples:

vecchio (*old man*)	**vecchi** (*old men*)
figlio (*son*)	**figli** (*sons*)

Sound or pronunciation of words is often key to remembering how to form the plural of Italian nouns. See Chapter 2 for a detailed explanation of Italian pronunciation.

Make the following singular nouns plural by changing the last letter(s) of each word. See the example.

Q. **orologio**

A. **orologi**

11. **fratello** _____

12. **idea** _____

13. **amico** _____

14. **cugino** _____

15. **zia** _____

16. **cane** _____

17. **valigia** _____

18. **medico** _____

19. **bacio** _____

20. **vecchio** _____

Forming Plurals of Irregular Nouns and Other Exceptions

Besides the three main endings (**-o, -a, -e**) for masculine and feminine nouns, Italian has various other, less common — but by no means rare — endings, or endings that appear to be masculine or feminine but aren't. I explain how to form the plural of these types of nouns in the following sections.

Nouns adopted from other languages

Words from other languages, especially words that end in consonants, never change their endings, whether they're singular or plural, masculine or feminine.

Here are some examples (these words mean the same in English and Italian): **film, computer, babysitter, meetings, tennis, club, stress, shock, smog, sport, weekend, jazz, Internet, e-mail.** The articles that accompany these nouns do change from singular to plural, however. See the later section "Using articles to determine plural or singular form" for details.

Nouns with stressed final syllables

Other nouns that don't change their endings are those with a stressed final syllable. These nouns carry an accent in written Italian and a stress in spoken Italian. Some examples are **tè** (**thè** in Florentine spelling) (*tea*), **caffè** (*café, coffee*), **tassì** (*taxi*), **città** (*city*), **università** (*university*), **gioventù** (*youth*), **virtù** (*virtue*), and **identità** (*identity*). All the weekdays also carry accents: **lunedì** (*Monday*), **martedì** (*Tuesday*), **mercoledì** (*Wednesday*), **giovedì** (*Thursday*), and **venerdì** (*Friday*). In general, **-à** and **-ù** are feminine words; **-è, -ì,** and **-ò** are masculine.

Nouns ending in -ista

Words that end in **-ista** (**turista** [*tourist*], **artista** [*artist*], and **dentista** [*dentist*], for example) have only the one singular form and are both masculine and feminine. The plurals, however, change their endings to show whether they're singular or plural, masculine or feminine: **turisti, turiste** (*male tourists, female tourists*); **artisti, artiste** (*male artists, female artists*); and **dentisti, dentiste** (*male dentists, female dentists*).

Nouns of Greek origin

Some words, usually of Greek origin (as opposed to Latin origin), end in **-a** but are masculine. The most common of these has to be **problema** (*problem*). Others include **dramma** (*drama*), **sistema** (*system*), **clima** (*climate*), **programma** (*program*), **cinema** (*cinema*), **fantasma** (*ghost*), **tema** (*theme*), and **pianeta** (*planet*). They all form plurals by changing the **-a** to **-i**.

Other words of Greek origin that are generally feminine end with the letters **-si** and include **tesi** (*thesis*), **crisi** (*crisis*), and **analisi** (*analysis*).

To make it a little more challenging, some words are masculine in the singular and feminine in the plural if they mean one thing, but may have a masculine plural form if they mean another. The following lists some examples.

Masculine Singular	Feminine Plural	Masculine Plural
dito (*finger*)	**dita** (*fingers*)	
braccio (*arm*)	**braccia** (*arms*)	**bracci** (*arms, of a cross*)
labbro (*lip*)	**labbra** (*lips*)	**labbri** (*rims, edges of a wound*)
ginocchio (*knee*)	**ginocchia** (*knees*)	
calcagno (*heel*)	**calcagna** (*heels*)	
ciglio (*eyebrow*)	**ciglia** (*eyebrows*)	**cigli** (*edges*)
osso (*bone*)	**ossa** (*human bones*)	**ossi** (*skeleton, carcass*)
paio (*pair*)	**paia** (*pairs*)	
centinaio (*hundred*)	**centinaia** (*hundred*)	
migliaio (*thousand*)	**migliaia** (*thousands*)	
miglio (*mile*)	**miglia** (*miles*)	
lenzuolo (*bedsheet*)	**lenzuola** (*bedsheets*)	
muro (*wall*)	**mura** (*walls of a town*)	**muri** (*walls of a house or garden*)
uovo (*egg*)	**uova** (*eggs*)	**uovi** (*crude use referring to male anatomy*)
riso (*rice*)	**rise** (*laughs*)	**risi** (*rice dishes, kinds of rice*)

Finally, you encounter nouns that simply defy logic in their gender and formation such as **mano, mani** (*hand, hands* [feminine, singular/plural]) and **uomo, uomini** (*man, men* [masculine, singular/plural]).

Nouns used primarily in the singular or the plural

A few nouns exist that you use only in the singular or the plural. In general, you use the following nouns only in the singular. Some are collective nouns, or nouns that speak of a group but are used with singular verbs, like **la gente** (*the people*).

- **l'argento** (*silver*)
- **la fame** (*hunger*)
- **la famiglia** (*family*)
- **la frutta** (*fruit*)
- **la gente** (*people*)
- **il miele** (*honey*)
- **l'onestà** (*honesty*)
- **l'oro** (*gold*)
- **la sete** (*thirst*)
- **la verdura** (*vegetables*)

Nouns that are used only in the plural are relatively few but include the following.

> ✔ **le forbici** (*scissors*)
>
> ✔ **le molle** (*tongs*)
>
> ✔ **le nozze** (*marriage*)
>
> ✔ **le spezie** (*spices*)
>
> ✔ **le stoviglie** (*dishes*)
>
> ✔ **le tenebre** (*darkness, shadows*)

Change the following singular nouns to their plural forms. Some nouns have two plural forms, one masculine and one feminine. If the nouns are already plural, change them to their singular forms.

0. **problema**

A. **problemi**

21. **stress** _____

22. **ottimista** _____

23. **tema** _____

24. **città** _____

25. **tennis** _____

26. **crisi** _____

27. **fantasma** _____

28. **paio** _____

29. **mano** _____

30. **gioventù** _____

Getting Specific or Speaking in General: A Primer on Articles

The, a, and *an* are articles. They appear often in language, perhaps more often in Romance languages than in English. In Italian, these articles, which are technically adjectives (see Chapters 5 and 13 for details on adjectives), must agree in number and gender with the nouns they accompany. This means that articles have masculine and feminine, singular and plural forms. Furthermore, they live right next to the nouns they modify, so the beginning letters of the noun may also change the form the articles take. In English, you say *a car* and *an elephant.* In Italian, you take the beginning of the noun into account (for formation of the article) as well as the ending (for gender and number). I explore articles and their uses in Italian in the following sections.

Dealing with the definite article, "the"

You can say *the* in Italian in eight ways: masculine and feminine, singular and plural, and variations on the articles according to the beginning letters of the word being modified. Table 3-1 shows you how the definite articles align with the nouns according to number, gender, and word beginnings.

Definite articles point you to specific things: *the car* as opposed to *a, any car* and *the book* as compared to *any old book.*

As I mention earlier in this chapter, Italian has five vowels: **a, e, i, o,** and **u.** Very occasionally, **j** replaces **i,** and then it's a vowel as well. All the other letters of the Italian alphabet, which doesn't include *j, k, w, x,* or *y,* are consonants. Table 3-1 shows how the definite articles align with vowels or consonants.

Table 3-1	Definite Articles Paired with Nouns		
Singular Article	*Plural Article*	*Where Used*	*Examples*
il (masculine)	**i** (masculine)	before a consonant	**il libro** (*the book*), **i libri** (*the books*)
l' (masculine)	**gli** (masculine)	before a vowel	**l'amico** (*the friend*), **gli amici** (*the friends*)
lo (masculine)	**gli** (masculine)	before **s** followed by a consonant, before **z, ps,** and **gn**	**lo studente** (*the student*), **gli studenti** (*the students*); **lo zio** (*the uncle*), **gli zii** (*the uncles, the aunts and uncles*); **lo psicologo** (*the psychologist*), **gli psicologi** (*the psychologists*); **lo gnocco** (*the dumpling*), **gli gnocchi** (*the dumplings*)
la (feminine)	**le** (feminine)	before a consonant	**la casa** (*the house*), **le case** (*the houses*)
l' (feminine)	**le** (feminine)	before a vowel	**l'entrata** (*the entrance*), **le entrate** (*the entrances*)

When you have all masculine nouns, you use the masculine article; when you have all feminine nouns, you use the feminine. However, when you have a mixed group — the men and women, for example — the masculine form dominates. This holds true even if the mixed group is composed of five women and one man. For example: **i padri e le madri** (*the fathers and the mothers*), **i ragazzi e le ragazze** (*the boys and the girls*), **i padri** (*the parents*), and **i ragazzi** (*the boys*).

Remember to look at both ends of nouns. The final letters give you gender and number. The beginning letters tell you whether you need to change the article from the basic masculine or feminine forms.

Stato (*state*), for example, is a masculine singular noun (because it ends in **-o**). But it begins with **s** followed by a consonant, so you use the article **lo** (**lo stato**). **Saluto** (*a greeting*), a masculine singular noun, begins with **s** followed by a vowel, however, so you use the article **il,** as in **il saluto.**

Studentessa (*female student*), a feminine singular noun, takes the article **la.** You know its gender because of the last letter, the vowel **a.** (Remember that all feminine nouns take **la** unless they begin with a vowel; then they take **l'.**)

Gn at the start of a word tells you that you may use **lo** but only if the word is masculine and singular (**gnocco** [*dumpling*]). If instead you look at the end of the word and find an **-a** ending, as in **gnucca** (*brain*), you use the article **la.**

Put articles with the following words, using masculine, singular or plural, or feminine, singular or plural, forms. Keep in mind the beginning and ending of the words and their inherent meanings.

0. **madri** (*mothers*)

A. le

31. amica (*girlfriend*) _____

32. casa (*house*) _____

33. errori (*mistakes*) _____

34. padri (*fathers*) _____

35. arance (*oranges*) _____

36. entrate (*entrances*) _____

37. gnocchi (*dumplings*) _____

38. signora (*lady*) _____

39. oche (*female geese*) _____

40. zii (*aunts and uncles*) _____

Saying "a" or "an" in Italian: Indefinite articles

Using the indefinite article (*a, an*) allows you to be vague. You can talk about *a house,* not about a specific house (*the house*). You can say *a* or *an* in Italian in four ways: **un, uno** (masculine, singular); **un', una** (feminine, singular). Technically, *a* and *an* don't have plural forms, although *some,* by extension, can be a plural of the indefinite articles. You can look over the formation and uses of *some* in Chapter 13 and in the later section "Understanding plural indefinite articles."

The indefinite articles also take gender into account, which you can figure out by looking at the beginning and ending of the noun it's modifying and considering the word's meaning. If the word begins with a vowel, you use a different form of *a* or *an* than if the word begins with a consonant.

Table 3-2 shows you how the indefinite articles appear with nouns.

Table 3-2	Indefinite Articles Paired with Nouns	
Article	*Where Used*	*Examples*
un (masculine)	before a consonant or a vowel	**un libro** (*a book*); **un amico** (*a friend*); **un elefante** (*an elephant*)
uno (masculine)	before **s** followed by a consonant, before **z, ps,** and **gn**	**uno studente** (*a student*); **uno zio** (*an uncle*); **uno psicologo** (*a psychologist*); **uno gnocco** (*a dumpling*)
un' (feminine)	before a vowel	**un'amica** (*a female friend*)
una (feminine)	before a consonant	**una casa** (*a house*)

You say **un anno** (*a year*), but **un'amica** (*girlfriend*). The only difference in the article is the apostrophe that follows the feminine **un. Un insegnante,** then, is *a male teacher;* **un'insegnante** is *a female teacher.*

Give the appropriate indefinite article for the following words.

Q. **nonna**

A. **una**

41. **zaino** _____

42. **aeroplano** _____

43. **errore** _____

44. **madre** _____

45. **arancia** _____

46. **finestra** _____

47. **studentessa** _____

48. **entrata** _____

49. **scuola** _____

50. **succo** _____

Understanding plural indefinite articles

Oddly enough, to form a "plural" indefinite article — and I put *plural* in quotes because technically you can't say *a cats* — you use a form of the *definite* article, *the,* and the preposition **di** (*of*). (For an overview of prepositions in general and of **di** in particular, see Chapter 12.)

When you combine **di** with a definite article (**il, l', lo, i, gli, la,** and **le**), it means *of the,* but it also means *some.* Table 3-3 shows how to combine **di** with the definite article. In the interests of sound and pronunciation, **di** changes to **de** when it combines with these definite articles.

Table 3-3	Combining Di with a Definite Article	
	Di + Article	*Example*
Masculine, Singular	**di + il = del**	**del vino** (*some wine*); **del caffè** (*some coffee*)
	di + l' = dell'	**dell'oro** (*some gold*)
	di + lo = dello	**dello spazio** (*some space*)
Masculine, Plural	**di + i = dei**	**dei libri** (*some books*)
	di + gli = degli	**degli studenti** (*some students*)
Feminine, Singular	**di + la = della**	**della carne** (*some meat*)
	di + l' = dell'	**dell'insalata** (*some salad*)
Feminine, Plural	**di + le = delle**	**delle donne** (*some women*)

For more details on using definite articles, see the earlier section "Dealing with the definite article, 'the'." Also check out Chapter 13 for other words that mean *some.*

Deciding when to include (or leave out) articles

When in doubt about whether a noun needs an article, use one. You can't go too far wrong because the majority of the time, Italian nouns need articles. For example, in English, you say *time flies* or *water is scarce;* in Italian, you say **il tempo vola** (*[the] time flies*) or **l'acqua manca** (*[the] water is scarce*). Here are several more situations where you use (or don't use) articles in Italian:

✔ To generalize, you use plural articles (and nouns): **Gli studenti sono il nostro futuro** (*[The] students are our future*).

✔ You use definite articles when you talk about places (except for cities) and people, as in these examples:

> **L'Italia è un bel paese.** (*Italy is a beautiful country.*)

> **Il signor Medici è famoso.** (*Mr. Medici is famous.*)

> **La signora Rossi è molto gentile.** (*Mrs. Rossi is very kind.*)

Note: Before a masculine name, you drop the final **e** from the term of address: **il signore**, **il signor Bianchi; il dottore**, **il dottor Alani,** and so forth. This rule doesn't hold true for feminine forms: **la signora Bianchi; la professoressa Alani.**)

On the other hand, if you're talking *to* a person, you don't use the article. For example:

Dottor Fanciulli, posso parlarLe francamente? (*Dr. Fanciulli, may I speak frankly to you?*)

Professor di Carlini, ha i compiti per gli studenti? (*Professor di Carlini, do you have the homework for the students?*)

✔ You use the definite article with dates and years — **il 4 settembre** (*September 4th*) and **il 2013** (*2013*) — but not with days of the week unless you're talking about every single Monday (**il lunedì** [*Mondays*]), Tuesday (**il martedì** [*Tuesdays*]), and so on. For example:

Questo weekend, sabato, non vado a scuola. (*This weekend, Saturday, I'm not going to school*).

Il lunedì vado a scuola. (*Mondays I go to school.*) Here, the use of the article tells you that you do this every single Monday.

✔ You can use the definite article instead of the possessive if you're talking about close relatives (**la mamma** [*my mom*], **lo zio** [*my uncle*]), clothing (**mi metto la cravatta** [*I'm putting on my tie*]), or body parts (**gli occhi sono stanchi** [*my eyes are tired*]).

✔ Many expressions that use the preposition **in** don't follow **in** with definite articles, for example, **in ufficio** (*at the office*), **in giardino** (*in the garden*), and **in Italia** (*in Italy*). (See Chapter 12 for details on the use of **in**.)

With geographic references, however, the minute you add an adjective, you bring back the article: **in Africa, nell'Africa equatoriale** (*in Africa, in Equatorial Africa*).

✔ The preposition **a** works similarly to **in** — that is, when you add an adjective, you use an article. For example:

Sono a scuola. (*I'm at school.*)

Sono alla scuola media. (*I'm at the middle school.*)

Vada a destra poi a sinistra. (*Go to the right then to the left.*)

✔ After the verb **essere** (see Chapter 7 for the complete **essere** story), you can forego both the definite and the indefinite article, as in these examples:

È mio. (*It's mine.*)

Lui è medico. (*He's a doctor.*)

Because the indefinite article makes generalized references to begin with, it's used more consistently. If you think about its meaning — *a, an* — retaining it makes sense.

You drop the indefinite article in statements like **che gelida manina** (*what a frozen little hand*), **che bell'uomo** (*what a handsome man*), and **che gioia** (*what a delight, what a joy*).

In general, you can dispense with articles when you make generalizations and after certain prepositions. Otherwise, you use it often.

Using articles to determine plural or singular form

Some words can be masculine or feminine, singular or plural. They have only one spelling. The only way you know what and how many of them these words represent is by the article that goes with them.

Imported words that end in consonants are usually masculine, but their singular and plural forms are the same; for example, **il film, i film** (*the movie, the movies*); **il computer, i computer** (*the computer, the computers*); and **lo sport, gli sport** (*the sport, the sports*) are all examples of the article telling you how many films, computers, or sports you're talking about. One exception to the gender of such words being masculine is **e-mail,** which is feminine.

Words with stressed final syllables tend to be masculine when they end in -**è**, -**ì**, or -**ò** and feminine when they end in -**à** or -**ù**. Only the articles tell you whether you're talking about more than one. Here are some examples: **il caffè, i caffè** (*the café, the cafes*); **il tassì, i tassì** (*the cab, the cabs*); **la virtù, le virtù** (*the virtue, the virtues*); and **la città, le città** (*the city, the cities*).

Nouns that end in -**si** — as in **tesi** (*thesis*), **crisi** (*crisis*), and **analisi** (*analysis*) — use articles to let you know that you're talking about one or more than one: **la tesi, le tesi; la crisi,** and **le crisi.**

Translate the following nouns into Italian. Don't forget to use the definite article that goes with each noun.

Q. *sports*

A. **gli sport**

51. *people* _____

52. *vegetables* _____

53. *movies* _____

54. *cities* _____

55. *marriage* _____

Using Suffixes and Prefixes with Nouns

Suffixes and prefixes are really adjectives in disguise. They modify the meaning of nouns by adding groups of letters (they're not individual words) to the end (suffixes) or beginning (prefixes) of words. In the following sections, I show you how to empha-size a word's meaning by adding suffixes and prefixes.

Suffixes and prefixes are especially colloquial, and like hand gestures, they can be misused. Be careful when you use them until you're comfortable with their precise meanings.

Looking at the way words end: Suffixes

Suffixes abound in Italian. They can make something larger or smaller, appreciated or denigrated; they can even change a noun's gender. Suffixes act the way adjectives do (find out more about adjectives in Chapters 5 and 13). Here, the focus is on nouns.

Because so many suffixes exist in Italian, Table 3-4 lists the seven that are most useful to you.

Table 3-4	Most Common Suffixes for Nouns	
Suffix	*Meaning*	*Examples*
-ino, -ina	*little, often sweet*	**una tavolina** (*a small table*); **un regalino** (*a small gift*)
-etto, -etta	*small*	**una casetta** (*a small house*)
-one, -ona	*large*	**un donnone** (*a large woman*) (note the gender change from **una donna** [*a woman*], feminine, to the masculine **donnone**)
-uccio, -uccia	shows contempt, ugliness unless used with a proper name, in which it's frequently a term of endearment	**una stanzuccia** (*a dirty or ugly little room*); **Carluccio** (*dear little Carlo*)
-accio, -accia	*degradation*	**un dottoraccio** (*an incompetent doctor*)
-icello, -icella	*small, nice*	**un venticello** (*a small wind or breeze*); **un fiumicello** (*a nice, little river*)
-astro, -astra	*bad, awful* unless talking about a step-relative	**poetastro** (*a really bad poet*); **fratellastro** (*stepbrother*), **sorellastra** (*stepsister*), **figliastra** (*stepdaughter*), **figliastro** (*stepson*)

Some suffixes can combine, such as the following: **un libro** (*a book*) becomes **un librettino** (*a nice, little book*); **un uomo** (*a man*) turns into **un uomaccione** (*a big, bad man*); **una zucca** (*a squash*) is more familiar as **le zucchine** (*zucchini*).

Use suffixes with care. They inject nuance into Italian and, when used sarcastically, can be tremendously offensive. In Italy, meaning and frequency of use vary by region.

Seeing how it all begins: Prefixes

Prefixes, which attach to the beginnings of words and change their meaning, aren't as numerous as suffixes but are perhaps used more frequently. Most often you see them attached to verbs and adjectives; Table 3-5 lists some that attach to nouns.

Table 3-5		Common Prefixes for Nouns
Prefixes	*Meaning*	*Example*
s-	usually makes a word opposite	**pregio** (*esteem*) becomes **spregio** (*disdain*)
dis-	*no, not*	**gusto** (*taste, enjoyment*) becomes **disgusto** (*disgust*)
mis-	*not*	**credente** (*believer*) becomes **miscredente** (*heretic*)
anti-	*against*	**antipolio** (*against polio* [like a vaccine])
ir-	*un*	**irrealtà** (*unreality*)
ri-, re-	*again*	**riconosciuto** (*familiar, a recognized person or thing*)
im-	*not*	**impossibile** (*impossible, not possible*)
pre-	*before*	**previsione** (*forecast, "pre-vision"*)

Give the English equivalent of the following nouns. Each has a suffix or a prefix. I include a translation of each *root* word — the original word as defined when it doesn't have a suffix or prefix.

Q. **una casuccia** (*house*)

A. *A little, squalid house*

56. Mariuccia (*Maria*) _____

57. mezz'oretta (*half hour*) _____

58. stradone (*street*) _____

59. reazione (*action*) _____

60. prenotazione (*notation*) _____

Answer Key

1	F
2	F
3	M
4	M
5	M
6	M
7	M
8	F
9	M
10	F
11	**fratelli**
12	**idee**
13	**amici**
14	**cugini**
15	**zie**
16	**cani**
17	**valigia**
18	**medici**
19	**baci**
20	**vecchi**

21 stress

22 ottimisti, ottimiste

23 temi

24 città

25 tennis

26 crisi

27 fantamsi, fantasme

28 paia

29 mani

30 gioventù

31 l'

32 la

33 gli

34 i

35 le

36 le

37 gli

38 la

39 le

40 gli

41 uno

42	**un**
43	**un**
44	**una**
45	**un'**
46	**una**
47	**una**
48	**un'**
49	**una**
50	**un**
51	**la gente**
52	**la verdura**
53	**i film**
54	**le città**
55	**le nozze**
56	*dear little Maria*
57	*bare half-hour*
58	*big road*
59	*reaction*
60	*reservation*

Chapter 4

Dealing with Numbers, Dates, and Time

. . . .

In This Chapter

▶ Counting to a billion

▶ Using ordinal numbers to indicate sequence

▶ Naming the days, months, and seasons

▶ Talking about the time

▶ Discussing the weather

▶ Getting familiar with the metric system

. . . .

Numbers crop up in all aspects of conversation, from counting, to telling someone your phone number, to putting things in order ("I went to Rome first, then Bologna second"). The good news is, in Italian, numbers are reliably straightforward, even though using them for dates, for example, may not seem so. This chapter gets you up-to-speed on counting, chatting about time and date, and using numbers with confidence in Italian.

Counting from Zero to a Billion: Cardinal Numbers

To express how many glasses of wine or scoops of gelato you want, you have to know your numbers. Table 4-1 provides some of the more useful cardinal numbers, from zero to a billion.

Table 4-1		Counting from Zero to a Billion	
Number	*Italian*	*Number*	*Italian*
0	zero	27	ventisette
1	uno	28	ventotto
2	due	29	ventinove
3	tre	30	trenta
4	quattro	40	quaranta
5	cinque	50	cinquanta
6	sei	60	sessanta
7	sette	70	settanta
8	otto	80	ottanta
9	nove	90	novanta
10	dieci	100	cento
11	undici	101	centouno
12	dodici	200	duecento
13	tredici	300	trecento
14	quattordici	400	quattrocento
15	quindici	500	cinquecento
16	sedici	600	seicento
17	diciassette	700	settecento
18	diciotto	800	ottocento
19	diciannove	900	novecento
20	venti	1,000	mille
21	ventuno	2,000	duemila
22	ventidue	10,000	diecimila
23	ventitré	100,000	centomila
24	ventiquattro	105,000	centocinquemila
25	venticinque	1,000,000	un milione (di)
26	ventisei	1,000,000,000	un miliardo (di)

Building numbers in Italian

Before you can get very far with using numbers in Italian, you have to know how to build them. For example, say you have a powerful appetite and want to order 12,640 scoops of gelato. How do you convey that specific number? You'll be happy to know that you build Italian numbers in a direct manner, similar to English. When building Italian numbers, you spell out large numbers as one word, without the use of *and* (**e**) to connect them. So *12,640* is written (and spoken) as **dodicimilaseicentoquaranta.**

To build numbers in Italian, simply add the larger number at the beginning, as in the following examples:

2	due
22	ventidue
122	centoventidue
422	quattrocentoventidue
1422	millequattrocentoventidue
3422	tremilaquattrocentoventidue

Here are some other specifics you need to know about using numbers in Italian:

✔ Some handwritten numbers, such as 1, 4, 7, and 9, look different in Italian from their English counterparts. See Figure 4-1.

Figure 4-1:
Handwritten
Italian
numbers 1,
4, 7, and 9.

✔ Italian uses periods and commas in numbers differently from English. For example, 1.200 in Italian is 1,200 in English. Remembering this difference is particularly important when looking at bills. A dinner that costs €36,00 differs greatly from one that costs €36.00!

✔ Telephone numbers are usually separated by periods instead of hyphens and are broken into units of two instead of three. Italian speakers often say the units of two digits as one number; for example, 21.30.52 would be said **ventuno, trenta, cinquantadue.** A seven-digit number may be given as 4.21.30.52, or **quattro, ventuno, trenta, cinquantadue.** However, nothing can stop you from simply saying each individual digit to relay a phone number, such as **due, uno, tre, zero, cinque, due.**

Speaking numbers like a native

When speaking numbers in general, you want to maintain the fluid nature of spoken Italian. To this end, from 20 through 90, the numbers 1 (**uno**) and 8 (**otto**) *contract,* meaning they drop the final vowel from venti, trenta, and so on, before adding **uno** or **otto**.

So, although some numbers follow the counting pattern, such as 22 (**ventidue**) or 75 (**settantacinque**), others, like 21 (**ventuno,** rather than "ventiuno") and 68 (**sessantotto,** not "sessantaotto"), drop the final vowel from the tens and flow directly into **uno** and **otto**.

Cardinal numbers with special meanings

Certain cardinal numbers, accompanied by the masculine singular definite article **il or l'**, have specialized meanings, particularly when making historical, literary, or art historical references. **Il Trecento, Il Quattrocento,** and so on, refer to the *1300s,* the *1400s,* and so on, which is certainly easier than the English naming of centuries, where the 14th century refers to the 1300s. For example, Petrarch (**Petrarca**), inventor of the sonnet form of poetry, lived during the **Trecento** (also written as '**300**). Michelangelo lived during both the **Quattrocento** *(1400s)* and the **Cinquecento** *(1500s).* The High Renaissance refers to that time in the **Cinquecento** *(1500s)* when the focus of effort and artists moved from Florence to Rome. A study of 20th-century literature would be a study of the literature of the **Novecento** *(1900s).*

Other nouns that derive from the cardinal numbers include references to large quantities *(hundreds =* **centinaia;** *thousands =* **migliaia**). Also, by dropping the final vowel from a number and adding **-enne,** you can refer to a person of a certain age. A **diciottenne** is an 18-year-old; a **ventenne** is a 20-year-old.

Read the following numbers, paying close attention to the *musicality,* or the flow of sound, in each example.

> **ventotto**
>
> **trentuno**
>
> **cinquantuno**
>
> **sessantotto**
>
> **novantuno**
>
> **quarantotto**

Also, numbers ending in 3 require the use of an accent when written out. Thus, the number tre when added onto one of the tens becomes tré: ventitré, and so on.

One (**uno**) is the only cardinal number that agrees in number and gender with words it modifies. It works in the same way as the indefinite article (see Chapter 3 for a quick review).

> **un ragazzo** (*a boy*)
>
> **una ragazza** (*a girl*)
>
> **uno studente** (*a male student*)
>
> **una casa** (*a house*)
>
> **uno zio** (*an uncle*)
>
> **un'amica** (*a girl friend*)

Making sense of addresses

Like dates, which I discuss later in this chapter, Italian reverses the order of street numbers and zip codes from the typical pattern in English. In Italian, numbers *follow* street names and *precede* city names, so an address may read something like this:

Dott. Duilio Falcone

Via Verdi, 86

20000 Firenze (FI), Italia

But that's not the only thing that can make street addresses confusing in Italian. Sometimes, business addresses include a number and a color (such as **rosso,** or *red*), and residential numbers are followed by a different color (**blu,** or *blue,* for example). A street may have two buildings with the same number but with a color added. For example, **Via Verdi, 86blu** may indicate a residence; **Via Verdi, 86rosso** may indicate a store. These same numbers can be on different buildings, blocks apart, with only the color indicating the correct site.

Write out the numbers in parentheses, following the example.

Q. *(464)* _____

A. **quattrocentosessantaquattro**

1. *(1,947)* _____

2. *(31)* _____

3. *(212)* _____

4. *(19)* _____

5. *(5,612,423)* _____

6. *(88)* _____

7. *(966)* _____

8. *(23)* _____

9. *(6,298)* _____

10. *(861)* _____

Putting Things in Order: Ordinal Numbers

To express the order, placement, or sequence of things (such as first, fourth, and eighth), you use *ordinal numbers*. Unlike cardinal numbers, ordinal numbers agree in gender with the nouns or pronouns they modify. For more on modifying nouns and pronouns, see Chapter 5.

Table 4-2 lists examples of ordinal numbers in Italian. Note that for numbers one through ten, the ordinal numbers are irregular, meaning they do not follow the pattern of simply adding **-esimo** to their cardinal form. You'll have to memorize these.

From 11 to infinity, you form ordinal numbers by dropping the final vowel of cardinal numbers and adding **-esimo,** with stress on the **-e**. Here are some examples:

> **dodicesimo** (*12th*)
>
> **trentaquattresimo** (*34th*)
>
> **centesimo** (*100th*)

The only exception to this rule is a cardinal number that ends in **-tré**. In this case, you retain the final vowel, but the stress doesn't change:

> **ventitreesimo** (*23rd*)
>
> **cinquantatreesimo** (*53rd*)

Table 4-2	Ordinal Numbers
Number	*Italian*
First	**primo/prima**
Second	**secondo/seconda**
Third	**terzo/terza**
Fourth	**quarto/quarta**
Fifth	**quinto/quinta**
Sixth	**sesto/sesta**
Seventh	**settimo/settima**
Eighth	**ottavo/ottava**
Ninth	**nono/nona**
Tenth	**decimo/decima**
Eleventh	**undicesimo/undicesima**
Fifteenth	**quindicesimo/quindicesima**
Twentieth	**ventesimo/ventesima**
twenty-first	**ventunesimo/ventunesima**
twenty-third	**ventitreesimo/ventitreesima**
Thirtieth	**trentesimo/trentesima**
Sixtieth	**sessantesimo/sessantesima**
Hundredth	**centesimo/centesima**
Thousandth	**millesimo/millesima**
Millionth	**milionesimo/milionesima**

Here are several things to keep in mind when using ordinal numbers:

✔ You want to make sure the ordinal number that precedes a noun agrees in number and gender with that noun. For example:

È la quarta persona nella fila. (*He is the fourth person in line.*)

Questo è il nono figlio! (*This is the ninth son!*)

Prima donna (*first lady*)

I primi libri (*the first books*)

✔ To indicate something that has happened for the umpteenth time, you can use **ennesimo/ennesima.** Note that in the following example, **ennesima** is feminine and singular, as is the noun it modifies, **volta.**

È l'ennesima volta che me ne parla. (*It's the umpteenth time he has talked to me about it.*)

✔ To refer to someone whose title carries a number (such as a king like Henry II), you use Roman numerals in English and say, "Henry the Second." In Italian, you may also use a Roman numeral, but you don't use the article.

Enrico Secondo (*Henry the Second, Henry II*)

Carlo Quinto (*Charles the Fifth, Charles V*)

✔ You can abbreviate ordinal numbers by placing an **o** or an **a** in a raised, or superscript, position to agree in gender with what you're talking about. For example:

1° piano (*1st floor*)

5ª casa (*5th house*)

In the following sentences, fill in the blanks with the correct ordinal number in Italian. Use the spelled-out form of the number rather than the abbreviation. Remember to make the ordinal number agree in number and gender with the noun being modified. (To review number and gender, see Chapter 3.)

Q. il _____ libro (*first*)

A. primo

11. I _____ cugini (*first*)

12. La _____ attrice (*second*)

13. Il _____ edificio (*ninth*)

14. La _____ città (*fourth*)

15. La _____ settimana (*sixth*)

16. L'_____ volta (*umpteenth*)

17. Il _____ cliente (*millionth*)

18. La _____ **casa** (*thousandth*)

19. Le _____ **scene** (*first*)

20. L'_____ **libro** (*eleventh*)

Looking at the Calendar: Days, Months, and Seasons

In this day and age, to keep track of appointments or social events, for yourself and others, you need a calendar. To talk about when an event occurs or what date marks a special anniversary, you need to know the days of the week and months of the year in Italian. This section provides all the info you need to know to navigate the calendar and the seasons in Italian.

Days of the week

In English, you generally start naming the days of the week with Sunday, and you end the week with Saturday. In Italian, however, you begin with *Monday* (**lunedì**) and end with *Sunday* (**domenica**), which is how I organized the days of the week in Table 4-3. Note that in Italian, the days aren't capitalized as they are in English, unless they begin a sentence.

Table 4-3	Days of the Week
Italian	*English*
lunedì	*Monday*
martedì	*Tuesday*
mercoledì	*Wednesday*
giovedì	*Thursday*
venerdì	*Friday*
sabato	*Saturday*
domenica	*Sunday*

All the days except **domenica** (*Sunday*) are masculine. Using the definite article with the day names changes their meaning, a specific day to "every" one of those days. For example:

La domenica andavamo dalla nonna. (*Every Sunday, we used to go to Grandmother's.*)

Il lunedì vado a scuola. (*Every Monday, I go to school.*)

Il sabato non lavorano. (*They don't work on Saturdays.*)

Chiuso il mercoledì. (*Closed Wednesdays.*)

Months and seasons of the year

Being able to express the day will get you only so far; you also need to know the months of the year, which are listed in Table 4-4. As with days of the week, the months aren't capitalized in Italian.

Table 4-4	Months of the Year
Italian	*English*
gennaio	*January*
febbraio	*February*
marzo	*March*
aprile	*April*
maggio	*May*
giugno	*June*
luglio	*July*
agosto	*August*
settembre	*September*
ottobre	*October*
novembre	*November*
dicembre	*December*

To remember which months have 31, 30, or 28 (sometimes 29) days, this children's rhyme can help:

Trenta giorni ha settembre, (*Thirty days hath September,*)

Con aprile, giugno e novembre. (*With April, June, and November.*)

Di ventotto ce n'è uno. (*With twenty-eight days there is but one.*)

Tutti gli altri ne han trentuno. (*All the others have thirty-one.*)

Half of the seasons in Italian are feminine, and the other half are masculine. And, like the days of the week and months of the year, they are not capitalized.

- ✔ **La primavera** (*spring*)
- ✔ **L'estate** (*summer*)
- ✔ **L'autunno** (*fall, autumn*)
- ✔ **L'inverno** (*winter*)

To say *during the summer,* or *winter,* or whichever season, you say:

✔ **In estate** (*during the summer,* or *in the summer*)

✔ **In inverno** (*during the winter,* or *in the winter*)

Specific dates

In Italian, you use cardinal numbers to express a specific date, except for the first day of the month. For example:

Oggi è il primo settembre. (*Today is September 1st.*)

Domani sarà il secondo. (*Tomorrow is the 2nd.*)

Il mio compleanno è il quattro settembre. (*My birthday is September 4th.*)

Loro si sposano l'otto giugno. (*They are getting married June 8th.*)

Here are a few more specifics on how to note dates in Italian:

✔ The day and numbers always precede the name of the month.

Lunedì, 12 maggio, è il suo compleanno. (*Monday, May 12th, is his birthday.*)

Ma il suo onomastico è il 4 novembre. (*But his Saint's Day is November 4th.*)

✔ When you make a date or an appointment in Italian, as in English, you want to specify the day, the month, and the date. For example:

Domenica, undici maggio, vado a una festa. (*Sunday, May 11th, I'm going to a party.*)

✔ To add a year to a date, put it after the day, number, and month.

giovedì, il 4 settembre 1947 (*Thursday, September 4, 1947*)

l'undici ottobre 2006 (*October 11, 2006*)

To place something *in* a specific year, you use the contracted preposition **nel** (*in the*).

Luisa è nata nel 1983. (*Luisa was born in 1983.*)

Generally, you abbreviate dates in the same order you write them. In Italian, that means day/month/year. You write December 10, 2012, then, as **10/12/2012.** Sometimes, you may see the month written with a Roman numeral, such as **10/XII/2012.** Also, periods are often used instead of slashes: **10.XII.2012.**

To ask questions about dates, the following expressions may prove useful.

Che giorno è oggi? (*What day is today?*)

E domani? (*And tomorrow?*)

E ieri? (*And yesterday?*)

E l'altro ieri? (*And the day before yesterday?*)

E dopo domani? (*And the day after tomorrow?*)

Qual è la data? (*What is the date?*)

Quando è il tuo compleanno? (*When is your birthday?*)

Translate the dates below (and the events) into English. Here's an example.

Q. **festa, domenica, undici**

A. *party, Sunday the 11th*

21. **dentista, giovedì, quindici**

22. **cena da Mario, tre**

23. **concerto, trenta**

24. **lezione, sei**

25. **lezione, venti**

26. **il compleanno del babbo, primo**

27. **in ufficio, lunedì**

28. **veterinario, ventotto**

29. **caffè con Giorgio, nove**

30. **il cinema, ventiquattro**

Telling Time

After getting familiar with the numbers in Italian (see the earlier sections in this chapter), you can use them to tell time. For telling time, you need to be able to count to 60. To ask the time, you can say, **Che ora è?** or **Che ore sono?** (*What hour is it?* or *What hours?*) For 1:00, noon, or midnight, the answers are **È l'una, È mezzanotte, È mezzogiorno,** respectively. All other hours need **sono** before the hour(s), as shown in the following examples.

Che ora è?	***What time is it?***
Sono le due.	*It's 2:00.*
Sono le tre.	*It's 3:00.*
Sono le quattro.	*It's 4:00.*
Sono le cinque.	*It's 5:00.*
Sono le sei.	*It's 6:00.*

Che ora è?	*What time is it?*
Sono le sette.	*It's 7:00.*
Sono le otto.	*It's 8:00.*
Sono le nove.	*It's 9:00.*
Sono le dieci.	*It's 10:00.*
Sono le undici.	*It's 11:00.*
Sono le dodici.	*It's 12:00.*
È mezzogiorno.	*It's noon.*
È mezzanotte.	*It's midnight.*
È l'una.	*It's 1:00.*

If you're following the 24-hour clock, used for anything official — office hours; train, bus, plane arrivals and departures; or theater opening times — continue counting through ventiquattro. Thus, 5:00 in the morning remains le cinque, but, 5:00 in the afternoon becomes le diciassette. Another way to make clear the difference between morning and afternoon or evening is to add di mattina (a.m.) or del pomeriggio (early afternoon) or di sera (evening). These divisions are somewhat arbitrary: Mattina (morning) usually lasts until lunch; pomeriggio (afternoon), until 4:00 or 5:00 p.m.; and sera (evening), until one goes to bed.

One easy way to convert time is to subtract it from 12. 19.00-12.00 will give you 7, which is the time on the 12 hour clock.

When times are written numerically, Italian uses a period to separate the hour from the minutes, so the English *2:15* becomes **2.15.**

Here are a few other considerations to keep in mind when telling time in Italian:

✔ In general, you add the first 30 minutes of the hour to that hour.

> **Sono le due e dieci.** (*It's 2:10.*)

> **Sono le quattro e venti.** (*It's 4:20.*)

✔ You subtract the second half hour's minutes from the top of the hour.

> **Sono le dieci meno venti.** (*It's 9:40* or *It's 20 until 10.*)

✔ Instead of saying **quindici** (*15 minutes*), you can add on **un quarto** (*a quarter of an hour*).

> **Sono le cinque e un quarto.** (*It's 5:15.*)

✔ When referring to half past the hour, you can say **mezzo** (*half*) instead of **trenta** (*30*), although more and more, one hears **mezza** instead of **mezzo**, evidently referring to the feminine **ora.**

> **È l'una e mezzo.** (*It's 1:30.*)

✔ You may hear times that continue counting past 30 minutes and not simply with reference to the 24-hour clock.

> **Sono le due e quarantacinque.** (*It's 2:45.*)

✔ To ask at what time something is to happen, you say, **A che ora . . . ?** (*At what time . . .?*) The reply is **all'** (for **una**), **a** (for **mezzanotte** or **mezzogiorno**), or **alle** (all mean *at*) and a number. You can also say **verso le due** (*around two*), for example.

✔ When talking about time, you often make reference to something that has already happened, is about to happen, or will happen as a result of something else. To that end, the following expressions may prove useful.

> **Prima** (*first*): **Prima mangiamo.** (*First, we'll eat.*)
>
> **Poi** (*then*): **Poi andiamo.** (*Then we'll go.*)
>
> **Dopo** (*after*): **Dopo parleremo.** (*Afterward, we'll talk.*)
>
> **Fra** (*within*): **fra mezz'ora** (*within half an hour*)
>
> **Più tardi** (*later*): **Piu tardi vedremo loro.** (*Later, we'll see them.*)
>
> **A più tardi** (*Until later*)

✔ **Il mezzogiorno** (*noon, midday*) also refers to the southern regions of Italy, including the islands of Sicily and Sardinia. It's frequently used in publications (newspapers, magazines, and so forth) to refer to the area, approximately, south of Rome.

Write the following times in Italian, spelling out the numbers. Some will require the 24-hour clock.

Q. It's 2:14 a.m.

A. **Sono le due e quattordici di mattina.**

31. *It's noon.* _____

32. *It's 3:30 p.m.* _____

33. *It's 9:15 a.m.* _____

34. *It's 1:25 p.m.* _____

35. *It's 7:45 a.m.* _____

36. *At 2:20 p.m.* _____

37. *Around 6:00 p.m.* _____

38. *At 17:00 hours* _____

39. *It's 15 minutes after midnight.* _____

40. *It's 5:45 p.m.* _____

Chatting about the Weather

Talking about the weather in Italian is as easy as talking about it in English: Is it hot? Is it cold? Is it muggy? Is it raining? It's snowing. It's hailing. You can express a great deal about the weather by using one verb, impersonally: **fa** (Literally: *it makes* or *it does*). Here are some examples for how to answer the question, **Che tempo fa?** (*What's the weather like?*)

Fa caldo (statement or question depending on your intonation)

(*It's hot. Is it hot?*)

Sì, abbiamo 35 gradi! (*It's 35 degrees!*) (Celsius 35 = Fahrenheit 95.)

Fa freddo (statement or question depending on your intonation)

(*It's cold. Is it cold?*)

Fa un freddo orribile, -20! (*It's terribly cold*) (Celsius -20 = Fahrenheit 0.)

Fa fresco, fa freschino (statement or question depending on your intonation)

(*It's chilly, it's a little chilly. Is it chilly?*)

In the section "Familiarizing Yourself with the Metric System", you can find conversion equations for temperatures and weights and measures. Intonation, obviously, makes your comments about the weather statements or questions. The following simple words allow you to remark on the weather in any condition.

Piove. (*It's raining.*)

Tira vento. (*It's windy.*)

Lampeggia. (*It's lightning.*)

Tuona. (*It's thundering.*)

Nevica. (*It's snowing.*)

Grandina. (*It's hailing.*)

Che afa! (*It's muggy!*)

Fa bel tempo. (*It's beautiful.*)

Fa brutto tempo. (*It's nasty weather.*)

Familiarizing Yourself with the Metric System

If you're like most Americans, the metric system quite simply defeats you. The decimal system is practically hard-wired into U.S. residents. It's used almost exclusively, outside of scientific fields. So what do you really need to know about the metric system? The temperature would be nice. So would knowing how much of something to buy in the food market or at the gas station. If you're cooking, being able to convert oven temperatures may be useful. Likewise, knowing how to figure out the body's temperature is helpful.

To convert Fahrenheit to Centigrade, or Celsius, degrees, and Celsius to Fahrenheit, the following formula will suffice:

Fahrenheit degrees

Subtract 32

Remainder

Multiply by 0.556

Celsius degrees

So, for example, say you want to figure out how many Celsius degrees 100 degrees Fahrenheit is. Just plug the numbers into the formula to find the answer:

$$
\begin{array}{r}
100 \\
-32 \\
\hline
68 \\
\times 0.556 \\
\hline
37.7
\end{array}
$$

Then to convert Celsius degrees to Fahrenheit, you use this formula:

Celsius degrees

Add 17.8

Total

Multiply by 1.8

Fahrenheit degrees

Using the result of the earlier example, you can convert the Celsius degrees back to Fahrenheit like this:

$$
\begin{array}{r}
37.7 \\
+17.8 \\
\hline
55.5 \\
\times 1.8 \\
\hline
99.9
\end{array}
$$

This conversion works for oven temperatures (it's probably useful to know that the ever popular 350-degree Fahrenheit is about 180 degrees Celsius); for body temperatures (an Italian thermometer is normal when it reads 37 degrees Celsius); and for discussing the weather (38 degrees Celsius is *hot;* minus 20 degrees Celsius is way too cold to be out and walking about).

A dual scale (in grams and ounces) and dual measuring cups are invaluable as you try to cook with metric measures. As for weights and measures, a *kilogram* is about 2.2 pounds. At the market, if you're buying meats, fish, or cheeses and want about a pound, then a **mezzo chilo** (*half kilo*) should be about right. Loaves of bread tend to weigh about the same, a **mezzo chilo.**

Vegetables are a little harder to measure, and I recommend you use the old standby **una manciata, due manciate** (*a handful, two handfuls*). Remember that you're not the one picking out the vegetables and fruits; that is, you're not handling them. That is up to the greengrocer. You simply *do not touch* the fruit and vegetables on offer. For cold cuts, knowing that **un etto** equals 100 grams, or about 3.5 ounces, should be sufficient information. If you're especially hungry, **due etti di prosciutto crudo** (*200 grams,* or *7 ounces, of prosciutto*) is about right.

If you need to buy gasoline for your car (**benzina,** *not* **gas-olio,** which refers to *diesel fuel*), you need to know how to convert liters to gallons. One liter multiplied by 0.26420 equals about a quarter of a gallon. So four liters are a little more than a gallon. Close enough?

To convert miles into kilometers, multiply the number of miles by 1.60934. For example, if you want to drive 60 miles per hour, that will come out to 96.6 kilometers per hour on your speedometer. In other words, if something is 100 kilometers away, it's only a little more than 60 miles. Finally, to know whether your weight is holding steady, 1 pound is 0.4536 kilos. If you're used to weighing 180 pounds, it can be a bit of a shock to see your weight "drop" precipitously, to its kilo equivalent of 82.

Answer Key

1 millenovecentoquarantasette

2 trentuo

3 duecentododici

4 diciannove

5 cinquemilioneseicentododicimilaquattrocentoventitré

6 ottantotto

7 novecentosessantasei

8 ventitré

9 seimiladuecentonovantotto

10 ottocentosessantuno

11 primi

12 seconda

13 nono

14 quarta

15 sesta

16 ennesima

17 milionesimo

18 millesimo

19 prime

20 undicesimo

21 *dentist, Thursday the 15th*

22 *dinner at Mario's, the third*

23 *concert, the 30th*

24 *class, the 6th*

25 *class, the 20th*

26 *Dad's birthday, the first*

27 *at the office, Monday*

28 *veterinarian, the 28th*

29 *coffee with Giorgio, the 9th*

30 *movies, the 24th*

31 **È mezzogiorno**

32 **Sono le tre e mezza; sono le tre e trenta del pomeriggio.**

33 **Sono le nove e un quarto; sono le nove e quindici di mattina.**

34 **È l'una e venticinque del pomeriggio.**

35 **Sono le otto meno un quarto; sono le sette e quarantacinque di mattina.**

36 **Alle due e venti del pomeriggio.**

37 **Vero le sei di sera.**

38 **Alle diciassette ore.**

39 **È mezzanotte e un quarto; è mezzanotte e quindici.**

40 **Sono le cinque e quarantacinque; sono le sei meno un quarto di sera.**

Chapter 5

Adding Dimension and Description with Adjectives

*A*djectives add color to your Italian. You use them to describe and modify nouns and pronouns in a variety of ways. Instead of saying you just met someone, you can say you met a *dynamic, interesting, elegant* someone. You can vividly describe the world around you; for example, "It was a *dark* and *stormy* night" is certainly more interesting than just saying "it was nighttime." With adjectives, you can convey your opinions and feelings, positive or negative.

In this chapter, I introduce you to Italian adjectives and show you how to make them agree with the words they modify and where to place them in sentences. I also help you liven up your Italian by expressing opinions and being both literal and figurative in your descriptions.

Getting to Know Common Italian Adjectives

Italian has many adjectives, as does English. As you get familiar with common Italian adjectives, a great way to remember their meaning is to pair them with their opposite. That way, if you can't remember how to say something is *boring,* for example, you may remember to say instead that it *isn't interesting.* I once asked students to give me opposites of a series of adjectives, including **buono** (*good*) and **vecchio** (*old*); they dutifully wrote **non buono** and **non vecchio.** Although these words are opposites, they weren't quite what I had had in mind. Table 5-1 lists some of the more common adjectives, organized in pairs of opposites.

In Italian, all adjectives must match the nouns they modify in both gender and number. All the adjectives in Table 5-1 appear in the masculine singular form (which is how they show up in dictionaries), but I show you how to change the endings so the adjectives agree in number and gender with the words they modify in the later section "Matching gender and number."

Table 5-1	Common Italian Adjectives and Their Opposites		
Masculine Singular Adjective	*English Translation*	**Masculine Singular Adjective**	*English Translation*
alto	*tall*	basso	*short*
bello	*beautiful/ handsome*	brutto	*ugly*
bravo	*good*	cattivo	*bad*
buono	*good*	cattivo	*bad*
difficile	*hard*	facile	*easy*
felice	*happy*	triste	*sad*
giovane	*young*	vecchio	*old*
grande	*large*	piccolo	*small*
intelligente	*smart*	stupido	*stupid*
lungo	*long*	corto	*short*
nuovo	*new*	vecchio	*old*
ordinato	*organized*	disordinato	*disorganized*
magro	*thin*	grasso	*fat*
onesto	*honest*	disonesto	*dishonest*
pigro	*lazy*	dinamico	*dynamic*
responsabile	*responsible*	irresponsabile	*irresponsible*
ricco	*rich*	povero	*poor*
sensibile	*sensitive*	insensibile	*insensitive*
simpatico	*nice*	antipatico	*not nice*
serio	*serious*	spiritoso	*funny*
stesso	*same*	diverso	*different*
vero	*true*	falso	*false*

Note: **Grande** means *great,* in the sense of *important* or *terrific* (**un grande uomo/un grand'uomo** [*a great man*]), as well as *large.* If someone says to you **Sei grande!** he or she is telling you that you're *terrific.*

Colors and past participles are also adjectives, as are ordinal numbers (see Chapter 4). Here, I present these adjectives in their masculine singular form.

✔ Basic colors include

azzurro (*blue*)	**nero** (*black*)
bianco (*white*)	**rosa** (*pink*)
giallo (*yellow*)	**rosso** (*red*)
grigio (*gray*)	**verde** (*green*)

Rosa (*rose*) is actually a noun masquerading as an adjective, so it has only one form (which you use as masculine and feminine, singular and plural). I describe other nouns you can use as adjectives later in the section "Looking at invariable adjectives."

Some colors are so commonly associated with a particular product that they've come into the Italian vernacular as nouns. For example, **giallo** (*yellow*) means *detective stories or mysteries* because of the yellow color used for the covers on a line of these books.

✔ Past participles used as adjectives are as numerous as the verbs they come from. The most useful one is probably **preferito** (*preferred, favorite*). See Chapter 16 for the nitty-gritty details on past participles.

Using and Forming Italian Adjectives

To use adjectives correctly and to their fullest potential in Italian, you need to know a few rules.

Gender and number agreement between the adjective and the noun it modifies is important in Italian (something you don't have to worry about in English). Making this agreement between adjective and noun/pronoun requires some spelling changes to regular adjectives. I show you how to make those changes and when in this section.

I also give you a rundown on irregular adjectives and a group of other exception words that never change form — called *invariable adjectives*. And to make things even a bit more confusing, some suffixes can change the entire meaning of the adjective you use. But don't worry; I walk you through the nuances.

Matching gender and number

In Italian, adjectives must agree in number and gender with the nouns they modify, so they'll be singular or plural and masculine or feminine, depending on the word you're describing. (See Chapter 3 for an overview of number and gender.)

Italian has two types of adjectives: those ending in **-o** and those ending in **-e.**

✔ With Italian masculine singular adjectives ending in **-o,** you change the **-o** to **-i** to make it masculine plural, to **-a** to make it feminine singular, and to **-e** to make it feminine plural. For example, the adjective for *red* changes from **rosso** (masculine, singular) to **rossi** (masculine, plural) and from **rossa** (feminine, singular) to **rosse** (feminine, plural).

✔ Adjectives ending in **-e** stay the same for both masculine and feminine singular, but you change the **-e** to an **-i** for masculine and feminine plural. Each adjective ending in **-e,** therefore, has two forms: masculine and feminine singular (**un libro importante** [*an important book*] and **una donna importante** [*an important woman*]) and masculine and feminine plural (**due libri importanti** [*two important books*] and **due donne importanti** [*two important women*]).

Many adjectives that tell a person's nationality end in **-e** (and aren't capitalized as they are in English), including **inglese** (*English*), **francese** (*French*), **olandese** (*Dutch*), **portoghese** (*Portuguese*), **irlandese** (*Irish*), **cinese** (*Chinese*), and **giapponese** (*Japanese*).

If you're talking about a number of people or things that includes both feminine and masculine people or objects, you use the masculine plural form, such as **i ragazzi e le ragazze seri** (*the serious boys and girls*).

Forming regular adjectives

You need to make some spelling adjustments to adjectives, especially when forming plurals, to maintain pronunciation conventions. You make the same spelling changes, for the same reasons, with nouns (see Chapter 3). To maintain the sound of the singular adjective — for example, **simpatica** (*nice* [feminine, singular]) — you add an **h** to keep the hard sound of the **c** — **simpatiche** (*nice* [feminine, plural]). This spelling change happens most frequently with words that end in **-ca** and **-ga, -cia** and **-gia,** as you see throughout this section.

Adjectives ending in **-o** match the nouns they modify in number, gender, and even endings, for example: **il libro rosso** (*the red book* [masculine, singular]), **i libri rossi** (*the red books* [masculine, plural]), **la casa rossa** (*the red house* [feminine, singular]), and **le case rosse** (*the red houses* [feminine, plural]).

That sounds easy enough, right? Here are a few other rules that address spelling changes to follow when changing the **-o** and **-e** endings of regular adjectives from singular to plural:

✔ If a masculine singular adjective ends in **-io,** you simply drop the **-o** to make it plural, as in **grigio/grigi** (*gray*), **vecchio/vecchi** (*old*), and **serio/seri** (*serious*).

✔ If an adjective ends in **-go** or **-ga,** you add an **h** between the **g** and the ending vowel to maintain the hard *g* sound, like so: **lungo/lunghi** (*long* [masculine, singular/plural]) and **lunga/lunghe** (*long* [feminine, singular/plural]).

✔ For adjectives ending in **-co** or **-ca,** only the feminine form adds an **h** between the **c** and the ending vowel, as in **simpatica/simpatiche** (*nice*). The masculine form simply changes the **-o** to an **-i,** going from **simpatico** to **simpatici,** and the **c** makes a soft sound. (Chapter 2 gives an overview of Italian sounds and pronunciation.) The spelling, however, depends on the stress (accentuation) of the word being used as an adjective. **Simpatico** has a "backed-up" accent — that is, the accent is on the third-to-last syllable, so you stress the **a.** The plural is **simpatici. Tedesco** (*German*), however, carries the normal second-to-last syllable accentuation, and its plural is **tedeschi.**

Choose adjectives from the word bank that agree in number and gender with the nouns and that make sense. You may have more than one answer in some cases. Occasionally, you may have to look at the article accompanying the noun to figure out gender.

alta	grandi
bello	importante
brutta	nuove
buone	piccoli
difficile	pigri

Q. l'università

A. difficile, brutta, importante

1. i ragazzi _____

2. le bimbe _____

3. Giuliano è _____

4. le scuole _____

5. gli insegnanti _____

6. i gatti _____

7. le camere da letto _____

8. le amiche _____

9. la madre _____

10. la foto _____

Using irregular adjectives

You find relatively few irregular adjectives in Italian. The most common ones are **buono** (*good*), **santo** (*saint*), and **bello** (*beautiful, handsome*). In English, you don't need to worry about irregular adjectives because you don't change adjectives according to number and gender and because you frequently omit definite articles (you say *time flies,* not *the time flies*).

Because the Italian irregular adjectives **buono, santo,** and **bello** usually come before the nouns they're modifying (find out more about adjective placement in the later section "Putting Adjectives in Their Proper Place"), they not only agree in number and gender with the words they're modifying, but they also adapt themselves to the beginning letter of that word. The closest practice to this in English is that you say *an* elephant but *a* big elephant. You form the articles *a* or *an* according to the beginning of the following word (if it begins with a vowel sound, you use *an*). (See Chapter 13 for demonstrative adjectives, which follow the same pattern that I describe here.) For example, in Italian you use indefinite articles to say **un libro** (*a book*) but **uno student** (*a male student*); **una casa** (*a house*) but **un'elefante** (*an elephant* [female]).

Buono (*good*) follows this same spelling pattern that the articles do, depending on whether a singular word is masculine or feminine. Here are examples:

> **buona casa** (*good house*)
>
> **buon'insalata** (*good salad*)
>
> **buon libro** (*good book*)
>
> **buono stato** (*good state*)

Note: The plural forms of **buono** (**buoni, buone**) don't change their spellings: **buone case** (*good houses*), **buoni ragazzi** (*good boys*).

Santo (*saint*) follows a pattern like that of **buono,** as you can see here:

Santa Caterina	Santo Stefano
Sant'Anna	Sant'Ambrogio
Sante Caterina ed Anna	Santi Stefano ed Ambrogio

Note that sometimes Santa and Santo are abbreviated as Sta or S^{to}.

With **bello,** instead of imitating the indefinite articles, you follow the pattern of definite articles (see Chapter 3). Here are some examples:

Definite Article	*Form of Bello*	*Example*
il	**bel**	**bel libro** (*beautiful book*)
lo	**bello**	**bello studente** (*handsome student*)
l'	**bell'**	**bell'edificio** (*beautiful building*)
i	**bei**	**bei libri** (*beautiful books*)
gli	**begli**	**begli studenti** (*handsome students*)
la	**bella**	**bella donna** (*beautiful woman*)
l'	**bell'**	**bell'amica** (*beautiful friend*)
le	**belle**	**belle donne** (*beautiful women*)

Fill in the appropriate forms of **buono, santo,** or **bello** in the following phrases. Remember to make **buono, santo,** or **bello** agree in number and gender with the word being modified.

0. (santo) _____ Clemente

A. San

11. (buono) _____ giorno

12. (bello) _____ abiti

13. (santo) _____ Apostoli

14. (buono) _____ studentessa

15. (bello) _____ montagne

16. (bello) _____ giornata

17. (buono) _____ anno

18. (santo) _____ Elisabetta

19. (**bello**) _____ **ragazzi**

20. (**buono**) _____ **notte**

The other common form of irregular adjectives ends in the letter **-a,** such as **egoista** (*egotistical*), **ottimista** (*optimistic*), **pessimista** (*pessimistic*), **razzista** (*racist*), **realista** (*realistic*), and **idealista** (*idealistic*). These adjectives have one form for masculine and feminine singular, as you see here:

> **un uomo realista** (*a realistic man*)
>
> **una persona ottimista** (*an optimistic person*)
>
> **un signore egoista** (*an egotistical man*)

When you make these adjectives plural, you change the **-a** to either an **-i** (masculine) or an **-e** (feminine), like so:

> **due uomini realisti** (*two realistic men*)
>
> **due persone ottimiste** (*two optimistic persons*)
>
> **due signori egoisti** (*two egotistical men*)

Looking at invariable adjectives

Some adjectives never change. If they have only one syllable, such as **blu** (*blue*), you use the same form to modify masculine, feminine, singular, and plural nouns, as in these examples: **un libro blu** (*a blue book*), **una casa blu** (*a blue house*), **due libri blu** (*two blue books*), and **due case blu** (*two blue houses*). Unfortunately, these adjectives are relatively rare.

More common are adjectives that aren't really adjectives; they're nouns, masquerading as adjectives. A true adjective can change, in English and in Italian. It can follow the verbs *to be* or *to seem,* like so: *A tall child. A taller child. The child is tall. The child seems taller.*

If you replace *tall* with a noun acting as an adjective (*school*, for example), you see that you can't change such an adjective or use it after *to be* or *to seem: A school child. A schooler child. The child is school. The child seems schooler.*

Still, nouns do serve as adjectives. They simply maintain their form with any noun, masculine or feminine, singular or plural, that they modify. Some examples include **limone** (*lemon, lemon-colored*), **marrone** (*chestnut, brown*), and **arancio** (*orange tree, orange-colored*), and **rosa** (*rose, rose-colored, pink*).

Adding adjectival suffixes to nouns and adjectives

Adding adjectival suffixes to nouns is common practice in Italian. No hard or fast rule exists for adding suffixes, and the use of them varies regionally. They tend to be informal and colloquial.

Such adjectival suffixes can appear a little strange to the English speaker, for example, **ti vedrò fra mezz'oretta** (*I'll see you in a dear little half hour*). You'd more likely say *scarcely a half hour* or even *about a half hour,* but you probably wouldn't make the half hour both *small and dear.*

Adjectives in all forms (as discrete words or as suffixes) agree in number and gender with the words they modify. Thus, they have one of four endings: **-o** (masculine, singular), **-i** (masculine, plural), **-a** (feminine, singular), and **-e** (feminine, plural).

Here, I list the most common adjectival suffixes used with Italian nouns, their meanings, and some examples:

- ✔ **-ino:** You use **-ino** to reduce the size or importance of things. You may give someone what you call a **regalino** (*a little present*), a way to downplay the gift. In English, you can say *Oh, it's nothing, really* and get the same effect. If you're watching the opera *La Bohème,* you hear Rodolfo refer to Mimi's **manina** (*little hand*). The suffix **–ina** makes the hand small and delicate.

- ✔ **-one:** You use **-one** to add size and substance. For example, **una minestra** is a simple *soup;* **un minestrone** is a little more substantial, including more ingredients.

  The suffix **-one** can also change a word's gender; for example, if **una donna** (*a lady*) is especially large, she may be called **un donnone** (*a large woman* [but now a masculine noun]). You may notice that **minestrone** undergoes the same gender change; **donnone** is perhaps just a little more startling.

- ✔ **-etto:** This suffix makes something little. The best-known example in Italian has to be the modified form of **spaghi** (*strings*), or **spaghetti** (*little strings, spaghetti*).

- ✔ **-issimo:** Adding **-issimo** is another way to add *very* to an adjective. For example, **bravissimo** means *very good,* as in **la ragazza è bravissima** (*the girl is very good*). Technically, **-issimo** is an adverb (see Chapter 15 for more details on how this suffix works), but because it attaches to adjectives, I include it in this list.

- ✔ **-uccio:** This suffix is usually positive, implying a dearness or affection for something or someone. For example, **Carluccio** is *little, sweet Carlo.*

- ✔ **-accio:** This suffix is definitely *not* positive, because you use it to denigrate something or someone. For example, **un dottore** (*a doctor*) as **un dottoraccio** becomes *a quack,* and **un ragazzo** (*a boy*) as **un ragazzaccio** becomes *a brat* or *a bad boy.*

Occasionally, suffixes change a word's meaning entirely: If you wrote Mimi's **manine** (*little hands*) as **manette,** it becomes *handcuffs.* I recommend using suffixes cautiously until you're sure they don't change a word's meaning entirely.

Putting Adjectives in Their Proper Place

In English, you place adjectives before the noun they're modifying; in Italian, you usually place them after. *A red house* thus becomes **una casa rossa** (Literally: *a house red*). But don't get too comfortable: There are exceptions to this rule, which I discuss throughout this chapter. (See also Chapter 13 for where to place possessive, demonstrative, and indefinite adjectives.)

Adjectives can move around in two instances. When adjectives move — that is, when they don't directly follow the noun they modify — they can change meaning.

The first instance occurs when you use the *BAGS* adjectives; that is, those that deal with *b*eauty, *a*ge, *g*oodness, and *s*ize. Here are a few examples, paired with their opposites for easier reference:

- ✔ **piccolo** (*small*), **grande** (*large*)
- ✔ **vecchio** (*old*), **giovane** (*young*)
- ✔ **vecchio** (*old*), **nuovo** (*new*)
- ✔ **bello** (*beautiful*), **brutto** (*ugly*)
- ✔ **bravo** (*good*), **cattivo** (*bad*)
- ✔ **buono** (*good*), **cattivo** (*bad*)
- ✔ **vero** (*true*), **falso** (*false*)
- ✔ **lungo** (*long*), **corto** (*short*) [horizontal]
- ✔ **alto** (*tall*), **basso** (*short*) [vertical]
- ✔ **caro** (*dear*) [both sweet and expensive]

If you say **una bella donna** (*a beautiful woman*), you're talking about beauty. You discuss age with **un giovane ragazzo** (*a young boy*), goodness with **un bravo studente** (*a good student*), and size with **un piccolo bambino** (*a small child*). In each case, the adjective precedes the noun being described.

Placing these adjectives so they precede or follow a noun determines whether you're speaking literally or figuratively. If you're describing someone literally as *old* or *tall,* you say **un amico vecchio** or **un uomo alto.** But if you're using the adjectives figuratively, **un vecchio amico** becomes someone you've known for a long time. **Un professore alto** is a professor who is *tall;* **un alto professore** is *highly placed,* or *important.* **Un caro amico** is a *dear* friend; **un amico caro** may be high maintenance.

Because adjectives that generally precede a noun can take on a figurative meaning when placed there, context becomes all important. The adjectives don't necessarily change their meaning, so context determines the meaning.

If you modify the adjective with, say, the word *very* (**molto**), then the adjective must follow the noun you're describing, for example, **una donna molto bella** (*a very beautiful woman*). Note that **molto** is an adverb, modifying the adjective **bella,** and it doesn't change. (See Chapter 15 for more on adverbs.)

The use of adjectival suffixes skirts the question of where to place adjectives because they attach to the end of the nouns they modify. See the earlier section "Adding adjectival suffixes to nouns and adjectives."

Place the adjective in parentheses either before or after the noun it modifies.

Q. (tedesco) ragazzo

A. ragazzo tedesco

21. (piccola) scuola

   _____

22. (interessante) libro

   _____

23. (grande) casa

   _____

24. (francesi) studenti

   _____

25. (care) gatte

   _____

26. (intelligente) donna

   _____

27. (simpatico) zio

   _____

28. (alto) edificio

   _____

29. (blu) macchina

   _____

30. (preferito) film

   _____

Answer Key

1 piccoli, grandi, pigri

2 buone

3 bello, difficile, importante

4 grandi, buone

5 piccoli, grandi pigri

6 piccoli, grandi, pigri

7 nuove, buone

8 nuove, buone

9 difficile, brutta, alta

10 difficile, brutta

11 buon

12 begli

13 santi

14 buona

15 belle

16 bella

17 buon

18 Santa

19 bei

20 buona

21 **piccola scuola**

22 **libro interessante**

23 **grande casa**

24 **studenti francesi**

25 **care gatte** (*sweet cats, expensive cats*)

26 **donna intelligente**

27 **zio simpatico**

28 **edificio alto**

29 **macchina blu**

30 **film preferito**

Part II

Forming Simple Sentences and Asking Questions

The Italian Alphabet

Italian Letter	Name of Letter	Italian Letter	Name of Letter
A	a	N	enne
B	bi	O	o
C	ci	P	pi
D	di	Q	cu
E	e	R	erre
F	effe	S	esse
G	gi	T	ti
H	acca	U	u
I	i	V	vu
L	elle	Z	zeta
M	emme		

Letters "Borrowed" from Other Languages

Letter	Name of Letter
J	i lungo
K	kappa
W	doppia vu
X	ics
Y	ipsilon

Find out ways to improve your Italian language skills at home (or in your supermarket) at www.dummies.com/extras/italiangrammar.

In this part . . .

✔ Discover how to express what you're doing, how you got some-where, how you're feeling, what you're thinking, and any other action you can imagine by using verbs. Understand how to con-jugate verbs — both regular verbs and their trickier irregular counterparts — to express who did something and when.

✔ Use pronouns — *he, she, him, her,* and so on — to replace nouns so your sentences don't become cumbersome and repetitive.

✔ Figure out how to connect verbs with their objects (or the person/thing doing the action). Also reflect back on the subject with reflexive verbs, such as *I wash myself.*

✔ Take your language beyond the basics by mastering ways to share your likes and dislikes, ask and respond to questions, and make requests. Look at ways to be commanding, inquisitive, and revealing in Italian to help you bridge the gap between merely communicating and becoming more like yourself in a new language.

Chapter 6

Jumping into Action with Italian Regular Verbs

In This Chapter

▶ Understanding how regular verbs work in Italian

▶ Conjugating regular verbs in the present indicative sense

▶ Building simple and compound sentences with regular verbs

*V*erbs bring language to life. Without them, you can't tell, question, evaluate, or comment. You can't share how you *enjoy learning* Italian. Verbs reflect actions, whether they're immediate, ongoing, or habitual. You use verbs to talk about what you've done, what you hope to do, and where you've been. Verbs let you state facts — and opinions, for that matter. In short, without using verbs, you can't fully express yourself in Italian or in any other language.

Verbs have many forms; you have to know how to say a verb, such as *eat,* in the present tense (I eat), the past tense (I ate), and the future tense (I will eat). Expressing a verb in various tenses is called *conjugation.* With some verbs, the rules for conjugation are always the same. For example, in English, you simply add *-ed* to the end of many verbs to express them in the past tense. Verbs that follow these rules are called *regular* verbs. Verbs that don't follow these rules are called *irregular* verbs, which I discuss in Chapter 7.

In this chapter, I look at Italian regular verbs and how to conjugate them so you can avoid being "all words and no action" in the past, present, and future. Here, you discover that Italian and English are remarkably similar in their use of verbs, and that, thankfully, Italian has more regular verbs than English.

Conjugating Regular Verbs in Italian

Italian verbs are categorized by type, according to their *infinitive* form — a verb's most basic form. In English, an infinitive is always preceded by *to* (to be, to do, to read). In its infinitive form, a verb has no subject and isn't conjugated. When you discover a new verb in Italian, you realize this "raw" form. To use the verb effectively, you need to understand the rules of conjugation.

To start, look at some infinitives. The three major types of Italian infinitives end in **-are, -ere,** and **-ire,** with the majority ending in **-are,** followed by **-ere** and then **-ire.** Here are some examples.

> **parlare** (*to speak*)
>
> **scrivere** (*to write*)
>
> **dormire** (*to sleep*)

A small number of verbs end in **-orre, -urre,** and **-arre,** such as **proporre** (*to propose*), **tradurre** (*to translate*), and **attrarre** (*to attract*). I don't discuss these in detail here because they are not very commonly used. Since **-are, -ere,** and **-ire** verbs make up a dominant proportion of Italian verbs, I focus on those instead. See Chapter 7 for an overview of the **-orre, -urre,** and **-arre** verbs.

To conjugate verbs, you need to know who or what the subject is. The subject tells you what to add to the verb *stem,* which you get by removing the identifying **-are, -ere,** or **-ire.** For example, the stem of **parlare** is **parl.**

To this stem, you add endings that are determined by the subject. Each subject, or subject pronoun, calls for a specific ending. For example: **io** means that you add an **o** to the verb stem: **io parlo,** or *I am speaking.* **Noi** (*we*) wants the ending **-iamo,** as in **Noi mangiamo** (*We eat*). While in English you can't say just *speaking* or *eating,* without naming the subject, in Italian the endings **o** and **iamo** tell you what the subject is. In a sense, the subject pronouns are redundant in Italian.

English also has a different verb ending depending on the subject. For example, *I eat, you eat, he/she/it eats.* But you must state the subject. Here is a list of Italian subject pronouns with their English equivalents (I discuss Italian subject pronouns in more detail in the later sections on individual verbs).

- **io** (*I*)
- **tu** (*you,* singular informal)
- **lui** (*he, it*)
- **lei** (*she, it; you,* singular formal)
- **noi** (*we; you,* plural informal)
- **loro** (*they,* masculine)
- **loro** (*they,* feminine)
- **loro** (*you,* plural formal)

In the following sections, I explain how to conjugate (or change the endings that attach to the stem) each verb type according to the subject pronoun that accompanies it.

Sometimes you can get away with using the infinitive form, when it follows a different conjugated verb. For more on how that works, see the section "Communicating quickly with verbs," later in this chapter.

Conjugating -are verbs

This largest category of Italian verbs is wonderfully dependable — and mostly regular in conjugation. A few **-are** verbs have pronunciations that are a bit different; they have the so-called **accento sdrucciolo** (*slippery accent*). Later in this section I show you their pronunciation peculiarities.

To conjugate or use an **-are** verb, first you remove the letters **-are** from the infinitive, which leaves you with the stem:

> infinitive: **parlare**
>
> stem: **parl**

To the stem, you add the endings (**-o, -i, -a, -iamo, -ate, -ano**) that reflect the subject (**io, tu, lui, lei, Lei, noi, voi, loro, Loro**). The following table shows a sample conjugation.

parlare (to speak)	
io parl**o**	**noi** parl**iamo**
tu parl**i**	**voi** parl**ate**
lui, lei, Lei parl**a**	**loro, Loro** parl**ano**

All regular **-are** verbs (the vast majority of them, in other words) follow this pattern of conjugation in the present tense. The subject pronouns and corresponding endings, then, are as follows: **io = o; tu = i; lui, lei, Lei = a; noi = iamo; voi = ate; loro, Loro = ano**.

Here are some of the more commonly used **-are** verbs. I use them throughout this book so you'll become accustomed to them. Each of these verbs follows the conjugation pattern just described for **-are** verbs.

- **abbracciare** (*to hug*)
- **abitare** (*to live*)
- **ascoltare** (*to listen*)
- **aspettare** (*to wait for*)
- **baciare** (*to kiss*)
- **ballare** (*to dance*)
- **cercare** (*to look for*)
- **cominciare** (*to begin*)
- **comprare** (*to buy*)
- **comunicare** (*to communicate*)
- **frequentare** (*to attend*)
- **giocare (a)** (*to play a sport or a game*)
- **guardare** (*to look at*)
- **guidare** (*to drive*)
- **imparare** (*to learn*)
- **incontrare** (*to meet, to encounter, to run into*)
- **indicare** (*to indicate*)
- **insegnare** (*to teach*)
- **inviare** (*to send*)
- **lavorare** (*to work*)
- **mangiare** (*to eat*)
- **negare** (*to deny*)
- **pagare** (*to pay for*)
- **parlare** (*to talk, to speak*)
- **pensare** (*to think*)
- **portare** (*to wear, to carry*)
- **ritornare** (*to return*)
- **salutare** (*to greet*)
- **sciare** (*to ski*)
- **spiegare** (*to explain*)
- **studiare** (*to study*)
- **suonare** (*to play a musical instrument*)
- **telefonare (a)** (*to call on the phone*)
- **visitare** (*to visit*)

Several verbs have built-in prepositions. **Pagare,** for example, means *to pay for,* without adding an additional preposition to the verb. **Aspettare** (*to wait for*), likewise, needs no additional preposition; **Io aspetto la posta.** (*I'm waiting for the mail.*) **Cercare** (*to look for*) follows the same pattern: **Lui cerca le chiavi.** (*He is looking for the keys.*)

Conjugate the verbs in parentheses so they reflect the subject. Refer to the earlier list of verbs for help. Follow the example.

Q. Io _____ (ascoltare) la radio.

A. ascolto

1. Noi _____ (abitare) in una vecchia casa.

2. Tu _____ (frequentare) una scuola molto famosa.

3. Loro _____ (insegnare) le lingue.

4. Lui _____ (imparare) molto.

5. Lei _____ (aspettare) un tassì.

6. Guido _____ (portare) sempre una cravatta.

7. Voi _____ (ritornare) tardi?

8. Loro _____ (parlare) spesso.

9. Angelo _____ (guidare) una macchina molto elegante.

10. Voi due _____ (ballare) assai bene.

Verbs ending in -care and -gare

To maintain the sound of the **-are** infinitives in their conjugated forms, you find a few verbs, specifically, those ending in **-care** and **-gare,** that require some spelling changes.

Instead of simply adding subject endings to the stems of the **tu** and **noi** forms, you need to insert the letter **h** to keep the hard *c* or *g* sound. For more on the why and when of making hard or soft consonant sounds, see Chapter 2.

The following tables show conjugations of **-care** and **-gare** verbs that have spelling changes.

cercare (to look for)	
io cerco	noi cerchiamo
tu cerchi	voi cercate
lui, lei, Lei cerca	loro, Loro cercano

pagare (to pay for)	
io pago	noi paghiamo
tu paghi	voi pagate
lui, lei, Lei paga	loro, Loro pagano

Other verbs with the **-care** and **-gare** endings include **comunicare** (*to communicate*), **giocare** (*to play a game or sport*), **indicare** (*to indicate, to point out*), **criticare** (*to criticize*), **negare** (*to deny*), and **spiegare** (*to explain*).

Conjugate the **-care** and **-gare** verbs in parentheses according to the subject pronouns in the following sentences. Follow the example.

Q. **Pago io o _____ (pagare) tu?**

A. **paghi**

11. **Noi _____ (cercare) il museo.**

12. **Tonio _____ (giocare) a calico ogni giorno.**

13. **Tu _____ (negare) questo?**

14. **La professoressa _____ (spiegare) tutto.**

15. **Noi _____ (pagare) oggi.**

16. **Lui _____ (criticare) tutto.**

17. **Tu _____ (indicare) la strada?**

18. **Tu, cosa _____ (cercare)?**

19. **Loro non _____ (comunicare) con il pubblico.**

20. **Tu _____ (giocare) a pallavolo?**

Verbs ending in -iare

In the interests of maintaining the sound of the **-are** infinitive, you make some spelling changes to verbs that end in **-care** and **-gare** and also those that end in **-iare**. These changes make the conjugated forms sound the way the infinitive does.

Some of the more common verbs ending in **-iare** include **cominciare** (*to begin*), **mangiare** (*to eat*), **abbracciare** (*to hug*), **baciare** (*to kiss*), and **studiare** (*to study*).

Dropping the **-are** from the infinitive leaves you with the letter **i** on the end of the stem. You don't want a double **i** in your conjugation, so the **tu** and **voi** forms drop the **i** from the stem. All the other forms keep it.

The following tables show the conjugated forms of **-iare** verbs.

cominciare (to begin)	
io comincio	noi cominciamo
tu cominci	voi cominciate
lui, lei, Lei comincia	loro, Loro cominciano

mangiare (to eat)	
io mangio	noi mangiamo
tu mangi	voi mangiate
lui, lei, Lei mangia	loro, Loro mangiano

studiare (to study)	
io studio	noi studiamo
tu studi	voi studiate
lui, lei, Lei studia	loro, Loro studiano

Usually, you drop the **i** from the **tu** and **noi** stems, unless the **i** is stressed: **comíncio**, **mángio**, **stúdio**. Compare those stressed syllables with **invío** and **scío**. If the stress or accent falls on the **i** in the **tu** form, then you keep the extra letter. Thus, the **tu** form of **inviare** is **invii**, and the **tu** form of **sciare** is **scii**. Note that this doesn't apply to the **noi** form because the stress doesn't fall on the **i.**

On these same lines, some **-are** verbs undergo a pronunciation change and use the **accento sdrucciolo** (*slippery accent*). This means that instead of stressing the second to the last syllable on the singular conjugations, or the third to the last on the third person plural, you back the stress up by one syllable. Thus **abito** has a stressed **a.** Here is a sample conjugation of such a verb, with the stressed syllable in bold face type. The **noi** and **voi** forms follow regular rules of pronunciation and stress the second to the last syllable.

Io **a**bito	noi abitiamo
Tu **a**biti	voi abitate
Lui, lei, Lei **a**bita	loro, Loro **a**bitano

Common verbs that carry this particular stress include **telefonare** (*to call*), **terminare** (*to end*), **preoccupare** (*to worry*), **partecipare** (*to participate*), **desiderare** (*to want*), **significare** (*to mean*), and **ordinare** (*to order*). There is no way you can predict which verbs use this stress. It truly is something you learn as you go.

Keeping pronunciation in mind, fill in the correctly spelled conjugation, according to the subject pronoun of the following verbs. Use the example as a guide.

Q. Io _____ (mangiare) molto.

A. mangio

21. Tu _____ (cominciare).

22. Voi _____ (cambiare).

23. Noi _____ (mangiare).

24. Io _____ (studiare).

25. Lui _____ (cercare).

26. Noi _____ (sciare).

27. Tu _____ (inviare).

28. Noi _____ (pagare).

29. Loro _____ (studiare).

30. Lei _____ (indicare).

Conjugating -ere verbs

The second largest category of Italian verb conjugations is as dependable as the first. The **-ere** verbs strictly follow the path of removing **-ere** from the infinitive and adding the subject endings specific to the conjugation. You have no spelling changes to remember here because only the **-are** verbs maintain the pronunciation of the infinitive. The following tables show the various ending for **-ere** verbs.

scrivere (to write)	
io scrivo	noi scriviamo
tu scrivi	voi scrivete
lui, lei, Lei scrive	loro, Loro scrivono

leggere (to read)	
io leggo	noi scriviamo
tu leggi	voi leggete
lui, lei, Lei legge	loro, Loro leggono

Notice that **leggere** in its conjugations has different sounds, some of which are *not* true to the sound of the infinitive. The **io** and **loro** forms both have a hard *g* sound, while all the other forms keep the soft *g* of the infinitive. For more on basic pronunciation, check out Chapter 2.

Because **-ere** verbs derive from two Latin conjugations, the infinitives may not follow the general Italian rule of placing stress on the next-to-last syllable. Compare the following infinitives' pronunciations. I indicate where the stress falls by adding accents. Many **-ere** verbs use the *slippery accent* (**accento sdrucciolo**), so the accent falls on the third-to-the-last syllable.

- ✔ **chiédere** (*to ask*)
- ✔ **chiúdere** (*to close*)
- ✔ **conóscere** (*to know a person or place, to be acquainted with*)
- ✔ **crédere** (*to believe*)
- ✔ **léggere** (*to read*)
- ✔ **préndere** (*to take, to eat, to drink*)
- ✔ **ripétere** (*to repeat*)
- ✔ **rispóndere** (*to reply*)
- ✔ **scrívere** (*to write*)
- ✔ **véndere** (*to sell*)
- ✔ **vívere** (*to live*)

Conjugate the verbs in parentheses according to the subject pronouns, as shown in the example.

Q. Mario _____ (leggere) molto.

A. legge

31. Io _____ (scrivere) cartoline agli amici.

32. Noi _____ (vivere) ad Arezzo.

33. Tu _____ (prendere) thè o caffè?

34. Lui _____ (chiudere) la porta.

35. Loro _____ (vendere) frutta e verdura.

36. Voi _____ (vedere) quello?

37. Mirella _____ (rispondere) subito.

38. Gli studenti _____ (ripetere) le parole.

39. Lei _____ (credere) di sì.

40. Noi _____ (prendere) sempre l'autobus numero 7a.

Conjugating -ire verbs

Although **-ire** verbs follow pronunciation rules reliably, they have a different surprise in store — they come in two types: The first is a regular, normal Italian verb, such as **dormire** (*to sleep*); the second is known as an **-isc** verb because all the conjugated forms, except for **noi** and **voi,** insert the letters **-isc** between the stem and the endings.

Compare the following conjugations.

dormire (to sleep)	
io dorm**o**	noi dorm**iamo**
tu dorm**i**	voi dorm**ite**
lui, lei, Lei dorm**e**	loro, Loro dorm**ono**

capire (isc) (to understand)	
io cap**isco**	noi capiamo
tu cap**isci**	voi capite
lui, lei, Lei cap**isce**	loro, Loro cap**iscono**

How do you know which verbs take **-isc** in their conjugation? You don't. You have to refer to the dictionary, which shows the conjugation right after the infinitive. I show you in this book by putting **-isc** after those infinitives that use it. The best thing is to memorize the most commonly used **-isc** verbs from the get-go. Only a few will be useful at this point, and they include the following:

- ✔ **capire (isc)** (*to understand*)
- ✔ **finire (isc)** (*to finish*)
- ✔ **preferire (isc)** (*to prefer*)
- ✔ **guarire (isc)** (*to heal*)
- ✔ **garantire (isc)** (*to guarantee*)
- ✔ **punire (isc)** (*to punish*)
- ✔ **pulire (isc)** (*to clean*)

Spedire (*to send*) is an **-isc** verb, but you can use the regular **-are** verbs **mandare** or **inviare** to mean the same thing. Other **-isc** verbs are truly arcane. **Barrire** is one of them. It means *to trumpet* (or to make the noise that elephants make, as in **Gli elefanti barriscono.** *The elephants trumpet/The elephants make elephant noises.*). **Garrire** is another, which means to *make a strident bird noise* (as in **Le rondini garriscono.** *The swallows are making their strident bird noise.*). However, these verbs will unlikely be a big part of your everyday vocabulary.

Here are the most common **-ire** verbs (without **-isc**):

- ✔ **dormire** (*to sleep*)
- ✔ **aprire** (*to open*)
- ✔ **partire** (*to leave, to depart*)
- ✔ **seguire** (*to follow*)
- ✔ **sentire** (*to hear, to feel*)
- ✔ **mentire** (*to lie*)
- ✔ **coprire** (*to cover*)

As there were fewer **-ere** verbs than **-are** verbs, so there are even fewer **-ire** verbs.

Conjugate the verbs in parentheses according to the subject, as shown in the example. Try to remember which ones take **-isc**, but look back at the list of **-ire (isc)** verbs if you need a reminder.

Q. Io non _____ (capire).

A. capisco

41. Tu _____ (sentire) qualcosa?

42. Riccardo _____ (dormire) fino a tardi.

43. Noi _____ (aprire) i libri.

44. Loro _____ (finire) le lezioni all'una.

45. Voi _____ (partire) domani, vero?

46. Francesca _____ (capire) sempre.

47. Loro _____ (seguire) gli altri.

48. Io _____ (preferire) i gatti ai cani.

49. Tu _____ (pulire) la casa il sabato, no?

50. Io non _____ (sentire) nulla.

After you figure out how to conjugate each of the three infinitive types, you immediately multiply your vocabulary by a factor of six — and that's just in the present tense.

Another element that multiplies your vocabulary exponentially comes with meanings in the present tense.

Parlo, for example, means *I speak, I do speak,* and *I am speaking.* You can use it to make statements or to ask questions. Still using **parlare**, the **tu** form, **parli**, can mean many things. **Parli italiano** is a statement: *You speak Italian. You are speaking Italian. You do speak Italian.* It can also be a question: *Do you speak Italian? Are you speaking Italian? You speak Italian?* All that comes in one five-letter word.

Moving Past the Present Tense

You can "get by" in a language by sticking to the present tense. With it, you can discuss what's actually happening: **Ora i bambini dormono.** (*Right now, the kids are sleeping.*) You can describe a permanent or continuing situation: **La mamma lavora senza sosta.** (*Mom works without stopping.*) To express something that's a given, you can say: **Il ristorante chiude il mercoledì.** (*The restaurant closes on Wednesdays.*)

You can even discuss the future, so long as it's the not too distant future and what you're talking about is a sure thing: **Questa settimana io lavoro ogni giorno.** (*This week I'm working every day.*) **Domani preparo il pollo.** (*Tomorrow, I'm fixing the chicken.*) **Ci vediamo domani.** (*We'll see each other tomorrow,* or *See you tomorrow.*)

Finally, you use the present after the preposition **da** (*from, since, by*) to express the English present progressive tense: **Abito qui da dieci anni.** (*I've been living here for ten years.*) **Marco studia l'inglese dal 2000.** (*Marco has been studying English since 2000.*)

Some conversational clues tell you that you can use the present tense, such as the following common words and phrases:

- ✔ **a mezzogiorno** (*at noon* or at any other specific time)
- ✔ **ogni giorno** (*every day*)
- ✔ **oggi** (*today*)
- ✔ **domani** (*tomorrow*)
- ✔ **stasera** (*this evening*)
- ✔ **mai** (*never*)
- ✔ **mai più** (*never again*)
- ✔ **sempre** (*always*)
- ✔ **il lunedì, il martedì . . .** (*Mondays, Tuesdays,* and so on)

When you tire of sounding like a precocious 4-year-old and are comfortable with the present tense, you can add in other tenses. (See Part IV of this book.)

Communicating quickly with verbs

No doubt you want to communicate in Italian, but maybe you feel that you don't yet have an adequate vocabulary. There's so much to remember. And verbs, the lifeline of any language, take work, practice, and patience.

Here are some verbs you can use to express yourself quickly and easily. As in English, they're followed by an infinitive. Rather than learning all the conjugations immediately, try these verbs, all of which are in the **io** conjugation, but not all of which are in the present tense, and attach infinitives that express your daily wants, needs, and actions. Remember that all are in the **io** form, so you can choose to use the subject pronoun or not.

- ✔ **preferisco** (*I prefer to*)

- ✔ **vorrei** (*I would like to*)

  Note: This isn't in the present tense; but it is much more polite than saying "I want."

- ✔ **mi piacerebbe** (*I would like to*)

  Again, in the interests of being polite, this isn't in the present tense.

- ✔ **devo** (*I must, I have to*)

- ✔ **posso** (*I am able to, I can*)

- ✔ **so, non so** (*I know how to, I don't know how to*)

- ✔ **ho bisogno di** (*I need to*)

- ✔ **ho voglia di** (*I feel like*)

- ✔ **sto per** (*I'm about to*)

Consider your daily movements. Which infinitives would you attach to these expressions? (If you need to, review the verbs already presented in this chapter.) Here are some examples:

Devo studiare. Mi piacerebbe guardare la televisione. Ma non posso. (*I have to study. I would like to watch television. But I can't.*)

So parlare italiano. Vorrei parlare italiano molto bene. Sto per studiare. Ma prima, vorrei mangiare e prendere un caffè. (*I know how to speak Italian. I would like to speak Italian really well. I'm about to study. But first, I'd like to eat and have a cup of coffee.*)

Posso ballare? No. Non so ballare. Posso cantare? No. Posso suonare uno strumento musicale? No. Ma posso scrivere belle poesie. (*Can I dance? No. I don't know how to dance. Can I sing? No. Can I play a musical instrument? No. But I can write nice poetry.*)

Ho voglia di andare al cinema. Vorrei vedere quel nuovo film di Benigni. Invece, devo lavorare. (*I feel like going to the movies. I'd like to see that new Benigni film. Instead, I have to work.*)

Sto per partire. Posso telefonare dopo? (*I'm about to leave. Can I call later?*)

Looking More Closely at Personal Subject Pronouns

Personal subject pronouns tell you who the subject of a verb is or who is completing an action. They also determine which form of a conjugated verb to use.

Italian formal *you* forms of address include the plural **loro**. But when addressing people, you often use **voi** instead.

In an attempt to make Italian more egalitarian, during the 1940s, the government abolished the distinction between the formal and informal singular forms and used **voi** instead. If someone addresses you (just you, one of you) as **voi**, it probably means that he or she is of an advanced age or is speaking "opera, where use of **voi** is ubiquitous.

Because verb endings always indicate the subject, personal subject pronouns aren't required in the present tense. However, if you want to be really clear, you should still use them. For example, the verb endings for *he, she, it,* and *you* (formal) are the same. **Giorgio e Mirella? Lui canta e lei balla.** (*George and Mirella? He sings and she dances.*) The pronouns make it clear that Giorgio is singing and Mirella is dancing.

Sometimes, to be particularly emphatic, you use a pronoun: **Oggi pago io** (*Today, I'm paying*). Another variation is to use **anche** (*too, also*): **Anche Lei?** (*You, too?*) or **Anch'io** (*Me, too*).

Combining pronouns takes practice. If you're referring to yourself and someone else, **Mario ed io** (*Mario and I*), but don't want to name names, you may use **noi** (*we*). Remember that the verb conjugation must agree with this double subject. **Mario ed io mangiamo insieme ogni giorno** (*Mario and I eat together every day*) is the same as **Noi mangiamo insieme ogni giorno** (*We eat together every day*).

Here are some other examples of double or compound subjects:

> **tu e Giuseppe cantate** (*you and Giuseppe = voi*)
>
> **voi ed io parliamo** (*you and I = noi*)
>
> **Marco, Beppe, e Margherita scrivono** (*Marco, Beppe, and Margherita = loro*)

When you see double or compound subjects, the verb needs a plural ending. Later in this chapter, I provide practice questions to help you master subject-verb agreement.

Until you're comfortable with the conjugations, you may want to use the personal subject pronouns. You'll notice, however, that you use them less and less frequently as your command of Italian grows.

Using the information from this chapter, you can start putting together simple sentences and conversations. Before you begin, you may want to review the verbs introduced in the previous sections of this chapter. Keeping the three conjugations separate helps you attach the correct endings to verbs and allows for subject-verb agreement.

Translate the following short sentences and phrases into Italian. Be sure the subject and verb agree. Don't worry if you haven't learned all the verbs from this chapter yet. After referring back to them, even more than once, you'll find them taking up permanent residence in your vocabulary.

Q. **Beppe is teaching.**

A. **Beppe insegna.**

51. *Luisa sings.*

_____

52. *I understand.*

_____

53. *We are reading.*

_____

54. *You (familiar, singular) eat.*

_____

55. *They pay.*

_____

56. *You (familiar, plural) are writing.*

_____

57. *I finish.*

_____

58. *He wears.*

_____

59. *He and she open.*

_____

60. *They follow.*

_____

To express more complicated thoughts and actions, you need a few basic *conjunctions* — words that join two or more parts of a sentence. To begin, you can use the most prevalent Italian conjunctions shown here.

> ✔ **e** (*and*)
>
> ✔ **ed** (*and;* used before a vowel)
>
> ✔ **ma** (*but*)
>
> ✔ **o** (*or*)
>
> ✔ **perché** (*because*)

For an in-depth look at conjunctions and other transitional elements, see Chapter 14.

Put the sentences into Italian, using the basic conjunctions. Here is an example:

0. *I don't understand, but he does, always.*

A. **Io non capisco, ma lui capisce, sempre.**

61. *Paolo phones Marisa and they talk.*

_____

62. *I'm leaving tomorrow, but I'm returning on Saturday.*

_____

63. *She is listening to the radio, and he is watching television.*

_____

64. *You are looking for Beatrice, and Beatrice is looking for Davide.*

_____

65. *They begin, but they don't finish.*

_____

66. *Edo and Giulia are sleeping because Rosa is reading.*

_____

67. *They know Florence but not Rome.*

_____

68. *He reads, she writes, and I study.*

_____

69. *They buy or sell books.*

_____

70. *Do you* (familiar, singular) *ski or play a sport?*

_____

For even more practice, try creating a series of short sentences of your own that tell about things you do and ask others what they do.

Translate the following short paragraph, as an example.

71. *I would like to learn Italian because I would like to visit Italy. I would like to eat pizza and spaghetti al ragù. I would like to see the museums. Do you speak Italian? Are you studying Italian?*

_____

_____

_____

Answer Key

1 abitiamo

2 frequenti

3 insegnano

4 impara

5 aspetta

6 porta

7 ritornate

8 parlano

9 guida

10 ballate

11 cerchiamo

12 gioca

13 nega

14 spiega

15 paghiamo

16 critica

17 indichi

18 cerchi

19 comunicano

20 giochi

21 cominci

22 cambiate

23 mangiamo

24 studio

25 cerca

26 sciamo

27 invii

28 paghiamo

29 studiano

30 indica

31 scrivo

32 viviamo

33 prendi

34 chiude

35 vendono

36 vedete

37 risponde

38 ripetono

39 crede

40 prendiamo

41 senti

42 dorme

43 apriamo

44 finiscono

45 partite

46 capisce

47 seguono

48 preferisco

49 pulisci

50 sento

51 Luisa canta.

52 Capisco.

53 Leggiamo.

54 Mangi.

55 Pagano.

56 Scrivete.

57 Finisco.

58 Porta.

59 Aprono.

60 Seguono.

61 Paolo telefona a Marisa e parlano.

62 Parto domani ma ritorno sabato.

63 Lei ascolta la radio e lui guarda la televisione.

64 Tu cerchi Beatrice e Beatrice cerca Davide.

65 Cominciano ma non finiscono.

66 Edo e Giulia dormono perché Rosa legge.

67 Conoscono Firenze ma non conoscono Roma.

68 Lui legge, lei scrive ed io studio.

69 Loro comprano o vendono libri.

70 Scii o giochi a uno sport?

71 Io vorrei imparare l'italiano perché vorrei visitare l'Italia. Mi piacerebbe mangiare pizza e spaghetti al ragù. Vorrei vedere i musei. Parli italiano? Studi l'italiano?

Chapter 7

Using Irregular Verbs in the Present Tense

*I*rregular verbs work the same way regular verbs do: You use them to tell, question, evaluate, and comment. They reflect actions (immediate, ongoing, or habitual). They enable you to state facts and opinions. In short, you need them to communicate.

Like all verbs, you conjugate irregular verbs so that the subject and verb agree in number. The difference is, irregular verbs aren't particularly straightforward about their conjugations, as are their regular verb counterparts (see Chapter 6). Although you can often trace the linguistic genealogy of irregular verbs, you frequently can't assign any logic to their formations. You could say that irregular verbs aren't entirely user-friendly, but they can be conquered — it just takes practice, repetition, and memorization.

Moreover, in Italian, irregular verbs frequently show up in idiomatic expressions. *Idiomatic expressions* are those language constructions that make little to no sense if translated word for word but that collectively convey an idea or make an allusion. For example, the English idiom "having a long face" means nothing if translated literally to another language, but English speakers know it means someone looks unhappy.

Idiomatic expressions are common in Italian as in most languages. Recognizing them allows you to sound more Italian and, perhaps more important, to understand what's being said to you. Idioms can also provide witty insights into the culture.

In this chapter, I explore common irregular verbs and show you how to conjugate them. I then discuss some idiomatic expressions that contain irregular verbs (as well as a dash of Italian culture). Later in this chapter, I talk about the most commonly used irregular verbs and how they team up with phrases and other words to make idiomatic speech possible.

To Be or Not to Be: Conjugating Essere

The most fundamental of verbs, **essere** (*to be*), is always irregular, across languages and across tenses. And, along with several other irregular verbs that I introduce later in this chapter, **essere** allows you to say almost anything. It will prove a mainstay in your linguistic wardrobe.

The following table shows the conjugation of **essere** in the present tense.

essere (to be)	
io **sono**	noi **siamo**
Tu **sei**	voi **siete**
Lui, lei, Lei **è**	loro, Loro **sono**

The verb **essere** is a good example of why you don't need personal subject pronouns all the time (for more on personal subject pronouns, see Chapter 6). The only duplicate form in the conjugated **essere** is **sono** (*I am, they are*), but context often makes its meaning clear.

You use **essere** to form compound verb tenses, of which there are seven in Italian.

No separate word for the English subject *it* exists in Italian. **È** means *it is,* the *it* being understood. *It,* however, does have a gender in Italian. For example: **È bello. È bella.** The first refers to a masculine subject; the second, to a feminine subject.

> **È lunedì.** (*It is Monday.*)

> **È una giornata splendida.** (*It's a gorgeous day.*)

Other basic expressions that include the invisible *it* are **Quanto è?** (*How much is it?*); **Dov'è?** (*Where is it?*); and **Chi è?** (*Who is it?*).

Use the appropriate conjugated form of **essere** in the following sentences, according to the subject. Here's an example:

Q. Marco _____ un bravo studente.

A. è

1. Loro _____ simpatici.

2. Tu _____ americana?

3. Voi _____ insegnanti?

4. Giulia e Chiara _____ cugine.

5. Io _____ felice.

6. I bambini _____ a casa.

7. Tu e Paola _____ amici.

8. Laura _____ molto giovane.

9. Io ed Emilio _____ in campagna.

10. Tu e loro _____ in montagna durante l'estate.

Essere appears in many idiomatic expressions in Italian. See the section "Using Irregular Verbs in Idiomatic Expressions," later in this chapter, for examples.

To Have and to Hold: Conjugating Avere

Avere (*to have*) rivals **essere** (*to be*) for being ubiquitous. In fact, it's used in many expressions that allow it to do double duty because it can also mean *to be*. I explain that further in this section. First, have a look at the conjugation of **avere**.

avere (to have)	
Io **ho**	Noi **abbiamo**
Tu **hai**	Voi **avete**
Lui, lei, Lei **ha**	loro, Loro **hanno**

Also, as with **essere,** *it* is included in the verb. For example: **Ha un aspetto meraviglioso.** (*It has a great look to it.*) This expression is frequently used to comment on a dish being served at table.

Often, Italians add **ci** (*here* or *there*) to conjugations of **avere.** This little two-letter word adds emphasis to what you're saying. **Hai le chiavi?** (*Do you have the keys?*) may get the response **Sì, c'ho le chiavi.** (*I have the keys, right here.*) The **ci** contracts with **ho** to produce a smoother sound.

Fill in the appropriately conjugated form of **avere** in the sentences that follow. Here's an example:

Q. Noi _____ molto da fare.

A. abbiamo

11. Luigi _____ un gatto che è vecchio vecchio.

12. Voi _____ una bellissima casa.

13. Lei, signora, _____ il biglietto?

14. Io non _____ una macchina.

15. Tu _____ un amico che si chiama Leonardo?

When accompanied by certain specific nouns, **avere** forms part of little units that, taken in their entirety, change its meaning from *to have* to *to be*. Table 7-1 shows some of these expressions.

Table 7-1	Avere Used to Mean *to Be*
Italian	*English*
avere fame	*to be hungry*
avere sete	*to be thirsty*
avere sonno	*to be sleepy*
avere caldo	*to be hot, personally*
avere freddo	*to be cold, personally*
avere fretta	*to be in a hurry*
avere ragione	*to be right*
avere torto	*to be wrong*
avere bisogno (di)	*to need*
avere voglia (di)	*to feel like*
avere paura (di)	*to be afraid of*
avere vergogna	*to be ashamed*
avere . . . anni	*to be . . . years old*

One rule for knowing when to use **essere** or **avere** to mean *to be* is that **essere** generally accompanies permanent states of being: "They are nice." "She is tall." "We are American." **Avere** tends to refer to temporary situations: "I'm hungry and thirsty." "She is in a hurry." "We're cold."

Using **avere** as your verb, translate the following short sentences into Italian. Don't be shy about looking back at the definitions as you work. The more you study them, the sooner they'll become natural to you.

0. *You're right.*

A. **Hai ragione.**

16. *I'm hungry.*

_____

17. *She is wrong.*

_____

18. *They are sleepy.*

_____

19. *He is in a hurry.*

_____

20. *Are you (formal plural) cold?*

_____

21. *Paolo is hot.*

_____

22. *I'm afraid.*

_____

23. *Nonna is 80 years old.*

_____

24. *Micia is thirsty.*

_____

25. *He has no shame.*

_____

Now decide whether to use **avere** or **essere** in the following phrases. Make sure whichever verb you choose agrees with the subject.

Q. Io _____ 24 anni.

A. ho

Q. Io _____ americana.

A. sono

26. Noi _____ studenti.

27. Il bambino _____ fame.

28. Tu _____ torto!

29. Lei _____ simpatica.

30. Io _____ freddo.

31. Loro _____ molto vecchi.

32. La maestra _____ intelligente.

33. Io _____ di mangiare.

34. Lui _____ molto ricco.

35. Voi _____ fretta?

To Make or Do: Conjugating Fare

In its most basic form, **fare** means *to make* or *to do*. With **essere** (*to be*) and **avere** (*to have*), it's one of the most versatile and useful Italian verbs.

Fare is also one of the most idiomatic verbs. Dozens of idiomatic expressions use **fare** as their base, and later in this chapter, in the section "Using Irregular Verbs in Idiomatic Expressions," I provide an admittedly incomplete but, I hope, useful list of **fare** expressions. See the following table for the conjugation of **fare**.

fare (to make or to do)	
Io **faccio**	noi **facciamo**
Tu **fai**	voi **fate**
Lui, lei, Lei **fa**	loro, Loro **fanno**

Fare can stand alone in its irregular state. For example: **Io non faccio nulla di interessante.** (*I'm not doing anything interesting.*) A common question used by a parent speaking to a child is **Cosa fai?** (*What are you doing?*), though friends also use it to ask, "What are you doing? What are you up to?"

Choose one of the following conjugated forms of **fare** to complete each sentence.

faccio   facciamo

fai   fate

fa   fanno

Q. Gli studenti _____ molte domande.

A. fanno

36. _____ brutto tempo oggi.

37. Mario, cosa _____?

38. Noi _____ pranzo fuori.

39. L'acqua gassata _____ male.

40. Voi _____ le valigie?

41. Emilio _____ una telefonata.

42. I turisti _____ molte fotografie.

43. I professori _____ la conoscenza degli studenti.

44. Lui _____ sempre lo spiritoso.

45. Dopo cena, io _____ la doccia.

To Give: Dare

Dare (*to give*) isn't terribly irregular. It follows the conjugation pattern of the **-are** regular verbs (see Chapter 6), with the exception of the **loro** forms, which double the consonant **n.**

dare (to give)	
io **do**	noi **diamo**
tu **dai**	voi **date**
lui, lei, Lei **dà**	loro, Loro **danno**

Dai (you give, are giving) can also mean "come on!" in Italian, and is pronounced like the English *die*. See Chapter 9 to understand this and other interjections.

The third person singular form of **dare** (**dà**, *he, she, it,* gives or *you formal* gives) carries an accent to distinguish it from **da** (*from, by*)**,** without an accent, which is a preposition. (See Chapter 12 for a discussion on prepositions.)

To Ask How Others Are: Stare

You use **stare** to ask how someone is. **Come stai?** (familiar, *How are you?*) or **come sta** (formal, *How are you?*). It can also mean *to stay,* physically, somewhere. **Sto all'Albergo Magnifico.** (*I'm staying at the Magnifico Hotel.*) **Sto a casa.** (*I'm staying home.*) Accompanied by the preposition **per,** it means *to be about to.* **Sto per mangiare.** (*I'm about to eat.*)

Like **dare, stare** isn't as irregular as some verbs, in that it follows the conjugation pattern of the **-are** verbs (see Chapter 6), with the exception of the **loro** forms, which double the consonant **n.**

stare (to be)	
io **sto**	noi **stiamo**
Tu **stai**	voi **state**
Lui, lei, Lei **sta**	loro, Loro **stanno**

Stare has one other extremely important use. It combines with a verb's present participle (-*ing* form, like eating, sleeping, or reading) to make up the *present progressive verb tense*. As serious and confusing as that sounds, it's pretty much still the present tense — it's simply a little more immediate. For example, if someone calls and asks whether he's interrupting, you may say: **Sto mangiando.** (*I'm eating* [*right now, in other words*].)

You form the participles of verbs by dropping a verb's traditional or identifying ending and substituting **-ando** for **-are** and **-endo** for **-ere** and **-ire**. Here are some examples:

Sto mangiando. (*I am eating.*)

Stiamo parlando. (*We are talking.*)

Stai leggendo. (*You are reading.*)

State partendo. (*You are leaving.*)

Sta pulendo. (*He, she, it is cleaning/You are cleaning.*)

Stanno vivendo. (*They/You are living.*)

To Come and Go: Venire and Andare

"What is all this coming and going?" asks a worried Rodolfo from the opera *La Bohème.* Coming and going are so much a part of daily activity that the verbs **venire** (*to come*) and **andare** (*to go*) are terrifically useful. And, grammatically speaking, it's safe to say that figuring out how to use both verbs is pretty straightforward — but still irregular.

Venire (*to come*) is the opposite of **andare. Vieni alla festa?** (*Are you coming to the party?*) **Vengono loro.** (*They are coming.*) Other verbs also mean *to go,* such as **partire** (*to go* as in *to leave*) and **uscire** (*to go out*). **Uscire** has its own section later in this chapter.

Andare (*to go*) refers to going to a particular destination or to leaving. For example, you can say: **Vado via.** (*I am going away.*) Or the emphatic, and slightly petulant, **Me ne vado.** (*I'm getting out of here.*) You can also say, simply, **Vanno a teatro.** (*They are going to the theater.*); **Vai in ufficio?** (*Are you going to the office?*); or **Non vado a scuola oggi.** (*I'm not going to school today.*)

A useful expression that takes **andare** is **andare di male in peggio** (*to go from bad to worse*). For example: **La situazione va di male in peggio.** (*The situation is going from bad to worse.*)

See the following conjugations for **venire** and **andare**.

venire (to come)	
io **vengo**	noi **veniamo**
tu **vieni**	voi **venite**
lui, lei, Lei **viene**	loro, Loro **vengono**

andare (to go)	
io **vado**	noi **andiamo**
tu **vai**	voi **andate**
lui, lei, Lei **va**	loro, Loro **vanno**

Venire has the added attraction of serving as a base verb; that is, when altered by the addition of prefixes, it noticeably expands your vocabulary — and you have only one irregular conjugation to remember. For example, **svenire** adds the letter **s,** which often changes a word into its opposite. In this case, **svenire** means *to come undone,* or *to faint.*

Declaring Your Needs, Wants, and Abilities: Dovere, Volere, and Potere

You use the verbs **dovere** (*to have to*), **volere** (*to want*), and **potere** (*to be able to*) to express your needs, desires, and abilities. They're very personal verbs, in that you use them to communicate intimate or personal ideas.

These verbs are also called semi-auxiliary or "sort of" helping verbs. You can use them with infinitives, and you often will. For example: **Devo andare.** (*I have to go.*) **Non posso studiare.** (*I can't study.*) **Vorrei mangiare.** (*I would like to eat.*)

For specific uses of these verbs in their semi-auxiliary role, see Chapter 6.

The following tables show the conjugations of **dovere, volere,** and **potere,** respectively.

dovere (to have to)	
io **devo**	noi **dobbiamo**
tu **devi**	voi **dovete**
lui, lei, Lei **deve**	loro, Loro **devono**

volere (to want)	
io **voglio**	noi **vogliamo**
tu **vuoi**	voi **volete**
lui, lei, Lei **vuole**	loro, Loro **vogliono**

potere (to be able to)	
io **posso**	noi **possiamo**
tu **puoi**	voi **potete**
lui, lei, Lei **può**	loro, Loro **possono**

The first person singular, or *I* form, of **volere** isn't terribly polite. Just consider the difference between *I want* (**voglio**) and *I would like* (**vorrei**). I don't mean to suggest that you never use **voglio**, but **vorrei** is much more polite and the form you may want to use in public (in a restaurant, for example).

In moods other than the indicative (the conditional shows the mood of **vorrei**), these verbs change their basic meaning and allow you to use *should, might, could,* and *ought to.* (See Chapter 18.) In other words, they add nuance, and occasionally sarcasm, to your Italian.

From the verbs listed, choose the one most appropriate to the context of each sentence. Be sure the subject and verb agree in number. Some sentences may have more than one correct answer.

dare	**dovere**
stare	**potere**
venire	**volere**
andare	

Q. Noi _____ all'albergo in centro città.

A. stiamo

46. Paola _____ da mangiare al gatto.

47. A che ora _____ loro?

48. Io _____ studiare.

49. Voi _____ a teatro domani?

50. Come _____, caro?

51. Tu _____ venire con noi?

52. I bambini non _____ mangiare tanti dolci.

53. Tu e Marco _____ molti regali ai bambini.

54. Noi _____ arrivare presto.

55. Io _____ stasera.

Do Tell: Dire

Dire (*to say, to tell*) is another verb that serves as the base for other common verb forms. After you know the conjugation of **dire,** you can add prefixes to change its meaning. **Disdire,** for example, means *to take back,* while **maledire** becomes *to curse.*

dire (to say, to tell)	
Io **dico**	Noi **diciamo**
Tu **dici**	Voi **dite**
Lui, lei, Lei **dice**	loro, Loro **dicono**

Dire gives you the chance to use conversational fillers. For example, after interrupting your flow of thought, you can return to your point by saying **dicevo** (*as I was saying*). You can sum something up by saying **questo detto** (*this having been said*), a form, the ablative absolute, taken directly from that most economical of languages, Latin. Or you can use (sparingly, and only with a close friend or relative) the phrase **non t'avevo detto** (*didn't I tell you*).

To go has shades of meaning, even in English. In Italian, more than one verb exists for *to go,* each with a particular sense. See the next section.

Stepping Out: Uscire

Uscire means *to go out.* For example: **Esco con degli amici.** (*I am going out with some friends.*) **Lui non esce mai.** (*He never goes out.*) **Andare,** as I mention earlier in this chapter, means to undertake the physical act of going somewhere. **Vado in giardino.** (*I'm going to the garden.*) **Vanno a Napoli.** (*They are going to Naples.*) **Partire** means *to leave, to depart.* It has a regular **-ire** conjugation (see Chapter 6). **Noi partiamo per l'Italia domani mattina.** (*We are leaving for Italy tomorrow morning.*)

Here's the irregular conjugation for **uscire.** (See the earlier section "To Come and Go: Venire and Andare" for the conjugation of **andare.**)

uscire (to go out)	
io **esco**	noi **usciamo**
tu **esci**	voi **uscite**
lui, lei, Lei **esce**	loro, Loro **escono**

Uscire shows up with the prefix **ri-** (Literally: *again*) and is a type of synonym to **potere** (*to be able to*). Should someone say to you **Non riesco a farlo,** it doesn't mean he or she isn't going out again; it means he or she is unable to do something.

Using conjugated forms of the verbs given here, complete the following sentences. Some sentences may have more than one appropriate answer. See the example.

   dire

   uscire

   andare

   partire

Q. Roberto non _____ la verità.

A. dice

56. Tu _____ dopo cena?

57. Loro _____ domani mattina per Milano.

58. Io non _____ a scuola.

59. Marco _____ sempre con gli amici.

60. Figlio mio, dove _____?

61. I parenti _____ oggi. Tornano a casa.

62. Noi _____ di sì.

63. Io _____ con un'amica.

64. Voi _____ di no.

65. Lui _____ che non vieni.

Bottom's Up: Bere

Bere (*to drink*) is another commonly used verb, and its conjugation is shown in the following table.

bere (to drink)	
io **bevo**	noi **beviamo**
tu **bevi**	voi **bevete**
lui, lei, Lei **beve**	loro, Loro **bevono**

You can use **bere** to **bere alla salute** (*drink to someone's health*), but for having a cup of coffee or tea or a glass of wine, you can just as easily use **prendere**, a regular **-ere** verb (see Chapter 6). For example: **Io bevo thè** and **Io prendo thè** mean *I'm drinking tea*. The difference in meaning is very slight. **Bevo** (*I'm drinking*) is perhaps more immediate. **Prendo** (*I'm drinking*) carries the sense of ordering, as in *I'm having tea*.

The -orre, -urre, and -arre Verbs

These three conjugations are distinctly in the Italian linguistic minority. They're most useful as base verbs from which you can construct other verbs with expanded meanings. See the following tables for their conjugations.

porre (to put)	
io **pongo**	noi **poniamo**
tu **poni**	voi **ponete**
lui, lei, Lei **pone**	loro, Loro **pongono**

tradurre (to translate)	
io **traduco**	noi **traduciamo**
tu **traduci**	voi **traducete**
lui, lei, Lei **traduce**	loro, Loro **traducono**

trarre (to pull, to lead)	
io **traggo**	noi **tra(ggh)iamo**
tu **trai**	voi **traete**
lui, lei, Lei **trae**	loro, Loro **traggono**

Other incarnations of these kinds of verbs are dependent on the addition of prefixes. **Porre** by itself means *to put;* add **pro-,** and it becomes *to propose;* add **com-,** and it becomes *to compose.* **Tradurre** means *to translate;* change the prefix from **tra-** to **de-,** and you have *to deduce.* **Trarre** means *to pull* (a cart, for example). But enhanced forms are more useful: **Attrarre** (*to attract*), **contrarre** (*to contract*), and **distrarre** (*to distract*) are a few examples.

Using Irregular Verbs in Idiomatic Expressions

While an English-speaker may be born with a silver spoon (or to wealthy parents), a similarly endowed Italian is born wearing a shirt. In English, it rains cats and dogs; in Italian, basins full of water. Cultural bias or proclivity also shows up in idiomatic expressions: In English, something can be ugly as sin; in Italian, something truly ugly is **brutto come la fame** (*as ugly as hunger*). In a similar vein, something or someone really good is **buono come il pane** (*as good as bread*).

Both idiomatic expressions and allusions make use of **essere.** When you follow **essere** with the preposition **di,** you indicate possession. **È il libro di Giulio.** (*It's Giulio's book.*) **La macchina? È di Luigi.** (*The car? It's Luigi's.*) You can also use **essere** with **di** to say where you're from. **Io sono di Firenze. Lui è di Roma.** (*I'm from Florence. He is from Rome.*)

Idiomatic expressions with essere

Many idioms use **essere**. The following is a sample:

> **essere in gamba** (*to be on top of things; to be clever*)
>
> **essere al verde** (*to be broke*)
>
> **essere in vena** (*to be in the mood*)
>
> **essere un Cincinnato** (*to be an honest, simple, humble person*)
>
> **essere una Cassandra** (*to predict disaster and not be believed*)

Using idiomatic essere expressions, put the following sentences into their Italian equivalents, as per the example. Remember to conjugate the verb when using it in a sentence.

Q. *He is ugly as sin.*

A. **Lui è brutto come la fame.**

66. *She is truly an honest person.*

_____

67. *They aren't in the mood.*

_____

68. *I'm flat broke.*

_____

69. *No one ever believes her.*

_____

70. *He's truly on top of things.*

_____

Idiomatic expressions with fare

Here are some of the most common **fare** idiomatic expressions.

> **fare la conoscenza di** (*to make the acquaintance of*)
>
> **fare colazione, pranzo, cena** (*to eat breakfast, lunch, dinner*)
>
> **fare una foto** (*to take a picture*)

fare una domanda a (*to ask someone a question*)

fare lo spiritoso (*to be funny*)

fare un viaggio (*to take a trip*)

fare le valigie (*to pack the suitcases*)

fare una telefonata (*to make a phone call*)

fare una passeggiata (*to take a walk*)

fare un bagno, una doccia (*to take a bath, shower*)

fare finta di (*to pretend*)

fare una bella figura (*to make a good impression*)

fare una brutta figura (*to make a bad impression*)

Ci fa il conto? (*Could you get us the check?*)

Non si fa. (*One doesn't do that.*)

Fa bene/male. (*It's good for you/bad for you.*)

Fallo pure! (*Just do it!*)

Fa bel/brutto tempo. (*It's nice weather/nasty weather.*)

Idiomatic expressions with dare and stare

As is the case with many of the irregular verbs, **dare** and **stare** both create idiomatic speech. For example, **dare noia a** and **dare fastidio a** both mean *to annoy or bother*. **Il fratellino mi dà fastidio!** (*My little brother annoys me!*) When you meet someone, **tu dai la mano a lui** (*you shake hands with him*).

You may begin conversations with new acquaintances, using the formal form of address (a wise move when dealing with anyone in a position of authority). One of you may say, probably sooner rather than later, **Ma ci diamo del tu.** (*Let's use the informal.*) To feed your pet, **Gli dai da mangiare.** (*You are giving him food.*) Perhaps you want a mechanic to look over your car's engine or a friend to look over something you've done. In both cases, that person **dà un'occhiata** (*looks over*) whatever you need evaluated. In a moment, that's probably counterintuitive to English speakers, to *take* an exam is, in Italian, to *give* an exam: **Loro danno un esame oggi.** (*They are taking an exam today.*)

Other idiomatic phrases or expressions with **stare** include the following:

stare fresco (*to be in trouble*)

stare sulle spine (*to be on pins and needles*)

stare attento a (*to be careful, to watch out for*)

Ci sto! (*I'm game!*)

Answer Key

1 sono

2 sei

3 siete

4 sono

5 sono

6 sono

7 siete

8 è

9 siamo

10 siete

11 Ha

12 Avete

13 Ha

14 Ho

15 Hai

16 Ho fame.

17 Lei ha torto.

18 Hanno sonno.

19 Ha fretta.

20 Ha freddo?

21 Paolo ha caldo.

22 Ho paura.

23 Nonna ha ottanta anni.

24 Micia ha sete.

25 Non ha vergogna.

26 Siamo

27 Ha

28 hai

29 è

30 ho

31 sono

32 è

33 ho voglia di, ho bisogno di

34 è

35 avete

36 fa

37 fai

38 facciamo

39 fa

40 fate

41 fa

42 fanno

43 fanno

44 fa

45 faccio

46 dà

47 vanno, vengono

48 devo, posso, vorrei

49 andate

50 stai

51 vuoi, puoi

52 devono, possono, vogliono

53 date

54 dobbiamo, possiamo, vogliamo

55 vado, vengo

56 esci, parti

57 partono

58 vado

59 esce

60 vai

61 partono

62 diciamo

63 esco

64 dite

65 dice

66 Lei è un Cincinnato.

67 Non sono in vena.

68 Sono al verde.

69 Lei è una Cassandra.

70 Lui è molto in gamba.

Chapter 8

Substituting Pronouns for Nouns

*P*ronouns let you talk about one thing without repeating a name or a noun monotonously. Pronouns are ubiquitous; how many times a day do you say *he, she, him, her, they, them, I, we,* and *you?*

Pronouns replace nouns and tell you who's doing what and to whom or to what they're doing so. Pronouns are everywhere in both English and Italian. Sometimes pronouns aren't really necessary; in fact, subject pronouns in Italian are included in the verb conjugations, as I explain in Chapter 6. Object pronouns and the nouns they're replacing often inhabit the same sentence. Some object pronouns that are direct in English are indirect in Italian; and some that are indirect in English become direct in Italian.

In this chapter, I focus on subject and object pronouns and show you where they go in a sentence, reveal how they change form, and describe when they're really necessary — and when they're not.

Replacing Nouns with Subject Pronouns

A subject pronoun replaces a *noun* — person, place, or thing — that carries out the action of a verb. Instead of saying, "Francesca is beautiful," you can say, "She is beautiful." *She* is a subject pronoun. *She* replaces *Francesca,* a noun.

In English, you always use a noun or pronoun with a verb so you know who or what is driving the verb, or carrying out the action of a sentence. In Italian, because the conjugated verb's endings tell what the subject is, you don't always need to state the subject separately. I explain in detail how verbs work in Chapters 6 and 7.

In the following sections, you discover what the Italian subject pronouns are and how to use them, both separately and attached to verbs.

Introducing the subject pronouns

Italian has seven subject pronouns in modern use; however, two of them (**lei** and **loro**) have more than one meaning. I list the subject pronouns here with their English counterparts. I include their archaic forms in parentheses when the pronouns have them, because you see them in written Italian.

Singular	Plural
io (*I*)	**noi** (*we*)
tu (*you* [familiar])	**voi** (*you all* [familiar])
lui (**egli, esso**) (*he*)	**loro** (**essi** [masculine]) (*they*)
lei (**ella, essa**) (*she*)	**loro** (**esse** [feminine]) (*they*)
Lei (*you* [formal])	**Loro** (*you* [formal])

You use familiar forms with family, friends, peers, children, and animals. You use formal forms with everyone else. If you're unsure which form to use, go for the formal so you don't risk offending someone. Soon enough, the person to whom you're speaking can say **Ci diamo del tu** (*Let's use the familiar*). In today's Italian, when speaking to groups, you often use the plural **voi** instead of **Loro** to mean *you* (formal).

You see the capitalization of **Lei** and **Loro** for the formal uses of *you* sometimes in writing, though this use is disappearing.

Although there's no pronoun for *it,* and *it* isn't stated separately (**è bello**, for example, means *it is beautiful*), the word itself is masculine or feminine, depending on what noun it replaces. For example, referring to a *book* (**libro**), *it* takes the **lui** form of a verb because *it* is replacing a masculine noun; if you're talking about a *house* (**casa**), *it* uses the **lei** form of a verb because *it* takes the place of a feminine noun.

This distinction becomes important when you add adjectives into the mix to modify the pronoun *it* (see Chapters 5 and 13). If you say **è bello** (*it's beautiful*), you're talking about a masculine thing, but if you say **è bella** (*it's beautiful*), you're talking about something feminine.

Putting pronouns with verbs

Subjects, even pronouns, need verbs. To show how the subject pronoun accompanies a verb, I use **parlare** (*to speak*) as an example, here conjugated in the present tense. (For detailed explanation of conjugating verbs in the present tense, see Chapters 6 and 7.)

parlare (to speak)	
io **parlo** (*I speak*)	noi **parliamo** (*we speak*)
tu **parli** (*you* [familiar] *speak*)	voi **parlate** (*you all* [familiar] *speak*)
lui, lei, Lei **parla** (*he, she, it speaks; you* [formal] *speak*)	loro, Loro **parlano** (*they speak; you all* [formal] *speak*)

The endings of the verb (**-o, -i, -a, -iamo, -ate,** and **-ano**) tell you who the subject of an Italian sentence is, so you don't technically need the subject pronouns. However, you use the pronoun to be clear. For example, if you say simply **parla,** you could mean that *he speaks, she speaks, it speaks,* or that *you* (formal) *speak.* Adding the pronoun clarifies who's doing the speaking: **Lui parla** makes it clear that *he* is speaking; **lei parla** makes it clear that *she* is speaking; and **Lei parla** makes it clear that *you* (formal) are speaking.

You also use subject pronouns to be emphatic. **Parlo io** (*I'm speaking*) tells someone that you're doing the speaking and probably don't want to be interrupted. As another example, you're out having lunch with friends and want to pay, so you say **Oggi pago io** (*Today I'm paying*). The use of the pronoun after the verb says that you're being emphatic. For more on this, see the later section "Putting Stress Where It's Due: Stressed and Unstressed Pronouns."

Keep in mind that you can combine two pronouns, for example, **tu ed io** (*you and I*); by doing so, you need to use **noi** (*we*). Another example is when you're talking to friends and say **tu e loro** (*you and they*); you use the **voi** (*you all*) to show that you're talking to all the people in a group.

Fill in the appropriate subject pronouns to replace the subjects in the following phrases. In each case, you're talking *about* the subjects, not *to* them, unless otherwise indicated.

Q. **Riccardo**

A. **lui**

1. **i bambini** (*the children*) _____

2. **Marco e Giulia** _____

3. **tu e gli altri** (*you and the others*) _____

4. **il signor Rossi** (*Mr. Rossi*) _____

5. (talking to someone) **Dottor Bianchi** _____

6. (talking to someone) **Signori e signore** (*ladies and gentlemen*) _____

7. **la gatta** (*the cat* [feminine]) _____

8. **io ed un gruppo di amici** (*I and a group of friends*) _____

9. (talking to someone) **Ragazzi** (*Kids*) _____

10. (talking to someone) **Mamma** (*Mom*) _____

Telling What or Who with Direct Object Pronouns

Direct object pronouns replace nouns and answer such questions as <u>Who</u> are you seeing? and <u>What</u> are you buying? For example: *Do you see Beppe? Yes, I see him.* The pronoun *him* replaces the noun *Beppe* and answers the question *who.* Also, *Did you buy the puppy? Yes, I bought it.* The pronoun *it* replaces the noun *puppy* and answers the question *what.* The eight direct object pronouns are listed here.

Singular	**Plural**
mi (*me*)	**ci** (*us*)
ti (*you* [familiar])	**vi** (*you all* [familiar])
lo (*him, it*)	**li** (*them* [masculine])
la (*her, it*)	**le** (*them* [feminine])
La (*you* [masculine/feminine, formal])	**Li** (*you all* [masculine, formal])
	Le (*you all* [feminine, formal])

The direct object pronouns **lo, la, li, le, Li** and **Le** agree in number (singular, plural) and gender (masculine, feminine) with the nouns they replace. (See Chapter 3 for details on number and gender of nouns.) Here's an example.

> *He sees them. Them* is the direct object pronoun. In Italian, *them* is **li** or **le**, depending on who *he sees.* If he sees a group of women, the direct object pronoun is **le** (feminine); if he sees a group of men or a group of men *and* women, the direct object pronoun is **li** (masculine).

The direct object pronoun **La** (*you* [singular, formal]) is both masculine and feminine. Consider the word used to say *good-bye* in a formal situation: **arrivederLa.** The pronoun **La** refers to both masculine and feminine persons.

Direct object pronouns help you not repeat yourself because they allow you to refer back to the subject without stating the subject repeatedly. Compare the following sentences.

> *I'm buying the car.* (**Compro la macchina.**) *I love the car.* (**Adoro la macchina.**) *I'll have the car tomorrow.* (**Domani ho la macchina.**)

Instead of repeating *the car* over and over again, you can say

> *I'm buying the car.* (**Compro la macchina.**) *I love it.* (**L'adoro.**) *I'll have it tomorrow.* (**L'ho domani.**) The direct object pronoun **la** is feminine and singular, as is the noun it replaces, **la macchina.**

As you see, the direct object pronoun precedes the verb in Italian but stays right next to it. When the verb begins with a vowel (**adoro**) or an **h** (**ho**), you drop the vowel from **mi, ti, lo, la,** and **vi** and add an apostrophe, like so: **l'adoro, l'ho.**

The direct object pronoun follows verbs in three instances.

✔ When you drop the final **e** from the infinitive (see Chapter 6) and attach the pronoun:

> **Vorrei comprarlo.** (*I'd like to buy it.*)
>
> **Devo farlo domani.** (*I have to do it tomorrow.*)
>
> **Preferisci mangiarlo ora?** (*Do you prefer to eat it now?*)

✔ When you use a command (see Chapter 9):

> **Dallo a lui.** (*Give it to him.*)
>
> **Non mangiarlo!** (*Don't eat it!*)

✔ When you attach the direct object pronoun to present participles (see Chapter 7):

> **Sto leggendolo.** (*I'm reading it.*)
>
> **Stiamo mangiandolo.** (*We're eating it.*)

Here are some other examples of direct object pronouns at work.

> **Lo leggerò il più presto possibile.** (*I'll read it as soon as possible.*)
>
> **Li vedo ogni settimana.** (*I see them every week.*)
>
> **La mangio volentieri.** (*I'll eat it willingly.*)
>
> **Le comprarono molti anni fa.** (*They bought them many years ago.*)
>
> **L'ho a casa.** (*I have it at home.*)

 Some verbs take direct objects in Italian but take indirect objects in English because the prepositions that go with them are built in to the Italian form. For example, **guardare** means *to look at, to watch* and is followed by a direct object: **Hai guardato la televisione? L'ho guardata** (*Did you watch TV? I watched it*).

The other most common verbs with built-in prepositions are **aspettare** (*to wait for*), **cercare** (*to look for*), and **ascoltare** (*to listen to*). All take direct objects instead of indirect objects.

 Replace the following words with a direct object pronoun. Make sure the pronoun agrees in number and gender with the noun you're replacing.

Q. **la casa**

A. la

11. l'albero (*the tree*) _____

12. i fiori (*the flowers*) _____

13. le ragazze (*the girls*) _____

14. tu e me (*you and me*) _____

15. gli studenti (*the students*) _____

16. i gatti e le gatte (*male cats and female cats*) _____

17. **signori e signore** (*gentlemen and ladies*) _____

18. **il museo** (*the museum*) _____

19. **Giovanni** (*John*) _____

20. **la mamma** (*mom*) _____

Using Indirect Object Pronouns

Like direct object pronouns, which I discuss in the previous section, indirect object pronouns answer questions. But indirect objects always follow the preposition *to* or *for,* even if you don't say *to* or *for* in English: *I'm giving [to] him the book. Give [to] her my greetings. I'm buying [for] them the gifts.*

Italian indirect object pronouns have *to* or *for* built in. You **don't** need to **add a preposition.** (See Chapter 12 for more on prepositions.)

Here are the Italian indirect object pronouns.

Singular	*Plural*
mi (*to/for me*)	**ci** (*to/for us*)
ti (*to/for you* [familiar])	**vi** (*to/for you all* [familiar])
gli (*to/for him*)	**loro (gli)** (*to/for them* [masculine/feminine])
le (*to/for her*)	**Loro (Gli)** (*to/for you* [formal])
Le (*to/for you* [formal])	

Indirect object pronouns agree in number (singular, plural) and gender (masculine, feminine) with the nouns they replace (see Chapter 3 for details). Here are some examples.

> **Le scrivo una lettera.** (*I'm writing her a letter.*) (*I'm writing you* [formal] *a letter.*)

> **Ti do la bicicletta.** (*I'm giving you the bike.*)

These pronouns precede the verb but stay close — in fact, right next to it. The exception is **loro,** which always follows the verb, as in this example: **Do loro i biglietti** (*I'm giving them the tickets*). Today, **loro** has been largely replaced by **gli,** and you're more likely to say **Gli do i biglietti.**

When the verb begins with a vowel or an **h,** you drop the **i** in the indirect object pronouns **mi, ti,** and **vi** and replace it with an apostrophe. For example: **M'hai scritto** (*you wrote me*); **T'ho dato il libro** (*I gave you the book*).

Ci drops its final letter and replaces it with an apostrophe *only* if the verb begins with **i** or **e,** as in **C'invia le cose** (*He's sending us the things*).

Indirect object pronouns stay close to the verb but sometimes don't precede it, and in these situations, they become part of another word:

✔ You can attach an indirect pronoun to an infinitive; just drop the final **e** of the infinitive before adding the pronoun.

> **Devo parlargli.** (*I have to speak to him.*)

> **Lui preferisce scrivervi.** (*He prefers to write you.*)

✔ You can attach the indirect object pronoun to a command.

> **Digli la verità.** (*Tell him the truth.*)

> **Dille di no.** (*Tell her no.*)

✔ You can attach the pronoun to the end of a present participle.

> **Sto parlandogli di questo.** (*I'm talking to him about this.*)

> **Stiamo dandoti una bicicletta.** (*We're giving you a bike.*)

Certain verbs in Italian take indirect objects even if they don't in English. **Telefonare** (*to call*) takes an indirect object in Italian (**le telefono** [*I'm calling (to) her*]), but not in English. In English, you can say *Who are you calling? I'm calling him.* And you use direct objects.

Other verbs that take indirect objects in Italian (though not necessarily in English) include **consigliare** (*to counsel*), **dare** (*to give*), **scrivere** (*to write*), **mandare** (*to send*), **insegnare** (*to teach*), **rispondere** (*to reply*), and **comprare** (*to buy*). Remember that the prepositions *to* and *for* are built into the indirect object pronoun and don't need repeating.

Piacere uses the indirect object pronouns to replace the English subject and to mean *to like*. See Chapter 10 on how **piacere** and indirect object pronouns work.

Put the English indirect object pronouns into Italian. Remember that each phrase needs just one word to replace it.

Q. *to Mom*

A. **le**

21. *to them* _____

22. *for me* _____

23. *to her* _____

24. *to us* _____

25. *for them* _____

26. *to you all* _____

27. *for you and me* _____

28. *to him* _____

29. *to you* (singular, familiar) _____

30. *for him and her* _____

Forming Double Pronouns

In the interests of not repeating yourself endlessly, you use direct object and indirect object pronouns together, at the same time and in the same sentence. Instead of replying to *Did you get the book for the kids?* with *Yes, I got the book for the kids,* using double object pronouns, you can say *Yes, I got it for them.*

Indirect object pronouns *always* precede direct object pronouns when they're used together. Compare the English and Italian sentences with both pronouns:

English: *I am giving it to them.*

Italian: **Glielo do.** (Literally: *To them it I am giving.*)

To keep the flow or sound of Italian as musical as it can be, you make changes to the indirect object pronouns when they combine with direct object pronouns.

For simplicity's sake, I use the direct object pronoun **lo** (*it*) in Table 8-1, which shows how indirect object and direct object pronouns combine. Notice that **glie** and the direct object pronoun **lo** combine to form one word.

Table 8-1	Combining Indirect and Direct Object Pronouns		
Original Indirect Object Pronoun	*Revised Indirect Object Pronoun*	*Direct Object Pronoun*	*Example*
mi	me	lo	**me lo** (*it to me*)
ti	te	lo	**te lo** (*it to you* [familiar])
gli	glie	lo	**glielo** (*it to him/it*)
le	glie	lo	**glielo** (*it to her/it*)
Le	glie	lo	**glielo** (*it to you* [formal])
ci	ce	lo	**ce lo** (*it to us*)
vi	ve	lo	**ve lo** (*it to you* [familiar])
gli	glie	lo	**glielo** (*it to them/it/you* [formal])

Me lo dai? (*Are you giving it to me?*) **Sì, te lo do.** (*Yes, I'm giving it to you.*)

Ce li leggi, Mamma? (*Mom, will you read them to us?*) **Sì, ve li leggo.** (*Yes, I'll read them to you.*)

Gliele compro. (*I'm buying them for them/him/her/it/you* [formal].)

Io glieli do. (*I'm giving it to them/him/her/it/you* [formal].)

The **gli** in **glielo** takes on a multitude of meanings in combination with a direct object pronoun. **Gli** (indirect object pronoun) + **lo** (direct object pronoun) = **glielo,** meaning *it to him/her/it/them/you* (formal). Context is all you need. If you want to be absolutely clear, you can use only the indirect object *noun* — or you can repeat the *noun* you replaced with the indirect object pronoun. For example: **Glielo scrivo a Mario** (Literally: *To him it I'm writing to Mario*).

Reflexive verbs, whose pronouns are **mi, ti, si, ci, vi,** and **si,** also change their pronouns' spellings from **i** to **e** when used with a direct object. Check out the following examples (and see Chapter 9 for more on reflexive verbs).

> **Mi** lavo i denti. (*I'm brushing my teeth.*) **Me** li lavo. (*I'm brushing them.*)

> **Si** mandano cartoline. (*They send each other postcards.*) **Se** le mandano. (*They send them to each other.*)

The indirect object pronoun comes first (**me, se**), followed by the direct object pronoun (**li, le**) and then the verb.

Translate the following double object pronouns into English. Keep in mind that some of the forms have more than one meaning.

Q. me la

A. *it to me*

31. ce li _____

32. ve la _____

33. me li _____

34. glielo _____

35. te li _____

36. ce lo _____

37. glieli _____

38. gliele _____

39. me lo _____

40. te la _____

Putting Stress Where It's Due: Stressed and Unstressed Pronouns

Most object and subject pronouns can be stressed or unstressed. When the pronoun is right next to the verb (**ti vedo** [*I see you*]), it's unstressed, or conjunctive. When the pronoun follows the verb (**vedo te** [*I see you,* with emphasis on the *you*]), or a preposition (**con te** [*with you,* with emphasis on the *you*]) it's stressed, or disjunctive.

You also use the stressed pronoun in interjections: **Fortunato me!** (*Lucky me!*) Note that subject pronouns can be stressed and still be next to the verb, as in this example: **Prendi te qualcosa?** (*Are you having anything?*) Pronouns that attach to the verb itself are unstressed: **Posso darti qualcosa?** (*Can I give you something?*)

Some stressed pronouns change the spelling of their unstressed forms. Here's how they look.

Singular	*Plural*
me (*me, myself*)	**noi** (*us, ourselves*)
te (*you, yourself*)	**voi** (*you all, yourselves*)
lui (*him*)	**loro** (*them*)
lei (*her*)	**Loro** (*you* [formal])
Lei (*you* [formal])	**sè** (*themselves, yourselves* [formal])
sè (*himself, herself, itself, yourself* [formal])	

Notice that **lui, lei, noi, voi,** and **loro** are the same as the subject pronouns (see the earlier section "Replacing Nouns with Subject Pronouns").

You can use stressed pronouns in the following four ways.

- ✔ In exclamations:

    Beato te! (*Lucky you!*)

    Povera me! (*Poor me!*)

    Fortunati voi! (*Lucky all of you!*)

- ✔ Following prepositions:

    Laura viene con me. (*Laura is coming with me.*)

    Fai da te! (*Do it yourself!* [used to refer to stores])

    I bambini l'hanno fatto da sè. (*The kids did it by themselves.*)

- ✔ For emphasis or contrast:

    Sento te. (*I hear you.*)

    Cosa prendi te? (*What are you having?*)

    Invitano noi? (*They're inviting us?*)

- ✔ After a verb with two or more pronouns:

    Ascolto te, non loro. (*I'm listening to you, not them.*)

    Cosa prendete voi e lui? (*What are you all and he having?*)

    Invitano te, non me? (*They're inviting you, not me?*)

Looking at Ubiquitous Italian Pronouns: Ci and Ne

The pronouns **ci** and **ne** wear many hats in Italian. In their work as pronouns (or as pronouns fulfilling a variety of roles), they often combine with other pronouns and with each other. When they do, they follow the rules of formation discussed in the earlier section "Forming Double Pronouns." **Ci** becomes **ce,** but because **ne** already ends in **e,** it doesn't change when you use it in combination with another pronoun. **Ne** always follows whatever pronoun it allies itself with. I explain the nitty-gritty details of each pronoun in the following sections.

Using **ci** and **ne** comfortably takes a good deal of practice. Often, they're redundant and you can express yourself comprehensibly without them. They are, however, eminently idiomatic, and they help you sound Italian.

Checking out the characteristics of ci

Ci is a reflexive pronoun (**ci chiamiamo** [*our name is*]), a direct object pronoun (**Ci credo** [*I believe it*]), and an indirect object pronoun (**Ci fa il conto?** [*Will you bring us the bill?*]). It can take the place of a prepositional phrase (**Ci penso** [*I'm thinking about it*]). It changes the meaning of some verbs entirely (**mettere** [*to put*], **metterci** [*to take time*]; **Ci metto mezz'ora** [*it takes me half an hour*]).

Ci appears in some useful phrases: **farcela** (*to stand something, to be able to do something*), **avercela** (**con**) (*to be angry* or *to have had it with someone*), and **tenerci** (*to matter, to be really important*). See these examples:

> **Non ce la faccio.** (*I can't stand it.*) (*I can't do it.*)

> **Se proprio ci tieni.** (*If it really matters to you.*)

> **Ce l'ho avuto con te!** (*I've had it with you!*)

Characterizing **ci** is difficult, but here you can focus on its use as an adverbial pronoun, or a pronoun with an adverbial function (see Chapter 15 for a review of adverbs in general and **ci** in particular). **Ci** means both *here* and *there* and is most frequently used in the expressions **c'è** (*there is*) and **ci sono** (*there are*). Check out these uses of **ci**:

> **C'è un ristorante che puoi raccomandare?** (*Is there a restaurant you can recommend?*)

> **Ci sono molti studenti stranieri all'università.** (*There are many foreign students at the university.*)

Often **ci** is redundant. You see a good illustration of just how unnecessary it can be in this sentence: **C'è l'ho qui il libro** (*Here it I have here the book*). Certainly, such redundancy leaves no doubt about what you're saying.

Noting the numerous uses of ne

Ne is no less prolific than **ci** in its uses. This section explores all the ways you can use **ne**. As is the case with **ci, ne** can be redundant. It can replace prepositional phrases that start with **di,** but it's often added in instead of being a true substitute. For example: **Cosa ne pensate di quello?** (*What [about that] do you all think of that?*) Here are the multiple uses of **ne** and examples:

- **Ne** can replace a prepositional phrase:

    Mario viene da Siena. Ne viene. (*Mario comes from Siena. He comes from there.*)

    Che ne pensi? (*What do you think of it?*)

- **Ne** changes some verbs' meanings and emphases:

    Andarsene (*to go away, to leave*) is an emphatic way of going: **Me ne vado!** (*I'm leaving!*)

    Valerne la pena (*to be worth it*) is an emphatic statement in itself. **Non ne vale la pena.** (*It's not worth the trouble [of it].*)

- When combined with **ci,** which it often is, **ne** follows **ci** (and **ci** becomes **ce**).

    Non ce n'è (*There isn't any*).

    As you can see, **ne** also contracts with the verb **è** (so you're not saying **non ce ne è**).

- As a pronoun, **ne** replaces a noun or stressed pronoun preceded by the preposition **di:**

    Devo parlargli di questo. (*I must speak to him about this.*) **Gliene parlerò domani.** (*I'll speak to him about it tomorrow.*) **Ne** replaces **di questo.**

    Che ne sarà di me? (*What will become of me?*) **Ne** and **di me** both say the same thing: *of me.*

- **Ne** also replaces pronouns that express quantity (see Chapter 13): *some, many, seven* (and other numbers).

    Hai figli? Ne ho tre. (*Do you have children? I have three [of them].*)

    La famiglia ha molte case. Ne ha sette. (*The family has many houses. It has seven [of them].*)

    Marco ha molti libri? Ne ha tantissimi! (*Does Marco have many books? He has so many [of them].*)

    Ci sono molti turisti nel Casentino? No, non ce ne sono tanti. (*Are there many tourists in the Casentino? No, there aren't so many.*) or **Sì, ce ne sono parecchi.** (*Yes, there are several.*)

Translate the following phrases and sentences into idiomatic English.

0. **C'è un medico qui?**

A. *Is there a doctor here?*

41. **Ci sono . . .**

   _____

42. **C'è Francesca?**

   _____

43. **Non c'è.**

   _____

44. **Vorrei averne due.**

   _____

45. **Non ce n'è.**

   _____

Answer Key

1 loro

2 loro

3 voi

4 lui

5 lei

6 loro or voi

7 lei

8 noi

9 voi

10 tu

11 lo

12 li

13 le

14 ci

15 li

16 li

17 li, Li, vi

18 lo

19 lo

20 la

21 **gli, loro**

22 **mi**

23 **le**

24 **ci**

25 **gli, loro**

26 **vi**

27 **ci**

28 **gli**

29 **ti**

30 **gli, loro**

31 *them to us*

32 *it/her to you all*

33 *them to me*

34 *it to him/her/it/you/them*

35 *them to you*

36 *it to us*

37 *them to him/her/it/you/them*

38 *them to him/her/it/you/them*

39 *it to me*

40 *it to you*

41 **voi**

42 **te**

43 **lei**

44 **noi**

45 **me**

46 *there are*

47 *Is Francesca there?*

48 *She/he/it isn't here.*

49 *I would like to have two of them.*

50 *There isn't any.*

Chapter 9

Using Reflexive Forms and Expressing Imperative Moods

In This Chapter

▶ Understanding reflexive verbs

▶ Using commands formally and informally

*V*erbs come in a variety of tenses (such as past, present, future), moods (imperative and indicative), and voices (passive or active). They tell you who is doing something and what is happening.

Sometimes verbs reflect the action right back onto the subject, by way of a pronoun. These are called *reflexive* verbs. They are more common in Italian than in English, and you will find yourself using them frequently to describe everyday actions.

This chapter will focus on how reflexive verbs are used throughout the day in Italian. It will also cover another type of verb used commonly: imperatives. Imperatives are used to issue commands, give orders, or deliver instructions.

Reflecting on Reflexive Verbs

Reflexive verbs are introverted. They direct the action characteristic of verbs back on their subjects by way of a pronoun. That means that the subject both gives and receives the action of the verb. In English, it's like saying, "I call myself Mary," instead of the more linear, "My name is Mary."

Reflexive verbs appear much more frequently in Italian than in English. From waking up (**svegliarsi**) to falling asleep (**addormentarsi**), in Italian, you use reflexive verbs all through the day.

These verbs are easy to recognize in the infinitive form because the standard **-are, -ere,** and **-ire** endings drop the final **e** and finish with **si.** For example, **chiamarsi** (*to be called*), **alzarsi** (*to get up*), **domandarsi** (*to wonder* or, literally, *to ask oneself*). (For more on the infinitive form, see Chapter 6.) The conjugations of reflexive verbs follow the normal pattern for **-are, -ere,** and **-ire** verbs, but they're preceded by reflexive pronouns.

In the following sections, I show you how to use reflexive pronouns and verbs, including how to pair them together, and I guide you through the reciprocal form and the impersonal **si.**

Pairing reflexive pronouns with reflexive verbs

To use a reflexive verb, you need the reflexive pronouns. (I discuss all the varied forms of pronouns in Chapter 8.) Table 9-1 lists the Italian reflexive pronouns.

Table 9-1	Reflexive Pronouns
Singular	*Plural*
mi (*me, myself*)	**ci** (*us, ourselves*)
ti (*you, yourself*)	**vi** (*you, yourselves*)
si (*himself, herself, itself; yourself* formal)	**si** (*themselves; yourselves,* formal)

When you're building a sentence with reflexive pronouns, you put the reflexive pronoun after the personal subject pronoun (if used, which you usually don't in this case) and before the conjugated verb form. For example, **io mi alzo** uses the subject pronoun **io** (*I*), follows it with the reflexive pronoun **mi** (*myself*) and the conjugated verb **alzo** (*get up*). The reflexive pronoun is part of the appropriate verb conjugation.

The following table shows the conjugation of the reflexive verb **chiamarsi** (*to call oneself*). This verb is the most common of reflexive verbs and is probably the first one you'll use when introducing yourself to strangers in **Italian**.

chiamarsi (to call oneself, to be named)	
io mi chiamo	noi ci chiamiamo
tu ti chiami	voi vi chiamate
lui, lei, Lei si chiama	Loro, Loro si chiamano

For example: Use **Come si chiama?** (*What is your name?* [formal]) and **Come ti chiami?** (*What's your name?* [familiar]) to begin conversations. And after you ask someone else's name, it's nice to be able to offer your own: **Mi chiamo . . .** (*My name is . . .*).

Come si chiama also means *What is his, her, its, your* (formal) *name?* For example: **Come si chiama quella signora?** (*What is that woman's name?*) **Che bel gatto! Come si chiama?** (*What a beautiful cat! What's its name?*) **Come si chiama quella trattoria?** (*What's the name of that restaurant?*)

Using reflexive verbs throughout the day

Reflexive verbs carry you through the day. Although they may be introverted, they're also responsible. All the actions they portray carry right back to the subject.

To begin the day, you can use these verbs:

- ✔ **alzarsi** (_to get up_)
- ✔ **farsi il bagno, la doccia** (_to take a bath/shower_)
- ✔ **lavarsi** (_to wash up_)
- ✔ **lavarsi i denti** (_to brush your teeth_)
- ✔ **mettersi** (_to get dressed, to wear_)
- ✔ **pettinarsi** (_to comb your hair_)
- ✔ **radersi** (_to shave_)
- ✔ **svegliarsi** (_to wake up_)
- ✔ **vestirsi** (_to get dressed_)

During the day, you may do any of the following things:

- ✔ **accorgersi (di)** (_to realize_)
- ✔ **affrettarsi** (_to hurry_)
- ✔ **arrabbiarsi** (_to get angry_)
- ✔ **avvicinarsi** (_to get near_)
- ✔ **divertirsi** (_to have a good time_)
- ✔ **divorziarsi** (_to get divorced_)
- ✔ **domandarsi** (_to wonder_)
- ✔ **fermarsi** (_to stop_)
- ✔ **innamorarsi** (_to fall in love_)
- ✔ **lamentarsi** (_to complain_)
- ✔ **laurearsi** (_to graduate_)
- ✔ **muoversi** (_to move [bodily]_)
- ✔ **preoccuparsi** (_to worry_)
- ✔ **prepararsi** (_to prepare_)
- ✔ **ricordarsi (di)** (_to remember_)
- ✔ **sposarsi** (_to get married_)
- ✔ **trasferirsi (isc)** (_to move_ [from one city to another, for example])

And, finally, you can finish your day by doing the following:

- ✔ **addormentarsi** (_to go to sleep_)
- ✔ **coprirsi** (_to cover up_)
- ✔ **spogliarsi** (_to undress_)

Another extremely important reflexive verb is **trovarsi.** It's a synonym for both **essere** and **stare,** another way to say _to be._ For example: **Mi trovo molto bene.** (_I'm very well._) **Dove ti trovi?** (_Where are you?_) **Si trovano in Italia.** (_They are in Italy._)

The importance of the reflexive pronouns becomes clear if you consider that almost all reflexive verbs have nonreflexive forms and functions. For example, it's possible that **svegli i bambini, lavi i piatti, domandi qualcosa** (*you wake the children, wash the dishes, ask something*).

Compare the use of the following verbs in their reflexive and nonreflexive forms.

> **Io mi sveglio alle sei, poi, sveglio i bambini.** (*I wake up at six, and then I wake up the children.*)

> **Mi vesto, poi vesto i bambini perché i bambini sono piccoli e non sanno vestirsi.** (*I dress, and then I dress the children because the children are little and don't know how to dress themselves.*)

> **Mi diverto quando diverto i bambini.** (*I have fun when I amuse the children.*)

Complete the following sentences with the appropriate conjugations of the verbs in parentheses. Here's an example:

O. Loro _____ (svegliarsi) alle sei.

A. si svegliano

1. Lui _____ (arrabbiarsi) facilmente.

2. Primo mi faccio la doccia, poi _____ (pettinarsi).

3. Quando siamo con loro, _____ (divertirsi).

4. Lei _____ (sposarsi) domani.

5. A che ora [voi] _____ (addormentarsi)?

6. Io _____ (preoccuparsi) troppo.

7. Prima di dormire, i bambini _____ (lavarsi i denti).

8. Francesca non _____ (lamentarsi) mai.

9. Il babbo _____ (radersi) ogni mattina.

10. Io _____ (domandarsi) se lui dice la verità.

Altering the position of reflexive pronouns

Sometimes the reflexive pronoun (**mi**, **ti**, **si**, **ci**, **vi**, **si**) can be attached to the verb, but only to infinitives and present participles. **Non voglio alzarmi presto** (*I don't want to get [myself] up early*), for example, attaches the reflexive pronoun **mi** to the infinitive **alzare**, after dropping the final **e** from the infinitive. You can also say **Sto alzandomi presto** (*I'm getting [myself] up early*) by using the present participle getting and attaching the reflexive pronoun **mi** to that participle. (See Chapter 7 for use of the present participle with **stare**.)

Using the semi-auxiliaries, or a kind of helping verb, **dovere**, **potere**, and **volere** (see Chapter 7 for a quick review of these verbs), you can construct sentences that are truly idiomatic.

In the present tense, you don't want two conjugated verb forms next to one another, though a conjugated form followed by an infinitive works.

For example, you say:

> **Io devo svegliarmi alle sette.** *(I have to wake up at 7.00.)*
>
> **Non puoi svegliarti alle otto perché la classe comincia alle 8.05.** *(You can't wake up at 8.00 because class starts at 8.05.)*
>
> **Vuole svegliarsi alle nove per andare al parco.** *(He wants to wake up at 9.00 to go to the park.)*
>
> **Io devo studiare ma preferisco divertirmi.** *(I have to study, but I prefer to have a good time.)*

Notice two things about this construction. First, infinitives follow **devo** and **preferisco.** English does the same. Second, the pronoun attached to **divertirmi** is the pronoun that reflects the subject.

Another example of an attached pronoun: **Voi potete affrettarvi?** *(Can you all hurry up?)* Again, the reflexive pronoun, **vi,** reflects the subject, **voi.**

You can also attach pronouns to the present participles. (See Chapter 7 for a quick review of present participles used with **stare.**)

> **Io sto divertendomi.** *(I'm having a good time.)*
>
> **Tu stai divertendoti.** *(You are having a good time.)*
>
> **Lui, lei, Lei sta divertendosi.** *(He, she, it is having a good time./You are having a good time.)*
>
> **Noi stiamo divertendoci.** *(We are having a good time.)*
>
> **Voi state divertendovi.** *(You are having a good time.)*
>
> **Loro stanno divertendosi.** *(They are having a good time./You are having a good time.)*

Notice that the subjects (**io, tu, lui, lei, noi, voi, loro**) are reflected in the attached reflexive pronouns (**mi, ti, si, ci, vi, si**) and that both are in agreement with the verb conjugations (**sto, stai, sta, stiamo, state, stanno**).

Giving and taking with the reciprocal form

Almost any verb can be reflexive. Reciprocal reflexives take the process one step further. They use everyday verbs and show how people interact. In other words, they throw the action back on more than one subject and state things people do to each other.

For example: **Paolo e Francesca si parlano.** (*Paolo and Francesca talk to each other.*) **Ci vediamo.** (*We'll see each other.*) **Cristina e Piero già si conoscono.** (*Cristina and Piero already know each other.*) *Each other* is the key phrase here.

Parlare, vedere, and **conoscere** aren't normally reflexive verbs, but when they become reciprocal reflexives, they show people interacting with each other.

Reciprocal verbs work only in plural forms. For example:

Vi conoscete, vero? (*You know each other, right?*)

Non vi ricordate? (*You don't remember each other?*)

Si innamorano. (*They are falling in love with each other.*)

Si sposano. (*They are marrying each other; they are getting married.*)

Ci sentiamo. (Literally: *We'll hear each other.* [This phrase is often used on the phone to mean that *we'll talk to each other again, perhaps tomorrow.*])

Using the impersonal "si"

The impersonal construction with the reflexive pronoun **si** comes across in English as passive. And although situations occur in which the passive voice actually works better than an active form, in general, you don't want to use passive. In English, you use active voice to say, "She bought the car." But if you say, "The car was bought by her," you're using passive construction. Which do you think sounds better?

A more useful remark in the passive would be something like this: **Qui si parla inglese.** (*English is spoken here.*) Notice that the subject follows the verb. Thus, **si servono biscotti.** (*Cookies are served.*) You have to keep track of the subject and make sure the verb agrees in number with it. Consider the following examples:

Si vendono francobolli. (*Stamps are sold.*)

Si vende caffè. (*Coffee is sold.*)

Si parlano italiano, francese, giapponese e inglese. (*Italian, French, Japanese, and English are spoken.*)

Fill in the appropriate form of the reflexive, reciprocal reflexive, and impersonal **si** verbs. An example follows:

Q. **Stasera sto _____ (addormentarsi) presto.**

A. **addormentandomi**

11. **In quel ristorante non _____ (servire) carne.**

12. **Loro _____ (conoscere) da anni ed anni.**

13. **Io non _____ (ricordarsi) di loro.**

14. **Io e la mamma _____ (parlare) ogni giorno.**

15. Tu e Giuseppe _____ (vedere) spesso?

16. I bambini _____ (divertirsi) al cinema.

17. Lui _____ (radersi) prima di dormire.

18. Il bus _____ (fermarsi) proprio qui.

19. Io vorrei _____ (alzarsi) tardi.

20. Dobbiamo _____ (prepararsi).

Giving a Commanding Performance with the Imperative

Nowhere is the divide between familiar and formal forms of address more evident than when you use the imperative. The very distinction between familiar and formal tells you something important about manners. If you wouldn't use a command (often a demand) in English, then you certainly wouldn't use it in Italian.

The imperative isn't a tense; it's a mood. Italian has four moods: indicative (used to indicate something); subjunctive (subjective); conditional (used when something is dependent on certain conditions, such as "what if"); and the imperative (used with a sense of immediacy, though it's often made to sound like a request).

You can buffer your commands by including yourself in them. For example, in English, you may say, "Let's do that," which is more gentle than saying, "Do that."

Most commands, however, are directed at other people. So you need to be familiar or formal, and you need to know how many people you're addressing. Because you'll probably use familiar commands more often than formal ones, surprisingly often in fact, the first part of this section focuses on those "friendly" forms. The rest covers irregular imperative forms, formal commands, and where to put pronouns that you are using with commands.

Constructing positive and negative commands (of the tu, noi, and voi variety)

Mangia! (*Eat!*) says the proverbial Italian restaurant advertisement. This command is directed specifically at you in an informal way. To create the **tu** form of a positive or affirmative command, you first need to figure out whether the infinitive belongs to the **-are, -ere,** or **-ire** family of conjugations.

For regular **-are** verbs, you switch the characteristic present indicative endings. For **-ere** and **-ire** verbs, you keep the **tu** endings you already know. Check out the affirmative **tu** commands in Table 9-2.

Table 9-2	Tu Commands in the Affirmative	
Infinitive	*Present Indicative Tu Form*	*Imperative Tu Form*
mangiare	mangi (*you eat/are eating*)	mangia (*eat!*)
parlare	parli (*you speak/are speaking*)	parla (*speak!*)
ascoltare	ascolti (*you listen/are listening*)	ascolta (*listen!*)
abitare	abiti (*you live/are living*)	abita (*live!*)
scrivere	scrivi (*you write/are writing*)	scrivi (*write!*)
leggere	leggi (*you read/are reading*)	leggi (*read!*)
dormire	dormi (*you sleep/are sleeping*)	dormi (*sleep!*)
capire (isc)	capisci (*you understand/are understanding*)	capisci (*understand!*)
finire (isc)	finisci (*you finish/are finishing*)	finisci (*finish!*)
servire	servi (*you serve/are serving*)	servi (*serve!*)

Notice anything? The only **tu** form that changes belongs to **-are** verbs. And you don't use the personal subject pronouns.

As for **-ere** and **-ire** verbs (including **isc** verbs), the indicative **tu** and the imperative forms are the same. **Scrivi una lettera** can mean *you are writing a letter,* or it can be *write a letter.* **Leggi un libro** can indicate that *you are reading a book,* or it can be a command, probably from a teacher (*read a book*).

I have more good news as far as the familiar commands go. The **noi** and **voi** present indicative and imperative forms are also identical. The **noi** form comes across as more of a suggestion. For example: **Mangiamo!** (*Let's eat!*) **Andiamo!** (*Let's go!*) **Finiamo!** (*Let's finish!*) You use the **voi** form to address friends because it can have a stronger edge to it: **Andate!** (*Go!*) But it also retains its present indicative conjugated form.

To make these commands negative, you simply put **non** before them, though only with **noi** and **voi.** For example: **Non mangiate.** (*Don't eat.*) **Non finite.** (*Don't finish.*)

To make a **tu** command negative, you start with **non** (*don't*), but then you follow it with the original infinitive, such as these examples.

> **Non mangiamo questo.** (*Let's not eat this.*)
>
> **Non mangiate quello.** (*Don't eat that.*)

But . . .

> **Non mangiare quello.** (*Don't eat that.*)
>
> **Non parliamo con loro.** (*Let's not talk to them.*)
>
> **Non parlate con loro.** (*Don't talk to them.*)

But . . .

> **Non parlare con loro.** (*Don't talk to them.*)

Use the subjects, indicated in brackets, to translate the following sentences in Italian. The sentences may seem somewhat stilted because you have no pronouns attached to them — yet. You will later in this section. Here's an example.

Q. [**noi**] *Let's read.*

A. **Leggiamo.**

21. [**tu**] *Don't talk.*

_____

22. [**noi**] *Let's eat.*

_____

23. [**voi**] *Sleep (go to sleep).*

_____

24. [**tu**] *Sing.*

_____

25. [**tu**] *Don't call.*

_____

26. [**noi**] *Let's talk.*

_____

27. [**voi**] *Buy the car.*

_____

28. [**noi**] *Let's not write.*

_____

29. [**tu**] *Don't look.*

_____

30. [**voi**] *Wait.*

_____

Dealing with irregular imperatives

To create commands with irregular verbs, the same rules apply as for regular forms. **Noi** and **voi** commands are the same as the present indicative tense conjugations, though perhaps said in a different tone of voice. The **tu** forms are different enough that they deserve a little more attention; Table 9-3 lists the familiar **tu** commands.

Table 9-3	Singular Familiar (tu) Commands in Irregular Verbs	
Infinitive	*Affirmative Command*	*Negative Command*
essere (*to be*)	**sii** (*be*)	**non essere** (*don't be*)
avere (*to have*)	**abbi** (*have*)	**non avere** (*don't have*)
fare (*to make, to do*)	**fa'** (*make, do*)	**non fare** (*don't make, don't do*)
dare (*to give*)	**da'** (*give*)	**non dare** (*don't give*)
dire (*to tell, to say*)	**di'** (*tell, say*)	**non dire** (*don't tell, don't say*)
stare (*to be, to stay*)	**sta'** (*be, stay*)	**non stare** (*don't be, don't stay*)
andare (*to go*)	**va'** (*go*)	**non andare** (*don't go*)

The apostrophes show that these commands are simply shortened versions of the **tu** form in the present indicative tense. Occasionally, you'll hear someone say **Dai!** This isn't a comment on your mortality but a way to say *Come on!* It's actually a form of encouragement. It's also used to mean *really?* in the sense of *oh, come on,* or *you're kidding, right?* In English, a similar phrase may be *Come off it!*

Use these **tu, noi,** and **voi** forms only with people whom you're familiar with, such as family, friends, peers, children, and pets.

Commanding politely: Forming the Lei and Loro forms of the imperative

Regular and irregular forms of the polite (formal) imperative change the characteristic vowel of the infinitive. **A** becomes **i,** and **e** and **ono** change to **a** and **ano.** So if you want to say **Lei parla** (*you* [formal] *are speaking*) as a command, you'd say **parli** (*speak*). Or **Loro finiscono** (*they are finishing,* or *you* [formal] *are finishing*) becomes **finiscano** (*finish*).

As a general rule, the **Lei** command for irregular verbs takes its form from the first-person singular of the verb's present indicative. You can see examples in Table 9-4.

Table 9-4	Lei Commands of Irregular Verbs	
Infinitive	*First-Person Singular Present Indicative*	*Lei Command*
venire (*to come*)	**io vengo** (*I come*)	**venga** (*come*)
andare (*to go*)	**io vado** (*I go*)	**vada** (*go*)
dire (to tell, to say)	**io dico** (*I tell*)	**dica** (*tell*)
fare (*to make, to do*)	**io faccio** (*I make*)	**faccia** (*make*)
porre (*to put, to place*)	**io pongo** (*I put*)	**ponga** (*put*)
tradurre (*to translate*)	**io traduco** (*I translate*)	**traduca** (*translate*)

Naturally, **avere** and **essere** continue to do their own idiosyncratic thing. The **Lei** command for **essere** is **sia;** for **avere**, it's **abbia.**

These days, people don't use the formal plural command **Loro** often. If you're speaking to a group of people, formally, chances are you're going to use the **voi** form instead of **Loro.** Instead of saying **Parlino** (*speak*), you'd say **Parlate.** Instead of saying **Ripetano** (*repeat*), say **Ripetete.** This increasingly common practice will simplify your linguistic life to no end.

When in doubt — such as when you're talking to someone you met at a conference, or to a bureaucrat, use the formal, just as you do in speaking English.

In some instances, you never use the familiar. For example, you'll probably always be formal with the butcher you've gone to for 20 years; likewise, you'll be formal with your doctor or a teacher. Every now and again, you can avoid the use of a command completely. When asking a waiter for the bill, you say, **Ci fa il conto?** (*Would you bring the bill?*) This isn't a direct translation, but you get the idea. It's polite without being demanding.

Adding pronouns to the imperative

Some general — even dependable — rules exist for adding pronouns to the imperative.

Before reading on in this section, I recommend reviewing all the pronouns, especially the direct and indirect object pronouns, in Chapter 8. Also, you may want to take a look at the earlier section of this chapter, "Pairing reflexive pronouns with reflexive verbs", on attaching pronouns to reflexive verbs.

Affirmative familiar commands attach pronouns to the end of the command. The indirect object always precedes the direct object pronoun. For example: **Alzati.** (*Get up.*) **Leggimelo.** (*Read it to me.*)

When using the one-syllable commands (refer to Table 9-3 for examples), you double the initial letter of the pronoun, except when the pronoun is **gli.** For example: **Dammelo.** (*Give it to me.*) **Fammi vedere.** (*Show me.*) **Diglielo** (*Tell it to him.*)

With negative familiar commands, you have a choice: You can either attach the pronouns to the ends of the commands (dropping the final **e** from the infinitive in the case of the **tu** form) or put the pronouns in front of the command, like this: **Non lo fare.** (*Don't do it.*) **Non mi parlare.** (*Don't talk to me.*) **Non me lo dare.** (*Don't give it to me.*) You can also say, **Non farlo, Non parlarmi,** and **Non darmelo.**

Formal commands, both affirmative and negative, always place the pronoun before the command itself. Therefore, you say **Non lo faccia.** (*Don't do it.*) or **Mi dica.** (*Tell me.*)

To visualize and compare all these forms, check out Table 9-5.

Table 9-5	**Familiar and Formal Commands**	
Person	*Affirmative Command*	*Negative Command*
tu	**mangia** (*eat*)	**non mangiare** (*don't eat*)
	scrivi (*write*)	**non scrivere** (*don't write*)
	scriviglielo (*write it to him, her, them*)	**non scriverglielo** (*don't write it to him, her, them*)
	dormi (*sleep*)	**non dormire** (*don't sleep*)
	fa' (*do, make*)	**non fare** (*don't do, don't make*)
	fallo (*do it*)	**non lo fare** (*don't do it*)
Lei (formal)	**mangi** (*eat*)	**non mangi** (*don't eat*)
	scriva (*write*)	**non scriva** (*don't write*)
	glielo scriva (*write it to him, her, them*)	**non glielo scriva** (*don't write it to him, her, them*)
	dorma (*sleep*)	**non dorma** (*don't sleep*)
	faccia (*do*)	**non faccia** (*don't do*)
noi	**mangiamo** (*let's eat*)	**non mangiamo** (*let's not eat*)
	scriviamo (*let's write*)	**non scriviamo** (*let's not write*)
	scriviamoglielo (*let's write it to him, her, them*)	**non scriviamoglielo** (*let's not write it to him, her, them*)
	dormiamo (*let's sleep*)	**non dormiamo** (*let's not sleep*)
	facciamo (*let's do*)	**non facciamo** (*let's not do*)
noi	**mangiate** (*eat*)	**non mangiate** (*don't eat*)
	scrivete (*write*)	**non scrivete** (*don't write*)
	scriveteglielo (*write it to him, her, them*)	**non scriveteglielo** (*don't write it to him, her, them*)
	dormite (*sleep*)	**non dormite** (*don't sleep*)
	fate (*do*)	**non fate** (*don't do*)
Loro	**mangino** (*eat*)	**non mangino** (*don't eat*)
	scrivano (*write*)	**non scrivano** (*don't write*)
	gielo scrivano (*write it to him, her, them*)	**non glielo scrivano** (*don't write it to him, her, them*)
	dormano (*sleep*)	**non dormano** (*don't sleep*)
	faccino (*do*)	**non faccino** (*don't do*)

As you're going about your day and practicing Italian, you may find yourself using some of the more commonly used commands, such as the following expressions.

✔ In formal situations:

- **Scusi.** (*Excuse me.*) This word is often the only one tourists know, and it's greatly overused. To get through a crowd, you can also say, **Permesso.** (*Permission.*) To get someone's attention (a ticket vendor, for example), you can use **Senta.** (*Listen.*)

- **Mi dica.** (*Tell me.*) If you're asking for information, this expression is especially useful.

- **Si accomodi.** (*Make yourself comfortable./Take a seat.*) You hear this often in an office, where you're waiting to meet with someone.

✔ In more familiar surroundings:

- **Figurati.** (*Thanks, don't mention it.*) It also appears as **figuriamoci** ([between two friends] *don't think anything of it*).

- **Fallo pure.** (*Just do it.*) If a friend is dithering about whether to do something, this is the common piece of advice.

- **Fammi sapere.** (Literally: *Make me know;* another way to say *Tell me everything.*)

- **Fammi vedere.** (Literally: *Make me see;* another way to say *Show me.*)

- **Ma dai.** (*Oh, come on.*)

- **Non facciamo complimenti.** (*Let's be frank with each other.*)

Answer Key

1 si arrabbia

2 mi pettino

3 ci divertiamo

4 si sposa

5 vi addormentate

6 mi preoccupo

7 si lavano i denti

8 si lamenta

9 si rade

10 mi domando

11 si serve

12 si conoscono

13 mi ricordo

14 ci parliamo

15 vi vedete

16 si divertono

17 si rade

18 si ferma

19 alzarmi

20 prepararci

`21` **non parlare**

`22` **mangiamo**

`23` **dormite**

`24` **canta**

`25` **non telefonare**

`26` **parliamo**

`27` **comprate la macchina**

`28` **non scriviamo**

`29` **non guardare**

`30` **aspettate**

Chapter 10

Declaring Your Likes (and Dislikes) with Piacere

. . . .

In This Chapter

▶ Combining indirect object pronouns with **piacere** to express likes and dislikes

▶ Using **piacere** in different tenses

▶ Familiarizing yourself with other verbs that work like **piacere**

. . . .

The key to expressing yourself in any language is being able to share what you enjoy and what you don't care for. Getting to know people without understanding what hobbies they enjoy or what activities they really don't like can be difficult. A waiter will be better able to recommend a dish for you if you can let him know you don't care for anchovies or that you're crazy about a particular type of cheese.

In this chapter, I explain how to express likes and dislikes across the verb tenses with **piacere,** and I show you other verbs that work in a similar fashion. To use **piacere,** you need to construct sentences backward — at least to begin with. In English, if you want to say that you like something, you simply say *I like coffee,* for example; in Italian, this phrases takes the form *Coffee is pleasing to me.* You build your sentence so it reads, literally, *To me* (**mi**) *is pleasing* (**piace**) *coffee* (**il caffè**).

Using **piacere** also requires indirect object pronouns (**mi** [*to/for me*], **ti** [*to/for you*], and so on), which I explain in this chapter. You use either the singular **piace** (*it is pleasing*) or the plural **piacciono** (*they are pleasing*) and the object(s) (one or many) of your desire.

Understanding How to Use Piacere

To say you like something in English, you use a direct manner, such as *I like to read.* In Italian, you explain that something pleases you: **Mi piace leggere** (Literally: *Reading is pleasing to me*). In other words, Italian reverses the subject and object; the English direct object (*to read*) becomes an Italian subject (*reading*). The English subject (*I*) turns into an indirect object pronoun (**mi**). Whatever is liked becomes the subject. Whoever is doing the liking becomes the object.

> **Mi** (*to me*) **piace** (*is pleasing*) **leggere** (*to read/reading*).

With **piacere,** indirect object pronouns reveal who is pleased by (or who likes) something, so I start this section with a discussion on indirect object pronouns then go on to talk about likes and dislikes across time and show you **piacere's** past, present, and future forms. (For more on pronouns, see Chapter 8.)

Working with indirect object pronouns

In general, pronouns replace nouns in sentences and help to avoid monotonous repetition. For example: "Giuseppe gives the twins the old car. He gives it to them." In the second sentence, *Giuseppe,* the subject, is replaced by the pronoun *he.* The direct object (or what is being given), *the car,* is replaced by the direct object pronoun *it.* And the indirect object (or who receives the gift), *the twins,* is replaced by the indirect object pronoun *them.* Here's another example:

> **Io ho mandato molte cartoline agli amici.** (*I sent a lot of postcards to friends.*) **Gli ho mandato molte cartoline.** (*I sent them a lot of postcards.*) Here, you replace **agli amici** (*to friends*) with **Gli** (*to them*).

In the same way, **piacere** uses indirect object pronouns to tell who likes something or to whom something is pleasing. For example:

> **Mi piacciono i fiori.** (*I like flowers.*) (Literally: *Flowers are pleasing to me.*)

> **Ti piacciono i fiori?** (*Do you like flowers?*) (Literally: *Do flowers please you?*)

Indirect objects are recognizable (and distinguished from direct objects) by the questions they answer: "To or for whom?" and "To or for what?" Indirect objects are preceded by a preposition (*to, for,* and so on). In English, this preposition is often understood rather than expressed, as in *Giuseppe gives [to] them the car.* In Italian, the preposition is built into the indirect object pronoun (**Giuseppe gli dà la macchina**).

Table 10-1 lists the indirect object pronouns in Italian and their English equivalents.

Table 10-1	Indirect Object Pronouns
Singular	*Plural*
mi (*to/for me*)	**ci** (*to/for us*)
ti (*to/for you*)	**vi** (*to/for you*)
gli (*to/for him*)	**loro/gli** (*to/for them* [masculine, feminine])
le (*to/for her*)	**Loro/Gli** (*to/for you* [formal])
Le (*to/for you* [formal])	

Loro has largely given way to **gli,** which can mean *to or for him, to or for them,* and *to or for you* (formal). If it's combined with a direct object pronoun (**lo, la, li,** or **le**), it becomes **glielo gliela, glieli,** or **gliele** and can also mean *to or for her.* So **Mario glielo dà** can mean *Mario gives it to her/him/it/you/them,* depending on context.

How do **piacere** and the indirect object pronouns combine to tell who likes something? Read on.

Conjugating piacere

The verb **piacere** conjugates irregularly. It doesn't use subject pronouns, so in the tables throughout this chapter, when I do include subject pronouns for reference, I put them in brackets. You can see the basic conjugation of **piacere** in the following table.

piacere (to please)	
[io] piac**cio**	[noi] piac**ciamo**
[tu] piac**i**	[voi] piac**ete**
[lui, lei, Lei] piac**e**	[loro, Loro] piac**ciono**

The forms you'll use almost exclusively in the present tense are **piace** and **piacciono**. If you like one thing, you use the singular **piace. Mi piace leggere,** for example, is *I like to read.* An infinitive is singular, and even when you add more than one infinitive, **piace** is the form to use: **Mi piace leggere, scrivere e mangiare.** (*I like to read, write, and eat.*)

When you're talking about two or more things that you like, you use **piacciono.**

> **Mi piacciono i gatti.** (*I like cats.*)

> **Gli piacciono gli sport.** (*He likes sports.*)

Notice that the second **gli** is an article, not an indirect object pronoun (see Chapter 3 for a review of articles). In Italian, you use the article before the thing that is liked.

Using piacere with indirect object pronouns

Using **piacere** is easy enough. You or someone likes one thing (**piace**) or more than one thing (**piacciono**). Table 10-2 shows how to use **piace/piacciono** with the indirect object pronouns. When combined with the indirect object pronouns, **piacere**'s meaning becomes *to like.*

Table 10-2	Piacere and Indirect Object Pronouns
Singular	*Plural*
mi piace/piacciono (*I like*)	**ci piace/piacciono** (*we like*)
ti piace/piacciono (*you like*)	**vi piace/piacciono** (*you like*)
gli piace/piacciono (*he likes*)	**gli piace/piacciono** (*they like*)
le piace/piacciono (*she likes*)	**Gli piace/piacciono** (*you* [formal] *like*)
Le piace/piacciono (*you* [formal] *like*)	

Most of the time, people use only the third person singular and plural forms of **piacere.** However, occasionally, you'll hear someone say **le piaccio** (*she likes me*) (Literally: *I am pleasing to her*). If someone says to you **mi piaci,** he or she is saying *I like you.* Keep in mind that you're building sentences backward (placing the indirect object *before* the subject).

Another oddity, if you will, about using **piacere** is that you don't have to state the Italian subject or what in English would be the direct object. Here are some examples:

> **I bambini? Sì, mi piacciono.** (*Children? Yes, I like [them].*) *Them* is understood, though not expressed in Italian.

> **Ti piace viaggiare? Sì, mi piace.** (*Do you like to travel? Yes, I like [it].*)

> **Le piace cucinare? No, non le piace.** (*Does she like to cook? No, she doesn't like [it].*)

Finally, what if you want to say that a specific person, such as Rodolfo likes something? That is, you specifically want to name whoever is doing the liking. Simply remember that **piace/piacciono** means *is/are pleasing,* and you need to indicate that something is pleasing *to* someone. Adding the preposition **a** before a person or a pronoun gives you that *to.* For example:

> **A Rodolfo piace scrivere.** (*Rodolfo likes to write.*) (Literally: *Writing is pleasing to Rodolfo.*)

> **A Laura piacciono i fiori.** (*Laura likes flowers.*)

If you're using pronouns that are a little more emphatic, you may say **A lui piacciono i fiori** (*He likes flowers*).

Some of the pronouns change form slightly when preceded by a preposition, such as the following:

a me piace questo	a noi piace
a te piace	a voi piace
a lui piace	a loro piace
a lei piace	

Only **lui** and **lei** remain the same as their original indirect object forms. I discuss the other pronouns, stressed or disjunctive pronouns, in Chapter 8.

Never use both the regular indirect object pronouns and the form that follows **a** together (such as **a me mi piace**). It's considered vulgar and is simply not appropriate in Italian — ever!

Choose either **piace** or **piacciono** to complete the following sentences. Remember that you use **piace** for one thing and **piacciono** for more than one thing. Here's an example:

Q. Mi _____ i libri.

A. piacciono

1. Gli _____ studiare.

2. Ti _____ i bambini?

3. Non mi _____ i ragni.

4. A loro _____ mangiare.

5. Ci _____ i fiori.

6. Le _____ scrivere poesie.

7. Vi _____ gli sport?

8. Gli _____ i vini italiani.

9. Ti _____ il caffè ristretto?

10. A Mario _____ la bistecca fiorentina.

After filling in the forms of **piace/piacciono** in Questions 1 through 10, translate the sentences into English, as per the example.

Q. Mi piacciono i libri.

A. *I like books.*

11. _____

12. _____

13. _____

14. _____

15. _____

16. _____

17. _____

18. _____

19. _____

20. _____

Expressing Likes (and Dislikes) in Any Tense

You can conjugate all verbs in all indicative and subjunctive moods across the tenses. **Piacere** is no exception. The present indicative, present subjunctive, and the past absolute tenses are irregular, but **piacere** turns regular for all other conjugated forms. I explore these conjugations and more in the following sections.

Working with the subjunctive and past absolute conjugations of piacere

Earlier, I conjugated **piacere** in the present indicative tense (refer to the section "Conjugating piacere"). Here, I show you how to conjugate **piacere** in the present subjunctive and the past absolute.

In other tenses and in the conditional mood, **piacere** follows regular rules of conjugation. See Chapters 6, 7, 9, and Parts IV and V for general rules about verbs.

Subjunctive

The subjunctive mood lets you express possibility, doubt, fear, emotions; it's ultimately subjective.

[io] piaccia	[noi] piac**ciamo**
[tu] piac**cia**	[voi] piac**ciate**
[lui, lei, Lei] piac**cia**	[loro, Loro] piac**ciano**

Nowhere is sound as important as in the subjunctive because one difference in the pronunciation lets you know that a different verb mood is being used. Because the subjunctive lets you express nuance, doubt, and emotion (among other things), pronunciation is important.

Mi piacciono (*I like them*) indicates that you definitely like something. **Credo che mi piacciano** (*I think I like them*) means that you're not entirely sure. To say that you don't like something, you simply say **No, non mi piace.** The word **non** makes the sentiment negative.

A variation on **piacere** is **dispiacere.** Don't get confused and think this means *not to like.* It means *to be sorry.* You bump into someone and say **Mi dispiace** (*I'm sorry*). You lose your passport, and a friend says **Mi dispiace tanto** (*I'm so sorry*).

For an overview of the subjunctive, see Chapters 19, 20, 21, and 22. Yes, it's so important that I dedicate four chapters to it!

Past absolute

You use the past absolute to describe things that happened long ago and far away.

[io] piac**qui**	[noi] piac**emmo**
[tu] piac**esti**	[voi] piac**este**
[lui, lei, Lei] piac**que**	[loro, Loro] piac**quero**

Use of the past absolute, or the **passato remoto,** varies depending on where you are. Some regions of Italy hardly ever use it; in other regions, people use it to talk about things that happened last week. See Chapter 16 for a complete overview of this tense.

The past absolute shows up most frequently in literature and opera. To read Dante's *Inferno,* or any of the classics for that matter, you need to be able to recognize the past absolute. For example, **com'altrui piacque** (*as pleased another*) achieves almost formulaic status in the *Inferno.* The past absolute is notoriously irregular, so much so that when you look at conjugated forms, you sometimes can't figure out what the source infinitive is.

Being able to recognize the past absolute and understanding the most irregular forms are generally all you need to get by. You probably don't need to study the past absolute too much or memorize its conjugations.

Checking out more conjugations for piacere

Piacere has different conjugations for the future, the conditional, the imperfect, the present perfect or past, and the pluperfect. I explain all of them in this section. *Note:* In the interests of giving you workable (read: useful) grammar, I use only the third person forms of these various tenses and moods.

Future

The future tense of **piacere** is **piacerà** (singular) and **piaceranno** (plural). If, for example, you're telling a friend about a movie you just saw that you think she'll like, you use the future tense and say **Ti piacerà** (*You'll like it*). You can also use this tense to introduce someone to friends that you think that person will like: **Ti piaceranno.** (*You'll like them.*)

You can use the future tense to indicate probability. So **ti piacerà** can also mean *you will probably like it.*

Conditional

You use the conditional (**piacerebbe,** singular, or **piacerebbero,** plural) to express something that may be. For example, say you're expressing reservations about something, so you say **Mi piacerebbe ma . . .** (*I would like it, but . . .*). Or you think someone would like something: **Ti piacerebbero.** (*You would like them.*) Frequently, this construction includes a follow-up clause, explaining just why you like or don't like something. The conditional is often part of a complex sentence that uses the subjunctive for its second half. (See Chapters 19, 20, 21, and 22 for more information on this construction.)

Present perfect/past and imperfect

Knowing when to use either the present perfect/past or the imperfect takes practice. You can simplify this decision by considering the following questions each tense answers.

✔ The **present perfect/past** (**è piaciuto, è piaciuta,** singular, or **sono piaciuti, sono piaciute,** plural) answers the questions, "What happened? What did you (or someone else) do?" In the case of **piacere,** I often add the question, "Did you like it/them?"

The present perfect/past refers to a completed past action, something you started and finished, something that's over.

✔ The **imperfect** (**piaceva,** singular, or **piacevano,** plural) answers different questions: "What was something like? What was going on? What used to (habitually) go on? What did you used to do, regularly?"

The imperfect is the ultimately descriptive tense. The reason fairy tales begin with **C'era una volta . . .** (*Once upon a time, there was . . .*) is because they're opening up a story about the past that isn't completed, that isn't yet perfected — that's imperfect.

For example, you give someone a book to read and want to know whether she liked it: **Ti è piaciuto il libro?** (*Did you like the book?*) Or you show a friend a house you're thinking of renting or buying and want to get his opinion: **Gli è piaciuta la casa.** (*He liked the house.*) In both cases, you're talking about something that has happened, so you use the present perfect/past tense: She read the book. She liked it. He liked the house. End of story.

The thing liked determines the gender of **piaciuto.** A book, being masculine, takes **piaciuto.** A house, feminine, takes **piaciuta.** The plural forms follow this suit, too.

> **Ti sono piaciuti i libri?** (*Did you like the books?*) **Gli sono piaciute le case.** (*He liked the houses.*)

Verbal clues that tell you an action is recent and completed include **ieri** (*yesterday*), **due settimane fa** (*two weeks ago*), and other phrases that fix a time.

On the other hand, the very meaning of **piacere,** *liking,* lends itself to the imperfect because liking tends to be ongoing, unconfined by time. Rarely do you like something only between 2 and 4 p.m. when it wasn't raining, for example. Once again, context is everything.

Take this example: **Da bambino, gli piaceva andare al cinema il sabato.** (*As a child, he liked going to the movies on Saturdays.*) This sentence has two clues that you want to use the imperfect: *As a child* indicates an ongoing time, and *Saturdays* indicates that this action was a habitual one.

Another word that indicates habitual action is **ogni** (*every*). **Ogni giorno ci piaceva guardare la televisione.** (*Every day, we liked to watch TV.*)

Ci piacevano gli animali. (*We liked animals; we have always liked animals.*) Here, the speaker is talking about something they've always liked, as opposed to the animals they saw at the zoo this afternoon. **Le piaceva nuotare.** (*She liked swimming.*) Again, you're saying that this is something she has always liked.

Pluperfect (past perfect)

The pluperfect, or past perfect (**era piaciuto, era piaciuta,** singular, or **erano piaciuti, erano piaciute,** plural), follows the same rules as the present perfect. The only difference is in the helping verb, which you use in the imperfect rather than the present (**era** instead of **è,** and **erano** instead of **sono**). The pluperfect refers to something that had happened, often before another event being discussed. In English, you may say, *He had finished the first book before he began the second.* The first verb, *had finished,* is in the pluperfect; the second, *began,* is in the present perfect.

Likewise, you distinguish the pluperfect from the imperfect by asking the same questions: "What had happened? What had he done?" In the case of **piacere,** "What had he liked?" It refers, in other words, to something that occurred and is over.

For example: **Non gli era piciuto il libro.** (*He hadn't liked the book.*) A further elaboration may include the phrase *when he read it the first time.* **Non gli erano piaciute le poesie di quello scrittore.** (*He hadn't liked that writer's poetry.*)

For Questions 21 through 30, use the tense or mood in parentheses to fill in the blank with the verb **piacere.** Here's an example:

Q. Ti _____ (future) la musica.

A. piacerà

21. Gli _____ (future) le macchine.

22. Mi _____ (conditional) andare.

23. A lei _____ (pluperfect) la casa.

24. Vi _____ (conditional) venire?

25. Ti _____ (future) le isole.

26. Vi _____ (conditional) le montagne qui.

27. Non mi _____ (pluperfect) i biscotti.

28. Ci _____ (conditional) fare una telefonata.

29. Gli _____ (future) i nuovi pantaloni.

30. Ma non le _____ (future) la casa.

Using piacere as a noun

Piacere does double linguistic duty. It isn't just a verb (although that would be noteworthy enough), but it's also a noun. You use it as a noun most frequently when you meet someone. Upon being introduced, you say **Piacere** (*It's a pleasure*). The person you have just met may respond with **Il piacere è tutto mio** (*The pleasure is all mine*).

At its most basic, the noun **piacere** means *a pleasure.* You can make something into a great pleasure by adding the suffix **-one**. **Un piacerone** refers to something that is **un vero piacere** (a *true pleasure*).

For Questions 31 through 40, choose between using the present perfect or the imperfect tense of **piacere**. Here's an example:

Q. **La domenica ci _____ leggere i fumetti.**

A. **piaceva**

31. **Questo ultimo disegno non ci _____.**

32. **Non le _____ l'opera di Michelangelo.**

33. **A Rodolfo _____ di solito mangiare presto.**

34. **Ieri ho letto un libro che mi _____.**

35. **Ogni estate ci _____ visitare la nonna.**

36. **Mentre gli _____ il computer, non l'ha comprato.**

37. **Ai bambini _____ mangiare dolci.**

38. **Da bambina mi _____ leggere e scrivere.**

39. **Mi _____ quel film.**

40. **Al gatto non _____ il nuovo cibo.**

Looking at Other Verbs that Work Backward

Several Italian verbs work the same way as **piacere** — that is, backward and with accompanying indirect object pronouns. Some of them make more sense than others.

Those that make the most sense are **bastare** (*to be enough*), **sembrare** (*to seem*), **importare** (*to be important*), and **interessare** (*to be of interest*). All these verbs in English carry the stated or unstated indirect object in their constructions. For example: *It's of no interest to me. It's not important to me. Two are enough for me.* And, of course, *it seems to me.*

Here are the most used forms of these verbs:

- **basta** (*it's enough*)/**bastano** (*they're enough*)
- **sembra** (*it seems*)/**sembrano** (*they seem*)
- **importa** (*it's important*)/**importano** (*they're important*)
- **interessa** (*it's of interest*)/**interessano** (*they're of interest*)

The indirect object pronoun is *always* stated with these verbs. As with **piacere,** it precedes the conjugated forms. The following examples show how they work. They really aren't so different from their English counterparts; the main difference is that, in English, you don't usually add the indirect object.

Mi basta uno. (*One is enough for me.*)

Ti bastano dieci? (*Are ten enough for you?*)

Non mi sembra sincero. (*He doesn't seem honest to me.*)

Non mi sembrano veri. (*They don't seem real to me.*)

Non mi importa. (*It's not important to me.*) (*It doesn't matter.*)

Non mi importano le regole. (*The rules don't matter to me.*)

Non gli interessa. (*He isn't interested in it.*) (*It's of no interest to him.*)

Non ci interessano. (*We're not interested in them.*) (*They're of no interest to us.*)

Questions 41 through 50 use the verbs in parentheses: **bastare, sembrare, importare,** and **interessare.** Fill in the blanks with the appropriate conjugated form of the verb. All the verbs are used in the present tense. Remember to make the verb agree in number with what's enough, important, interesting, or seems to be. Here is an example:

Q. Ci _____ (interessare) le sue idee.

A. interessano

41. I film di lui non mi _____ (interessare).

42. Mi _____ (bastare) tre tuorli.

43. Loro ci _____ (sembrare) onesti.

44. Queste cose non le _____ (importare).

45. La ragazza non gli _____ (sembrare) sincera.

46. Questo posto mi _____ (sembrare) ideale.

47. C'è soltanto uno. Non ci _____ (bastare) questo.

48. Non gli _____ (interessare) le idee degli altri.

49. A me _____ (interessare) la moda.

50. A Paolo e Giuseppe _____ (importare) gli sport.

One other fairly common verb that works backward is **mancare** (*to miss*). I may miss my friends; you may miss your family; the cat misses his owner. The conjugation of the basic verb **mancare** is regular, as you can see in the following table. But the translation includes the added prepositions *to* or *by,* as in *I am missing to* or *I am missed by.*

mancare (to miss)	
[io] man**co**	[noi] man**chiamo**
[tu] man**chi**	[voi] man**cate**
[lui, lei, Lei] man**ca**	[loro, Loro] man**cano**

In other words, you, they, I, he, and we, for example, are missing *to* someone. To put it more idiomatically, they're missed *by* someone. If I miss my friends **Mi mancano** (*I miss them*) or (*They are missed by me*). If you say to someone **Ti manco**, you may sound more coy than you want because it means *You miss me* or *I am missed by you*.

To know who is doing the actual missing, you plug in the appropriate indirect object pronoun. For example:

Mi mancate. (*I miss you* [plural])

Mi manchi. (*I miss you.*)

Gli mancano i bambini. (*He misses the kids.*)

Ci manca la spiaggia; ti mancano le montagne. (*We miss the beach; you miss the mountains.*)

Admittedly, this verb takes some getting used to. Just remember that the indirect object pronoun, which precedes the verb, reveals who the subject is.

Using the appropriate form of **mancare,** translate the following sentences into Italian. Here's an example.

0. *He misses them.*

A. **Gli mancano.**

51. *I miss them.*

52. *You miss her.*

53. *They miss me.*

54. *We miss you* (plural).

55. *They miss them.*

Answer Key

1 **piace**

2 **piacciono**

3 **piacciono**

4 **piace**

5 **piacciono**

6 **piace**

7 **piacciono**

8 **piacciono**

9 **piace**

10 **piace**

11 *He likes to study.*

12 *Do you like children?*

13 *I don't like spiders.*

14 *They like to eat.*

15 *We like flowers.*

16 *She likes to write poems.*

17 *Do you like sports?*

18 *They like Italian wines. He likes Italian wines.*

19 *Do you like strong coffee?*

20 *Mario likes Florentine steak.*

21 **piaceranno**

22 **piacerebbe**

23 **era piaciuta**

24 **piacerebbe**

25 **piaceranno**

26 **piacerebbero**

27 **erano piaciuti**

28 **piacerebbe**

29 **piaceranno**

30 **piacerà**

31 **è piaciuto**

32 **piaceva**

33 **piaceva**

34 **è piaciuto**

35 **piaceva**

36 **piaceva**

37 **piacevano**

38 **piaceva**

39 **è piaciuto**

40 **è piaciuto**

41 **interessano**

`42` **basta**

`43` **sembrano**

`44` **importano**

`45` **sembra**

`46` **importano**

`47` **basta**

`48` **interessano**

`49` **interessa**

`50` **importano**

`51` **Mi mancano.**

`52` **Ti manca.**

`53` **Gli manco.**

`54` **Ci mancate.**

`55` **Gli mancano.**

Chapter 11

Asking and Responding to Questions

. . . .

In This Chapter

▶ Understanding how to ask and answer questions in Italian

▶ Knowing how to request what you need

▶ Sharing information with others

▶ Answering questions in the negative

. . . .

*W*ho? What? When? Where? Why? How? These basic questions, and variations on them, allow you to get the information you need in any language. Knowing how to ask questions is essential in the Italian world (and beyond). Here are some simple questions that can be answered with *yes, no,* or one or two words.

Vieni con noi? (*Are you coming with us?*) **Sì.** (*Yes.*)

È già arrivata? (*Has she already arrived?*) **No.** (*No.*)

Come stai? (*How are you?*) **Bene, grazie.** (*Fine, thanks.*)

Chi parla? (*Who's speaking?*) **Elisabetta.** (*Elizabeth.*)

But questions become more open-ended as you dig deeper and want more details and as you gain confidence and build your vocabulary. Such questions lead to conversation, discussion, even disagreement — all forms of your ultimate linguistic goal: communication.

In writing, you can recognize a question because it's followed by a question mark. In speech, you have to depend on other signs. Do you end the sentence on an up note? Do you put the subject at the end of the sentence?

The question words *who, what, when, where, why,* and *how* are basic to reporters, police officers, and parents. Questions with these words require more than a yes or no answer. In this chapter, you discover how to ask questions and, by doing so, how to listen carefully to questions you're asked so you can answer them appropriately.

Looking at Ways of Asking Questions in Italian

"Curiouser and curiouser" is the language-learner's motto. To satisfy your curiosity and to understand both a different language and a different culture, you need to be able to ask questions. You have relatively easy ways to do this: You can change your tone (or pitch) of voice, you can add a word like *right?* to the end of a sentence, or you can move the subject from the beginning to the end of a sentence. I explore these variations on asking questions in the following sections.

Adjusting your intonation

Language is musical, and nowhere do you see that better than in crafting sentences to make a statement, to exclaim, or to ask a question.

With a statement, you keep your voice pretty level. For example: **Carlo parla italiano** (*Carlo speaks Italian*) has a level tone with a slight drop at the end. To make this statement into a question, you raise your tone (think of it as going up a couple of notes on the musical scale) on the next-to-last syllable and then drop back a note on the very last syllable: **Carlo parla ital /ia \no?** (*Does Carlo speak Italian?*) If you listen to yourself, you discover that you make this same tone change in English.

Another option is to leave the sentence as a statement but finish it off with words like **no? non è vero?** or just **vero?** All translate, more or less, into *right?* or *isn't that so?* You can also say **ok?** or **va bene?** Both of which mean *okay?* When you use these words, you again go up a note or two on the musical scale. Here are some examples

> **Ho comprato i biglietti, va bene?** (*I've bought the tickets, okay?*)

> **Andiamo al cinema domani, no?** (*We're going to the movies tomorrow, right?*)

> **Tuo padre lavora sempre a Milano, vero?** (*Your father still works in Milan, right?*)

Flipping the word order: Inversion

Another way to turn a statement into a question is to move the subject from the beginning to the end of the sentence. **Carlo parla italiano** (*Carlo speaks Italian*) is a statement; **Parla italiano, Carlo?** (*Does Carlo speak Italian?*) is a question.

This technique works only if you have a stated subject. Here's another example:

> **Il gatto ha mangiato tutto il cibo.** (*The cat has eaten all the food.*) **Ha mangiato tutto il cibo, il gatto?** (*Has the cat eaten all the food?*)

Getting started with some common questions

In this section, I list some standard questions that will get you into the practice of asking about things. Some are more open-ended (like those that ask where something is) and may elicit a longer response than you can understand at first. You can anticipate an answer to a *where* question by using props — a street map, for example, allows someone to show you what they're talking about.

✔ **Come sta?** (*How are you?* [formal])

✔ **Come stai?** (*How are you?* [familiar])

✔ **Come va?** (*How are things going?*)

✔ **Come si chiama?** (*What is your name?* [formal])

✔ **Come ti chiami?** (*What is your name?* [familiar])

✔ **Chi è?** (*Who is it?*)

✔ **Che tempo fa?** (*What's the weather?*)

✔ **Come si dice** _____? (*How do you say* _____ *[in Italian]?*)

✔ **Cosa vuol dire** _____? (*What does* _____ *mean?*)

✔ **Dove, dov'è, dove sono** _____? (*Where, where is, where are* _____?)

✔ **Quanto costa?** (*How much is it?*)

✔ **Come?** (*Huh? What did you say?*)

✔ **Perché?** (*Why?*)

✔ **Pronto?** (*Hello?* [used to answer the phone])

Change the following statements into questions by moving the subject from the beginning to the end of the sentence. I underline the subject so it's easily recognizable. Don't forget to add a question mark.

Q. <u>Marisa</u> studia molto.

A. Studia molto, Marisa?

1. <u>Michele</u> ha mangiato tutti i biscotti.

   _____

2. <u>I ragazzi</u> sono a scuola.

   _____

3. <u>Tua madre</u> è impegnatissima.

   _____

4. <u>Giuseppe</u> parla inglese.

   _____

5. <u>Le nuove macchine</u> sono molto belle.

   _____

6. <u>Tu</u> prepari da mangiare.

   _____

7. <u>Marco e Lorenzo</u> sono andati in centro.

   _____

8. <u>Giulia</u> sarà a casa.

   _____

9. <u>Le donne</u> visitano i musei fiorentini.

   _____

10. <u>Io</u> leggo ogni giorno.

    _____

Digging Deeper: Asking More Complex Questions

To ask more complicated questions, beyond the most basic ones that require only a *yes, no,* or brief one- or two-word response, you need the interrogative adjectives, adverbs, and pronouns that lead to more profound conversations, which I discuss in the following sections. (See Chapters 5 and 13 for an overview of adjectives, Chapter 15 for adverbs, and Chapters 8 and 13 for pronouns.)

Here are some examples:

<u>Who</u> is that handsome man?	**Chi è quel bell'uomo?**
<u>What</u> do you know about him?	**Cosa ne sai?**
<u>When</u> did the accident happen, and <u>where</u>?	**Quando è successa l'incidente e dove?**
<u>Why</u> didn't you go to the party?	**Perché non sei andato alla festa?**
<u>How</u> many children do they have?	**Quanti figli hanno?**
<u>Which</u> cheese do you prefer?	**Quale formaggio preferisci?**

Any one of these questions is guaranteed to elicit an answer with details.

Calling for specifics in number: Interrogative adjectives

You use two adjectives to ask questions: **quanto** (*how much*) (*how many*) and **quale** (*which*).

Adjectives modify a noun or pronoun; because **quanto** and **quale** are adjectives, you need to make them agree in number (singular, plural) and gender (masculine, feminine) with the words they modify. (See Chapters 5 and 13 for more on adjectives, and Chapter 3 for details about number and gender.)

Finding how much/how many with quanto

Quanto (*how much*) (*how many*) has four forms: **quanto** (masculine, singular), **quanti** (masculine, plural), **quanta** (feminine, singular), and **quante** (feminine, plural). These words allow you to find out how much or how many of something you're asking about. Here are some examples, using the four forms of **quanto:**

Quanto denaro hai con te? (*How much money do you have with you?*)

Quanto tempo sarà necessario? (*How much time will be needed?*)

Quanti libri hai letto quest'anno? (*How many books have you read this year?*)

Quanti studenti ci sono in classe? (*How many students are there in class?*)

Quanta carne mangi? (*How much meat do you eat?*)

Quanta gente c'è? (*How many people are there?*)

Quante ragazze sanno ballare? (*How many girls know how to dance?*)

Quante macchine sono nuove? (*How many cars are new?*)

Determining which one with quale

Quale (*which*) has only two forms: **quale** (masculine/feminine, singular) and **quali** (masculine/feminine, plural). It means *which* and, like **quanto,** agrees in number with the thing you're asking about. Here are a few examples:

Quale libro preferisci? (*Which book do you prefer?*)

Quale casa è la più moderna? (*Which house is the most modern?*)

Dei documenti, qual è più importante? (*Of the documents, which is more important?*)

When **quale** precedes the verb **è** (*is*), you drop the final **e** from **quale.** You do not, however, pull **qual** and **è** together with an apostrophe, such as **Qual è la risposta giusta?** (*Which is the correct response?*) Though this use of **qual** serves as a pronoun, it's important that you see this spelling now because you'll encounter words that begin with **e** and **i** that make you want to contract **quale.** I go into detail about using **quale** as a pronoun in the later section "Inquiring about who, what, which one, and how many: Interrogative pronouns." The following examples show the plural form of **quale:**

Quali studenti vanno alla partita? (*Which students are going to the game?*)

Quali sedie sono comode? (*Which chairs are comfortable?*)

Choose the form of **quanto** (**quanto, quanti, quanta,** or **quante**) or **quale** (**quale** or **quali**) that best completes the following questions.

Q. _____ **libri ha letto?** (*How many books did he read?*)

A. **Quanti**

11. _____ **ragazze ci sono nel liceo Leonardo da Vinci?** (*How many girls are there at Leonardo da Vinci high school?*)

12. _____ **vino vorresti?** (*How much wine would you like?*)

13. _____ **macchina preferisci?** (*Which car do you prefer?*)

14. _____ **gatti ha?** (*How many cats does she have?*)

15. _____ ingrediente fa speciale il dolce? (_Which_ ingredient makes the dessert special?)

16. _____ ragazza è la più bella? (_Which_ girl is the prettiest?)

17. _____ ragazzo studia con te? (_Which_ boy is studying with you?)

18. _____ stoffa ci vuole? (_How much_ cloth does it take?)

19. _____ materia è la tua preferita? (_Which_ subject is your favorite?)

20. _____ scarpe dovrei comprare? (_Which_ shoes should I buy?)

Requesting the location and time: Interrogative adverbs

Where (**dove**) and _when_ (**quando**) do you use interrogative adverbs? Evidently, here and now. These interrogative adverbs keep you up-to-date on events. For example:

Dove andiamo? (_Where are we going?_)

Quando partiamo? (_When are we leaving?_)

Come arriviamo, in treno o in macchina? (_How are we going: by train or by car?_)

You put all interrogative adverbs right next to the verb in your question. (For the basics on adverbs, see Chapter 15.)

Because **dove, quando,** and **come** are adverbs, they're invariable. You don't have to think about number and gender.

Determining where with dove

With **dove** (_where_), you often use **è** (_is_) or **sono** (_are_). To produce the singular form (_where is_), you drop the final **e** from **dove** and use an apostrophe to connect it to the verb **è**. For example: **Dov'è la stazione?** (_Where is the station?_); **Dov'è il ristorante?** (_Where's the restaurant?_)

The plural is simply **dove sono** (_where are_): **Dove sono le chiavi?** (_Where are the keys?_) **Dove sono i turisti?** (_Where are the tourists?_)

Finding out when with quando

Quando (_when_) stays the same whether you use it with a singular or a plural verb. See the following examples:

Quando arrivano gli ospiti? (_When are the guests arriving?_)

Quando parte il treno? (_When does the train leave?_)

Quando vieni a trovarmi? (_When are you coming to see me?_) (Literally: _When are you coming to find me?_)

Knowing how and what with come

The third interrogative adverb, **come**, has two meanings: *how* and *what.* If you don't catch what someone is saying, you ask **Come?** (a nicer form than the English *Huh?* but with the same meaning). It also means *what* when used with **essere** (*to be*). When used with **è** (*is*), you drop the final **e** and use an apostrophe to form **com'è** (*what is something or someone like* [permanently]).

> **Com'è Elena? È bionda con gli occhi azzurri.** (*What is Elena like? She's blond, with blue eyes.*)

> **Come sono gli studenti? Sono intelligenti.** (*What are the students like? They're bright.*)

You use **come** as *how* most frequently to ask after someone's health, a temporary condition.

> **Come sta, Signorina?** (*How are you, Miss?*)

> **Come stai, Cinzia?** (*How are you, Cinzia?*)

Remember that you always put **come** right next to a verb.

> **Come hanno giocato?** (*How did they play?*)

> **Come ti senti oggi?** (*How are you feeling today?*)

Choose from the following words to complete the questions. Use each word only once.

dove   dove sono   come
dov'è   quando

Q. _____ **arriva il treno?** (*When does the train arrive?*)

A. **Quando**

21. _____ **i musicisti?** (*What are the musicians like?*)

22. _____ **la scuola elementare?** (*Where is the elementary school?*)

23. _____ **vai?** (*Where are you going?*)

24. _____ **parti?** (*When are you leaving?*)

25. _____ **le chiavi?** (*Where are the keys?*)

Inquiring about who, what, which one, and how many: Interrogative pronouns

When question words can stand alone, or not necessarily be tied to a verb, they're called interrogative pronouns. They replace nouns and must agree in number (singular/plural) and gender (masculine/feminine) with those nouns. I don't mean that they stand alone exclusively, but they can. Also, not all interrogative pronouns change. **Chi** (_who_) and **che, che cosa, cosa** (_what_) are invariable; **quale** (_which one_) and **quanto** (_how much_) (_how many_) aren't. Here are some example questions with these interrogative pronouns:

> **Chi mi ha telefonato?** (_Who called me?_)
>
> **Chi è?** (_Who is it?_)
>
> **Chi sarà?** (_Who could it be?_)
>
> **Che fai?** (_What are you doing?_)
>
> **Che cosa studi?** (_What are you studying?_)
>
> **Cosa è?** (_What is it?_)
>
> **A che ora mangiamo?** (_What time are we eating?_)

Quale (_which one_) uses only two forms: **quale** (_which one?_ [masculine/feminine, singular]) and **quali** (_which ones?_ [masculine/feminine, plural]).

> **Quale preferisci?** (_Which one do you prefer?_)
>
> **Quali compri?** (_Which ones are you buying?_)
>
> **Qual è tuo?** (_Which one is yours?_)

When you use **quale** with **è**, you drop its final **e.** You do not, however, connect **qual** with **è** by adding an apostrophe.

Only **quanto** (_how much_) (_how many_) has four forms: **quanto** (masculine, singular), **quanti** (masculine, plural), **quanta** (feminine, singular), and **quante** (feminine, plural).

> **Quanti compri?** (_How many are you buying?_)
>
> **Quante portano uno zaino?** (_How many [girls] are carrying a backpack?_)
>
> **Quanto costa un telefonino?** (_How much does a cellphone cost?_)
>
> **Quanta vuoi?** (_How much do you want?_)

Fill in the appropriate interrogative pronoun to complete the following sentences.

_0._ _Which ones do you prefer?_ _____ **preferisci?**

_A._ **Quali**

26. _What are you doing, Mario?_ _____ **fai, Mario?**

27. _Who is going tomorrow?_ _____ **va domani?**

28. _Girls, how many of you have cellphones?_ **Ragazze, _____ di voi avete telefonini?**

29. _How much time do we have?_ _____ **tempo abbiamo?**

30. _Which one should we order?_ _____ **dovremmo ordinare?**

Providing More Detailed Answers to Questions

To answer information questions (as opposed to yes/no questions), you need to listen very carefully. You have the vocabulary you need for your answer in the question. Keep in mind that the question word (*who, what, when, where, why, how*) is likely to begin the sentence; the content of the question (whose vocabulary you can appropriate) follows. Here, I break down a sample information question with steps to answer it.

1. **List carefully to the question:** <u>Quando partiamo domani?</u>

2. **Break the question into two parts:**

   Quando (question word: *when*) **partiamo domani** (content: *are we leaving tomorrow*)?

3. **Start your answer with the vocabulary from the content.**

   Partiamo domani _____.

4. **Fill in your answer to the question <u>quando</u> (*when*).**

   You can answer this question in several ways; here are a couple of examples:

   Non partiamo domani. Partiamo dopodomani. (*We're not leaving tomorrow. We're leaving day after tomorrow.*)

   Partiamo domani a mezzogiorno. (*We're leaving tomorrow at noon.*)

   You can even answer with a question of your own:

   Partiamo domani? (*We're leaving tomorrow?*)

Sometimes, you need to reverse the word order so that the subject precedes the verb in your answer.

   Dovè il museo? Il museo è all'angolo. (*Where's the museum? It's on the corner.*)

   Quando partono loro? Loro partono domani. (*When are they leaving? They are leaving tomorrow.*)

To answer a question involving quantities, you replace the question word with an amount or a number, as in these examples:

   Quante persone vanno alla spiaggia? Tre persone vanno alla spiaggia. (*How many people are going to the beach? Three people are going to the beach.*)

   Quanti ponti ci sono a Firenze? Ci sono cinque ponti a Firenze. (*How many bridges are there in Florence? There are five bridges in Florence.*)

Answer the following questions by using vocabulary from the question itself.

Q. **Dove studia Elena?** (*Where is Elena studying?*)

A. **Elena studia in biblioteca.** (*Elena is studying in the library.*)

31. Come sono i professori? (*What are the professors like?*)

_____ **molto gentili.** (*The professors are very nice.*)

32. Quanti studenti mangiano nella mensa universitaria? Molti? (*How many students eat at the university cafeteria? Many?*)

_____ **nella mensa universitaria.** (*Many students eat at the university cafeteria.*)

33. Che cosa fanno gli studenti? (*What are the students doing?*)

_____ **i compiti.** (*The students are doing their homework.*)

34. Quando apre il museo? (*When does the museum open?*)

_____ **alle 9.00.** (*The museum opens at 9:00.*)

35. Dove sono i biglietti? (*Where are the tickets?*)

_____ **sul tavolo.** (*The tickets are on the table.*)

For questions designed to elicit specific answers from you (about you), you need to change the verb in the question before using it in the answer. In English, when someone asks <u>*Are you*</u> *a student?* you answer with a different form of the verb, <u>*I am*</u> *a student.* (See Chapters 6 and 7 to review verbs in general and especially subject-verb coordination.)

The following questions are directed to you. Fill in the correct verb form in the answer, as in the example.

Q. **Quanti figli hai?** (*How many children do you have?*)

A. **Ho tre figli.**

36. Come <u>sei</u> tu? (*What are you like?*)

_____ **intelligente e felice.** (*I'm smart and happy.*)

37. Da dove vieni? (*Where are you from?*)

_____ **da Chicago.** (*I'm from Chicago.*)

38. Come stai oggi? (*How are you today?*)

_____ **bene, grazie.** (*I'm fine, thanks.*)

39. Quanti anni hai? (*How old are you?*) (*Literally: How many years do you have?*)

_____ **34 anni.** (*I am 34 years old.*)

40. Quale ristorante preferisci? (*Which restaurant do you prefer?*)

_____ **La Ginestra.** (*I prefer the Ginestra.*)

Answering Questions in the Negative

Answering questions in the negative requires the use of negative adverbs. In Italian, you can use two, even three, negative words in the same sentence without incurring the wrath of your teacher. Double negatives are the norm, not a broken rule. For example:

Non ho mai fatto nulla di cattivo. (Literally: *I have not never done nothing bad.*) (*I've never done anything bad.*)

The following lists some of the most common negative adverbs. The spaces indicate that a verb is needed for the adverb to cozy up to.

- **non _____ mai** (*never*)
- **non _____ nessuno** (*no one*)
- **non _____ niente, nulla** (*nothing*)
- **non _____ più** (*no more, no longer*)
- **non _____ neache, nemmeno, neppure** (*not even*)
- **non _____ né . . . né . . .** (*neither . . . nor . . .*)
- **non _____ mica** (*not really*)
- **non _____ affatto, per nulla, per niente** (*not at all*)

You can also put the adverb (without **non**) at the beginning of a sentence, making your meaning more emphatic.

Here are some examples using the negative adverbs.

Non sono mai andato in Italia. (*I've never gone to Italy.*)

Non c'è nessuno. (*No one is there.*)

Non c'è niente da fare. (*There's nothing to be done for it.*)

Non abito più in quella città. (*I don't live in that city any longer.*)

Non è neanche italiano. (*He's not even Italian.*)

Non è né pesce né carne. (*It's neither fish nor fowl.*)

Lei non è mica magra. (*She's not really thin.*)

Non è affatto grasso. (*He's not fat at all.*)

Non mi piace affatto. (*I don't like it at all.*)

Mai ci vado. (*I never go there.*)

Mica male. (*Not bad.*)

Neanche lui lo farebbe. (*Not even he would do it.*)

Answer Key

1 Ha mangiato tutti i biscotti, Michele?

2 Sono a scuola, i bambini?

3 È impegnatissima, tua madre?

4 Parla inglese, Giuseppe?

5 Sono molto belle, le nuove macchine?

6 Prepari da mangiare, tu?

7 Sono andati in centro, Marco e Lorenzo?

8 Sarà a casa, Giulia?

9 Visitano i musei fiorentini, le donne?

10 Leggo ogni giorno, io?

11 quante

12 quanto

13 quale

14 quanti

15 quale

16 qual

17 quale

18 quanta

19 qual

20 quali

`21` come

`22` dov'è

`23` dove

`24` quando

`25` dove sono

`26` cosa, che, che cosa

`27` chi

`28` quante

`29` quanto

`30` quale

`31` I professori sono molto gentili.

`32` Molti studenti mangiano nella mensa universitaria.

`33` Gli studenti fanno i compiti.

`34` Il museo apre alle 9.00.

`35` I biglietti sono sul tavolo.

`36` Sono

`37` Vengo

`38` Sto

`39` Ho

`40` Preferisco

Part III

Beefing Up Your Sentences

Build Sentences in Italian by Answering Who, What, When, Where, and Why

Question Word	Answer Example
Chi *(Who)*	**Questo è il mio gatto.** *(This is my cat.)*
Che *(What)*	**Questo è il mio gatto che dorme.** *(This is my cat who sleeps.)*
Quando *(When)*	**Questo è il mio gatto che dorme sempre.** *(This is my cat who sleeps always.)*
Dove *(Where)*	**Questo è il mio gatto che dorme sempre sulla mia poltrona preferita.** *(This is my cat who sleeps always on my favorite chair.)*
Perché *(Why)*	**Questo è il mio gatto che dorme sempre sulla mia poltrona preferita perché si trova al sole.** *(This is my cat who sleeps always on my favorite chair because it's in the sun.)*

Hand gestures are a key part of Italian communication. Learn how to form and interpret some common hand gestures at www.dummies.com/extras/italiangrammar.

In this part . . .

✔ Use adjectives and adverbs to describe how something felt, tasted, looked, or seemed, when and where something happened, who was involved, and so on.

✔ Discover the idiosyncrasies of prepositions in Italian and how to use them correctly to link nouns to other elements in a sentence — be it another noun, a verb, or an adjective or adverb.

✔ Talk about specific and general concepts or objects with *qualifiers* — words that modify nouns — such as *that* and *this.*

✔ Express possession in Italian by using articles — no apostrophe + *s* here! — and making sure words match in gender and number.

Chapter 12

Prepositions: Little Words, Big Challenges

In This Chapter

▶ Forming contracted prepositions

▶ Discovering Italian prepositions and their meanings

*P*repositions are little words that link nouns and pronouns to adjectives, verbs, and other nouns, so prepositions have a huge impact on language. For example, you put a book *on* the table; you take the dog *for* a walk. Both *on* and *for* act as prepositions here because they link words together.

Such little words are unsuspectingly difficult to master. They're the linguistic wild card of any language. They're exceedingly idiosyncratic and are the chameleon of languages, changing meaning according to their surroundings.

Italian has dozens of prepositions, and they appear everywhere and have different meanings. Take **a**, for example; it has at least four basic meanings: *at, to, in,* and *on.*

> **Vado a Roma.** (*I'm going to Rome.*)
>
> **Abito a Firenze.** (*I live in Florence.*)
>
> **Sono a scuola.** (*I'm at school.*)
>
> **Noi passiamo l'estate a Capri.** (*We spend the summer on Capri.*)

In this chapter, I introduce you to the most commonly used Italian prepositions and show you how to apply them to a variety of linguistic structures. But before I get into the details of Italian prepositions, I show you how some prepositions and the definite articles combine (called *contracted prepositions*). This approach may seem a bit like putting the cart before the horse, but you see these contracted prepositions throughout Italian, and it's next to impossible to speak Italian without them. If you're already aware of these contracted prepositions and want to review only their spellings, feel free to just glance over the first section, "Combining Prepositions with Articles." If you feel better reviewing the prepositions first, skip to the section "Looking at the Common Connectors: Italian Prepositions." To make life easier, I include the parts of these contracted prepositions in parentheses, such as **del** (**di + il**) **vino** (*some wine*).

Combining Prepositions with Articles

As I mention in the chapter introduction, prepositions often combine with definite articles (**il, l', lo, i, gli** [masculine] and **la, l', le** [feminine] — all mean *the*) to result in a smoother flow of language. (To review definite articles, see Chapter 3.)

When the prepositions **a, di, da, in,** and **su** (which have various meanings, depending on their use; see the individual sections throughout this chapter) are followed by the definite articles, they combine to become **preposizioni articolate** (*contracted preposi-tions*). Sometimes, the prepositions **con** (*with*) and **per** (*for*) combine with articles but not regularly and not with all articles. **Tra** (*between*) and **fra** (*among*) don't combine with the articles.

Table 12-1 shows these combinations in their basic forms. Notice that **di** (*of*) and **in** (*in*) change their form slightly to allow for reasonable pronunciation.

Table 12-1	Prepositions and Articles Combined	
Preposition	*Contracted Prepositions (Masculine)*	*Contracted Prepositions (Feminine)*
a	al, all', allo, ai, agli	alla, all', alle
di (de)	del, dell', dello, dei, degli	della, dell', delle
da	dal, dall', dallo, dai, dagli	dalla, dall', dalle
in (ne)	nel, nell', nello, nei, negli	nella, nell', nelle
su	sul, sull', sullo, sui, sugli	sulla, sull', sulle
con	col	coi
per	pel	

The one preposition that has another use is **di.** Combined with the definite articles, as Table 12-1 shows, it takes on the meaning of *some.* For example, **del vino** means *some wine;* **delle donne,** *some women;* **dei libri,** *some books;* and so on.

While *the* in Italian comes in many forms (depending on whether it accompanies a masculine, feminine, singular, or plural noun), by definition, the indefinite articles *a* and *an* don't have plural forms, unless you count *some* as an extension of one thing: *a house, some houses; a car, some cars.* I cover this use of **di** and an article, as well as other ways to say *some,* in Table 12-1 and in Chapter 3 as well.

Looking at the Common Connectors: Italian Prepositions

Prepositions give new meaning to the idea that there's an exception to every rule. The minute you think you can use prepositions regularly (or even logically), you encounter what may seem like an illogical application of them. In fact, you may think that they have a complete disregard for logic, at least compared to the way you use prepositions in English. Case in point: Some prepositions in Italian are included in verbs, such as **aspettare** (*to wait for*), **pagare** (*to pay for*), and **ascoltare** (*to listen to*). But don't fret: In this section, I show you all the ins and outs of Italian prepositions.

Each of the following sections treats a different preposition, in isolation from other members of the preposition family, so you can understand and use them better. At the end of each section, I provide idioms specific to the preposition just explained.

The various functions of a

As I said in the introduction to this chapter, the preposition **a** has at least four meanings: *to, at, in,* and *on*. Sometimes, it appears between verbs to indicate forward motion. And sometimes it precedes certain verbs as a matter of course. How can you sort all of this out? The following list and examples can help:

- ✔ **A** as *to:* You use **a** if you're going to a city, a small island, home, school, and other venues.

  Vado a Firenze. (*I'm going to Florence.*)

  Vado a Capri. (*I'm going to Capri.*)

  Vado a casa. (*I'm going home.*)

  Vado a scuola. (*I'm going to school.*)

  Vado a teatro. (*I'm going to the theater.*)

  You include the preposition **a** in the word **ci** to replace the prepositional phrase *to somewhere*. For example:

  Vai a Firenze? Sì, ci vado. (*Are you going to Florence? Yes, I'm going there.*)

- ✔ **A** as *at:* This usage applies to time, meals, and age.

  A mezzanotte hanno mangiato le uva. (*At midnight, they ate the grapes.*)

  Sono tornati alle tre. (*They returned at three.*)

  A cena parliamo del giorno. (*At the table, we talk about the day.*)

  A quindici anni voleva fare un viaggio in Francia. (*At 15, she wanted to take a trip to France.*)

- ✔ **A** as *in:* You use **a** to mean *in* a town.

  Abito a Firenze. (*I live in Florence.*)

  Si trova a Venezia. (*She is in Venice.*)

- ✔ **A** as *on:* To talk about a television program or a visit to a small island, you use **a**.

  C'è un programma interessante alla (a + la) televisione. (*There is an interesting program on TV.*)

  Sono stati ad Ischia. (*They have been on Ischia.*) (Note that in this case, you add a **d** to **a** so you have a differentiation between the **a** sound and the following vowel. If you were to say that you lived in Arezzo, for example, you'd say **abito ad Arezzo**. But if you lived in Roma, you'd say **a Roma**.)

✔ **A with verbs:** In general, you add **a** after conjugated verbs (usually forward-looking verbs, such as **cominciare** [*to begin*], **provare** [*to try*] and **imparare** [*to learn*]) if they're followed by an infinitive. Here are some examples.

> **Comincia a studiare.** (*He is beginning to study.*)
>
> **Continua a dormire.** (*He is continuing to sleep.*)
>
> **Prova a mangiare.** (*He is trying to eat.*)
>
> **Riesco a farlo.** (*I'm succeeding in doing it.*)

A also appears after conjugated verbs and before some pronouns and nouns. In this case, it's not translated as meaning *at* or *to,* for example; it simply occurs — without a discernibly logical reason.

> **Gioco a tennis.** (*I play tennis.*)
>
> **Loro partecipano ad una manifestazione.** (*They are participating in a demonstration.*) (Again, you add a **d.**)

Some idiomatic expressions with **a** include the following:

✔ **a due a due** (*two by two*)

✔ **suonano a quattro mani** (*they are playing a duet* [or using four hands])

✔ **ad alta voce** (*aloud*)

✔ **facciamo alla** (**a + la**) **romana** (*let's go Dutch*)

✔ **a destra, a sinistra** (*to the right, to the left*)

Expressing possession with di

At its most basic, **di** means *of.* But it doesn't always translate into English that way. Here are the more specific uses of **di:**

✔ It refers to possession (remember that Italian doesn't use *'s*).

> **È la casa di Mario.** (*It's Mario's house.*)
>
> **Sono i gatti della** (**di + la**) **vecchia signora.** (*They are the old lady's cats.*)
>
> **Vorrei un bicchiere di vino.** (*I would like a glass of wine.*)

✔ It tells where someone is from.

> **Richard è di Parigi.** (*Richard is from Paris.*)
>
> **Sono degli** (**di + gli**) **Stati Uniti.** (*I'm from the United States.*)
>
> **Di dove sei?** (*Where are you from?*)

✔ It precedes a description.

> **È un uomo di brutto carattere.** (*He is a man lacking integrity.*)
>
> **È di seta.** (*It's made of silk.*)
>
> **Sono libri di ricette.** (*They're books of recipes.*)

✔ It's used with expressions of time.

> **Vengono di mattina.** (*They come in the morning.*)
>
> **Arrivano di buon'ora.** (*They arrive on time.*)
>
> **Di estate, andiamo al mare.** (*In the summer, we go to the seaside.*)

✔ After indefinite pronouns, **di** precedes adjectives. (See Chapter 3 for details about indefinite pronouns.)

> **Ho qualcosa di bello da dirti.** (*I have something terrific to tell you.*)
>
> **Non c'è niente di nuovo.** (*There is nothing new.*)

✔ It accompanies certain verbs that are followed by infinitives. Again, there's no visible logic to this practice (in general, though, **di** follows verbs of "ending," like **finire** [*to finish*]). Examples of this practice follow.

To show the ending of something:

> **Ho smesso di fumare.** (*I quit smoking.*)
>
> **Hanno finito di leggere il libro.** (*They finished reading the book.*)

To express feelings:

> **Sono contenta di averlo conosciuto.** (*I'm happy to have met him.*)
>
> **Si è innamorato di lei.** (*He fell in love with her.*)

Other verbs that are followed by **di**, before a noun, pronoun, or infinitive, include **dimenticarsi** (*to forget*), **ricordarsi** (*to remember*), **interessarsi** (*to be interested in*), **trattarsi** (*to deal with*), and **ridere** (*to laugh*).

> **Mi sono dimenticata di farlo.** (*I forgot to do it.*)
>
> **Mi sono ricordato di comprare il latte.** (*I remembered to buy milk.*)
>
> **Marco si interessa del (di + il) lavoro.** (*Marco is interested in the job.*)
>
> **Si tratta della (di + la) politica.** (*It deals with politics.*)
>
> **Ridono di lui.** (*They're laughing at him.*)

Just as an **a** phrase can be included in **ci** (see previous section), a **di** phrase can be included in **ne,** like in these examples:

> **Ne parliamo.** (*We'll talk about it.*)
>
> **Cosa ne pensi?** (*What do you think of it?*)

Idiomatic expressions with **di** include

✔ **di nuovo** (something used frequently, meaning *again*)

✔ **Penso di sì.** (*I think so.*)

✔ **Credo di sì.** (*I believe so.*)

Choose **a** or **di** alone or combined with a definite article to fill in the blanks in the following sentences. Here's an example.

Q. La famiglia abita _____ Firenze.

A. a

1. Vanno a scuola _____ sette.

2. Paola è romana, è _____ Roma.

3. C'è un bel film _____ televisione.

4. Tu, Giulio, hai partecipato _____ manifestazione?

5. Sono i guanti _____ Laura.

6. Tornano _____ mezzogiorno.

7. Prendo sempre un bicchiere _____ latte.

8. L'abito è _____ lana.

9. Cominciano _____ sciare.

10. _____ dove sei?

The multiple uses of da

Da is the workhorse of prepositions. It indicates function, time since something else, distance, where someone is from, place, and more. In a general sense, it means *from* or *by*.

✔ **Da** means *from* when combined with the verb **venire** and indicates your place of origin.

> **Io vengo da Chicago.** (*I'm from Chicago.*)

✔ When accompanied by a noun or pronoun, **da** means *by*.

> **L'edificio è stato costruito da Michelangelo.** (*The building was constructed by Michelangelo.*) (For this and other passive constructions that use **da**, see Chapter 19.)

Here are a few more specific uses and examples of **da**:

✔ **Da** shows the functions and purposes of things.

> **una macchina da cucire** (*a sewing machine*)
>
> **un bicchiere da vino** (*a wine glass*) (compare this with **un bicchiere di vino** [*glass of wine*])
>
> **sala da pranzo** (*dining room*)
>
> **costume da bagno** (*swimming suit*) (Literally: *a bathing costume*)
>
> **Gli do da mangiare.** (*I'm giving him something to eat.*)

✔ **Da** tells you what is or has to be done.

> **Abbiamo un sacco di lavoro da fare.** (*We have a bunch of work to do.*)

> **Hanno una casa da vendere.** (*They have a house to sell.*)

> **Una commedia da fare** (*a play to make, create,* or *stage*) is the subtitle of Nobel laureate Luigi Pirandello's most famous play **Sei personaggi in cerca d'autore.**

✔ **Da** tells you where you are or where you're going.

> **Vado da Giuseppina.** (*I'm going to Giuseppina's.*)

> **Vado dal (da + il) medico.** (*I'm going to the doctor's office.*)

> **Loro mangiano da noi.** (*They're eating at our house.*)

✔ **Da** can describe your manner, behavior, or style.

> **Ti parlo d'amica (da amica).** (*I'm speaking to you as a friend.*)

> **Lui farà da guida.** (*He'll act as a guide.*)

> **Scialo da gran signore.** (*I live as though I were a great lord.*) (This is a line that the poor poet Rodolfo sings in the opera *La Bohème.*)

> **Guarda quella ragazza dai tatuaggi.** (*Look at that girl with the tattoos.*)

✔ **Da** plus a disjunctive pronoun (see Chapter 8) can mean *by ___self.*

> **Preferisco farlo da me.** (*I prefer to do it by myself.*)

✔ **Da** indicates worth or value.

> **francobolli da due Euro** (*stamps worth 2 Euro*)

✔ **Da** indicates an age and triggers use of the imperfect indicative verb (see Chapter 16).

> **Da bambina, mi piaceva visitare i nonni.** (*As a small girl, I loved visiting my grandparents.*)

> **Da ragazzo, frequentava una scuola privata.** (*As a boy, he went to a private school.*)

The seemingly all-purpose preposition **da** also shows time since something happened or since something has been going on, distance, and covering that distance, specifically in these situations:

✔ When followed by a present tense verb:

> **Da quanto tempo abiti a Firenze? Da dieci anni.** (*How long have you lived in Florence? Ten years.*)

> **Loro abitano a 2 kilometri da noi.** (*They live 2 kilometers from us.*)

✔ When followed by an imperfect tense verb:

> **Pioveva da sempre.** (It has been raining forever.)

Finally, **da** appears with **di** to create expressions that follow indefinite pronouns:

> **Non c'è niente di buono da mangiare.** (*There is nothing good to eat.*)

Idiomatic expressions with **da** include **da capo** (*from the top*) and **da oggi in poi** (*from today on*).

Using either **da** by itself or **da** combined with a definite article, fill in the missing prepositions in the following sentences. Here's an example.

Q. **Lui viene _____ Washington.**

A. **da**

11. **Noi veniamo _____ stato di Washington.**

12. **Ha comprato dodici bicchieri _____ vino.**

13. **Gli studenti hanno molti compiti _____ fare.**

14. **Domani vanno _____ barbiere.**

15. **È un disegno fatto _____ Raffaello.**

16. **Mangiano nella sala _____ pranzo.**

17. **_____ bambino, leggeva tanto.**

18. **Io, invece, vado _____ dentista.**

19. **Ho qualcosa di bello _____ darti.**

20. **Quando torni _____ centro?**

Using in to mean more than just in

Often **in** means just what it seems to, *in*. But not always. The following cases use **in** to mean *in:*

- When talking about general locations, **in** translates as *in* or *in the.*

    Vado in città. (*I'm going to the city.*) (*I'm going into town.*)

    Loro abitano in periferia. (*They live in the suburbs.*)

    Vivere in centro è impossibile. (*To live downtown is impossible.*)

    Studiamo in biblioteca. (*We study in the library.*)

- You can use **in** to talk about working or spending time in specific locations:

    in ufficio (*in the office*)

    in cucina (*in the kitchen*)

    in campagna (*in the country*)

    in bagno (*in the bath*)

    When you modify these places, that is, add adjectives or names to them, you then follow **in** with the definite article. Compare the following: **in ufficio** (*in the* office), **nell'ufficio postale** (*in the post office*); **in centro** (*in the center [of town]*), **nel centro storico** (*in the historic center*).

✔ **In** shows field of endeavor or profession.

> **Lui si è specializzato in ingegneria.** (*He works in engineering.*)

Here are some other meanings for **in**:

✔ *To:* when talking about countries and continents, and big islands (often big is defined politically, "bigness" somehow equating with importance).

> **Vado in Italia.** (*I'm going to Italy.*)

> **Vado in America.** (*I'm going to America.*)

> **Vado in Sicilia.** (*I'm going to Sicily.*)

When you add descriptors, you must add definite articles, and the preposition **in** combines with the articles.

> **Vado nell'Italia (in + l') centrale.** (*I'm going to central Italy.*)

> **Loro vanno negli (in + gli) Stati Uniti.** (*They're going to the United States.*)

✔ *By*: This meaning applies to any form of transportation.

> **Andiamo in treno.** (*We're going by train.*)

> **. . . in macchina** (*. . . by car*)

> **. . . in aereo** (*. . . by plane*)

> **. . . in barca** (*. . . by boat*)

✔ *On:* **In** means *on* when used with street names.

> **Abita in Via Pinti.** (*He lives on Pinti Street.*)

Translate the following phrases into Italian. Here's an example.

Q. *to Sicily*

A. **in Sicilia**

21. *at school* _____

22. *in Florence* _____

23. *at the doctor's* _____

24. *in central Asia* _____

25. *by train* _____

26. *at Giorgio's house* _____

27. *a wine glass* _____

28. *a glass of wine* _____

29. *in Italy* _____

30. *in the suburbs* _____

Idiomatic expressions with **in** include the following:

- ✔ **In bocca al lupo!** (*into the mouth of the wolf*) (*good luck!*)

- ✔ **in orario, in ritardo** (*on time*) (*late*)

- ✔ **in primavera** (*in the spring*), **in estate** (*in the summer*), **in autunno** (*in the fall*), **in inverno** (*in the winter*) (As I state earlier in this chapter, you can also use **a** to create these expressions.)

- ✔ **in erba** (*in the making, aspiring*) as in **Sono giornalisti in erba.** (*They're aspiring journalists.*)

Expressing physical position with su

Su can mean *on, upon, in, up,* and *about.* **Su** usually indicates a physical position. Here are some examples of the multiple uses of **su:**

- ✔ **Su** as *in, on:*

     Il gatto si è seduto sul (su + il) televisore. (*The cat is sitting on the television.*)

     Lui ha pubblicato un libro su Internet. (*He has published a book on the Internet.*)

     Ha pubblicato un articolo sul (su + il) giornale. (*He published an article in the newspaper.*)

- ✔ **Su** as *up* (although this use isn't as common, it's perhaps one of the better known uses):

     tiramisù (*pick me up*) (yes, like the dessert!)

     Su! (*Buck up!*)

- ✔ **Su** as *about:*

     Lei sarà sulla (su + la) cinquantina. (*She's probably about 50.*)

     Costa sui (su + i) cento euro. (*It costs about 100 euro.*)

- ✔ **Su** can sometimes mean *over* or *onto:*

     La camera dà sul (su + il) giardino. (*The room looks over the garden.*)

     dieci su cento (*ten over hundred,* or *ten percent*)

Idiomatic expressions with **su** include some that are especially useful:

- ✔ **sul serio** (*seriously*)

- ✔ **su per giù** (*roughly, approximately*)

- ✔ **su e giù** (*up and down*)

- ✔ **i su e giù** (*the ups and downs*)

- ✔ **Conto su di te.** (*I'm counting on you.*)

Using con and senza

Con (*with*) and its opposite **senza** (*without*) are pretty literal. **Con** is sometimes more felicitously translated as *in* but in general stays with its basic meaning.

> **Andiamo con loro.** (*We're going with them.*)
>
> **Anche con la neve, i bambini escono.** (*Even with [in] the snow, the kids go out.*)
>
> **Con chi studi stasera?** (*With whom are you studying tonight?*)
>
> **Non ce la faccio senza soldi.** (*I can't do it without money.*)

Idiomatic expressions for **con** and **senza** include

- ✔ **Non c'è rosa senza spine.** (*There are no roses without thorns.*)
- ✔ **Pigliare due piccioni con una fava** (*to catch two birds with one stone*)

Expressing for and through with per

Per means *for* and by extension *for that reason* or *in order to*. It can also mean *through*. Here are some examples:

> **L'ho comprato per il suo compleanno.** (*I bought it for his birthday.*)
>
> **Sono qui per un periodo lungo.** (*They are here for an extended period.*)
>
> **Ho studiato per poter parlare bene l'italiano.** (*I studied in order to speak Italian well.*)
>
> **Ci guardava per la finestra.** (*He was looking at us through the window.*)

Here are a few idiomatic expressions with **per:**

- ✔ **per amore o per forza** (*by hook or by crook*)
- ✔ **Perbacco!** (*My goodness!*)
- ✔ **per piacere** (*please*)
- ✔ **per carità** (*please*)
- ✔ **per favore** (*please*)

The somewhat interchangeable tra and fra

Meaning *between* or *among*, **tra** and **fra** are essentially interchangeable. Often, you choose to use one over the other because it sounds better. Instead of saying **tra Trapani e Palermo** (*between Trapani and Palermo*), you'd probably use **fra** to avoid a kind of stuttering effect. See these other examples:

> **Tra gli alberi si vedeva il sole.** (*Between the trees, you saw sunlight.*)
>
> **fra tutti i popoli** (*among all peoples*)

Here are a couple idiomatic expressions with **tra** and **fra**:

* ✔ **fra di noi** (*just between us*)
* ✔ **fra (tra) poco** (*in a little while*)

Translate the following expressions into Italian. Here's an example.

0. *about thirty*

A. **sulla trentina**

31. *over the garden*

_____

32. *by hook or by crook*

_____

33. *good luck*

_____

34. *aspiring*

_____

35. *I am at the office.*

_____

36. *on the Internet*

_____

37. *I'm counting on you.*

_____

38. *[in love] with Chiara*

_____

39. *[going] with Chiara to the theater*

_____

40. *seriously*

_____

Answer Key

1	alle
2	di
3	alla
4	alla
5	di
6	a
7	di
8	di
9	a
10	di
11	dallo
12	da
13	da
14	dal
15	da
16	da
17	da
18	dal
19	da
20	dal

21. a scuola

22. a Firenze

23. dal medico

24. nell'Asia centrale

25. in treno

26. da Giorgio

27. un bicchiere da vino

28. un bicchiere di vino

29. in Italia

30. in periferia

31. sul giardino

32. per amore o per forza

33. in bocca al lupo

34. in erba

35. sono in ufficio

36. su Internet

37. conto su di te

38. di Chiara

39. con Chiara a teatro

40. sul serio

Chapter 13

Qualifying Nouns with Demonstrative, Indefinite, and Possessive Words

*Q*ualifiers, like all adjectives, modify or describe something or someone. The types of qualifiers discussed in this chapter — demonstrative, indefinite, and possessive — differ from other adjectives, however, in that they do double (and sometimes triple) duty. They can act as pronouns or adjectives, and some can even be adverbs (see Chapter 15).

Because of their multitasking nature, I give these particular adjectives their very own chapter. You find information on the less versatile (single duty), but no less useful, adjectives in Chapter 5.

Demonstrative adjectives are words that make it clear exactly which thing is being discussed, that can indicate a type of thing rather than a specific one, and that often clarify to whom a thing belongs. Demonstrative adjectives indicate specifically which noun or group of nouns you're referring to, for example, *this* book is my favorite, *that* train is leaving soon, *those* children are noisy. Demonstrative pronouns go a step further and replace the noun outright: *This* is my favorite, *that* is not nice, and *those* are beautiful.

Possessive adjectives and pronouns tell to whom something belongs. It's *mine, his, yours,* or *ours*. You can use the possessive to stake a claim (yours or someone else's).

Indefinite adjectives and pronouns, on the other hand, allow you to be a little vague. *Some, various, any,* and *many* don't name specific people or things necessarily but encompass a varying amount of something: *many people, some animals, any politician.*

In this chapter, I show you how to use the adjective and pronoun forms of qualifiers to point out, describe, and express ownership of nouns in Italian.

Talking About Questo (This) and Quello (That)

Questo (*this*) and **quello** (*that*) are commonly used demonstrative adjectives. They always precede the nouns they modify, and they must match the nouns in number and gender.

Questo uses four forms to agree in number and gender with words it modifies: masculine singular (**questo ragazzo** [*this boy*]), feminine singular (**questa casa** [*this house*]), masculine plural (**questi ragazzi** [*these boys*]), and feminine plural (**queste case** [*these houses*]).

Here are a few examples of **questo** in action:

Questo giorno sarà lungo lungo. (*This day is going to be really long.*)

Questa casa mi piace molto. (*I like this house a lot.*)

Questi studenti sono bravi. (*These students are good.*)

Queste macchine sono bellissime. (*These cars are gorgeous.*)

Sometimes **questo** shortens to **sta-** as a prefix to nouns. You use it to say, for example, **stasera** (*this evening*) or **stamattina** (*this morning*).

Quello uses more than four forms, though they all reflect gender and number. **Quello** uses the definite articles (see Chapter 3 for more on that) to form a new word.

What form **quello** takes depends on the definite article, as you can see here:

Definite Article	Form of Quello	Example
il	quel	**quel libro** (*that book*)
lo	quello	**quello studente** (*that student*)
l'	quell'	**quell'edificio** (*that building*)
i	quei	**quei libri** (*those books*)
gli	quegli	**quegli studenti** (*those students*)
la	quella	**quella donna** (*that woman*)
l'	quell'	**quell'amica** (*that friend*)
le	quelle	**quelle donne** (*those women*)

The following examples contrast **questo** and **quello** as they're used:

Questi ragazzi sono simpatici. Quei ragazzi sono antipatici. (*These boys are nice. Those boys are not nice.*)

Questi stivali sono comodi. Quegli stivali non sono comodi. (*These boots are comfortable. Those boots are not comfortable.*)

Questa scuola manda molti studenti a quell'università. (*This school sends lots of students to that university.*)

> **Quell'appartamento in periferia è molto grande, ma questo appartamento in centro non lo è.** (*That suburban apartment is really big, but this apartment in the downtown isn't.*)

But perhaps you want to avoid repeating the subject. As long as **questo** and **quello** agree in number and gender with the word they're replacing, they can act as pronouns, fulfilling the most basic function of pronouns — that is, replacing a noun. In this case, **quello** uses the four adjective endings (**-o, -a, -i,** and **-e**) that **questo** does. For example:

> **Questi stivali sono comodi, ma quelli, no.** (*These boots are comfortable, but those aren't.*) **Quelli** refers to **stivali** and is thus masculine plural.

> **Quell'appartamento in periferia è molto grande, ma questo in centro non lo è.** (*That suburban apartment is really big, but this one downtown isn't.*) **Questo** refers to the **apartamento** and is thus masculine singular.

Complete the phrases or sentences with the word in parentheses (in Italian, of course).

0. (*This*) _____ **direttore è molto esigente.**

A. **Questo**

1. **Non mi piace** _____ (*that one*).

2. (*That*) _____ **edificio è famoso.**

3. (*This*) _____ **professoressa è intelligente.**

4. (*That*) _____ **professoressa è vecchia.**

5. **Le case nuove? Lui preferisce** (*those*) _____ **vecchie.**

6. (*This*) _____ **è il mio amico Stefano.**

7. (*Those*) _____ **stati sono vicino a Messico.**

8. **Sono** (*those*) _____ **le ragazze di cui mi hai parlato?**

9. **Questi fiori? Preferisco** (*those*) _____.

10. (*These*) _____ **biscotti sono deliziosi.**

Keeping It Vague with Indefinite Adjectives

Indefinite adjectives are nonspecific. You use them to allude to people or things without saying who or what precisely. And here's some good news: Many commonly used indefinite adjectives and pronouns are invariable.

Whether you're talking about something masculine or feminine, singular or plural, the indefinite adjectives **ogni** (*every*), **qualche** (*some*), **qualunque** (*any*), and **qualsiasi** (*any*) never change their forms. They're also always followed by singular nouns (though these nouns sometimes translate into English as plurals). Here are some examples:

> **Ogni giorno io mi alzo alle cinque.** (*Every day I get up at 5:00.*)
>
> **Ogni studente è impegnato.** (*Every student is committed.*)
>
> **Qualche volta mi dimentico di mangiare.** (*Sometimes I forget to eat.*)
>
> **Qualunque libro che lei legga, le piace.** (*Any book she reads, she likes.*)
>
> **Qualsiasi giocatore di calcio è famoso.** (*Any soccer player is famous.*)

Other indefinite adjectives do change endings and agree in number and gender with the nouns they modify. Table 13-1 lists frequently used indefinite adjectives.

The indefinite adjectives (**ciascuno** [*each*] and **nessuno** [*no*]) can be followed only by a singular noun. *One* (**alcuni, alcune**) is followed only by plural nouns.

Tutto is followed by the definite article appropriate to the noun being modified: **tutti gli studenti** (*all the students*) and **tutta la famiglia** (*the whole family*).

Table 13-1	Indefinite Adjectives	
Italian	*English Translation*	*Example*
alcuni	*some*	**alcuni libri** (*some books*)
altro	*other*	**altre persone** (*other people*)
certo	*certain*	**certi casi** (*certain cases*)
* **ciascuno**	*each*	**ciascuna ragazza** (*each girl*)
diverso	*different*	**diverse donne** (*different women*)
molto	*many, much*	**molti studenti** (*many students*)
* **nessuno**	*no*	**nessun biglietto** (*no ticket*)
parecchio	*some, several, many, much*	**parecchio tempo** (*some time*)
poco	*few, little*	**pochi studenti** (*few students*)
tanto	*so many*	**tanti studenti** (*so many students*)
troppo	*too many*	**troppi studenti** (*too many students*)
tutto	*all*	**tutto il gruppo** (*all the group*)
vario	*various*	**vari cani** (*various dogs*)

* These two adjectives follow the formation pattern of the indefinite article: un, uno, un', and una. See Chapter 3 for an overview of the way the indefinite article forms.

Translate the following phrases into Italian, using indefinite adjectives. If you can translate the phrase in more than one way, do so. I provide the nouns in parentheses so you don't have to look up that vocabulary.

Q. *every car* (**macchina**)

A. **ogni macchina, qualsiasi macchina, qualunque macchina**

11. *some books* (**libri**)

   _____

12. *too many boys* (**ragazzi**)

   _____

13. *so many tourists* (**turisti**)

   _____

14. *few students* (**studenti**)

   _____

15. *much (a lot of) wine* (**vino**)

   _____

16. *any girl* (**ragazza**)

   _____

17. *various politicians* (**politici**)

   _____

18. *several houses* (**case**)

   _____

19. *other words* (**parole**)

   _____

20. *no reason* (**ragione**)

   _____

Conveying Something Indefinite with Pronouns

You can use most of the indefinite adjectives discussed in the previous section as pronouns, too, enabling you to replace the noun with the pronoun. Table 13-2 lists the pronoun forms of common indefinite adjectives.

As you can see in Table 13-2, the pronouns agree in number (singular, plural) and gender (masculine, feminine) with the words they replace. (See Chapter 3 to review the details of number and gender.)

Table 13-2	Indefinite Pronouns	
Indefinite Adjective	*Example As an Adjective*	*Example As a Pronoun*
molti	**molti studenti** (*many students*)	**Molti vengono a scuola.** (*Many are coming to school.*)
poche	**poche ragazze** (*few girls*)	**Poche si sposano oggi.** (*Few are getting married today.*)
tutti	**tutti i ragazzi** (*all the kids*)	**Tutti vanno al mare.** (*They're all going to the seaside.*)
troppi	**troppi biscotti** (*too many cookies*)	**Troppi fanno male.** (*Too many are bad for you.*)
tanti	**tanti regali** (*so many gifts*)	**Ho ricevuto tanti.** (*I received so many.*)
ciascuna	**ciascuna persona** (*each person*)	**Ciascuna riceve un regalo.** (*Each one receives a gift.*)
nessuno	**nessuno studente** (*no student*)	**Nessuno è arrivato.** (*No one came.*)
alcune	**alcune madri** (*some mothers*)	**Alcune non sono d'accordo.** (*Some don't agree.*)
altri	**altri padre** (*other fathers*)	**Altri dicono di no.** (*Some said no.*)
certi	**certi racconti** (*certain stories*)	**Certi fanno un'impressione.** (*Certain ones make an impression.*)
diverse	**diverse poesie** (*different poems*)	**Diverse sono brutte.** (*Different ones are ugly.*)
parecchi	**parecchi film** (*several films*)	**Ne ho visti parecchi.** (*I've seen several.*)
vari	**vari cibi** (*various foods*)	**Vari sono strani.** (*Some are strange.*)

Some indefinite adjectives can't be used as pronouns — that is, they can't stand alone to replace a noun — including **qualunque** (*whichever*) and **qualsiasi** (*whichever*).

Some indefinite adjectives have to change their spelling to become pronouns. For example, **ogni** (*every*) becomes **ognuno** (*everyone, each*), and **qualche** (*some*) becomes **qualcuno** (*someone*). **Ognuno** and **qualcuno** agree in number and gender with the nouns they replace; **ogni donna** (*every woman*) is replaced by **ognuna** (*everyone* [the *one* being feminine]); **qualche giorno** (*some days*) is replaced by **qualcuno** (*someone*). You use both **ognuno** and **qualcuno** only in the singular, though they may translate as plurals in English.

Indefinite pronouns that are used only in the singular and that are invariable (they're masculine and used generically, the way you use *he* in English to mean *everyone,* masculine or feminine) include **qualcosa** (*something*), **chiunque** (*whoever*), and **nulla** or **niente** (both of which mean *nothing*). Here are some examples:

Ognuno è differente. (*Everyone is different.*)

Qualcuno mi ha mandato una lettera d'amore. (*Someone has sent me a love letter.*)

Qualcosa non è giusto. (*Something isn't right.*)

Chiunque sia . . . (*Whoever it is . . .*)

Nulla (niente) le interessa. (*Nothing interests her.*)

The other indefinite pronouns, the ones you've seen so far in this chapter, continue to agree in number and gender with whichever noun they replace.

Both **qualcosa** and **niente** (**nulla**) show one other idiosyncratic use: When they're followed by adjectives or infinitives, they require a preposition. If you try to translate phrases with **qualcosa di, qualcosa da,** or **niente di,** literally, they won't make sense. This is one of those constructions that simply exists, and no rational reason really exists for it. Here are some examples:

Ho qualcosa di bello da dirti. (*I have something terrific to tell you.*) Note that **qualcosa** (*something*) is followed by the adjective **bello** (*terrific*); this use of the indefinite **qualcosa** requires the addition of the preposition **di** (*of*) before the adjective **bello**.

Do qualcosa da mangiare ai gatti selvatici. (*I'm giving something to eat to the feral cats.*) In this case, the indefinite pronoun **qualcosa** (*something*) is followed by **mangiare** (*to eat*), an infinitive. This use requires you to add the preposition **da** (*by, from*) between the two words.

Non c'è niente di buono da mangiare. Niente di nuovo. (*There is nothing good to eat. Nothing new.*) Here **niente** (*nothing*) takes the preposition **di** (*of*) before the adjective **buono** (*good*) and also before the adjective **nuovo** (*new*).

Nulla da dire! (*There's nothing to say!*) In this case, **nulla** (*nothing*) takes the preposition **da** (*from, by*) before the infinitive **dire** (*to say*).

Translate the following phrases or sentences from Italian into idiomatic English. Here's an example.

Q. **Mamma, non c'è niente da fare.**

A. *Mom, there's nothing to do.*

21. **Pochi sono venuti oggi.**

   _____

22. **Non mi piacciono tanti.**

   _____

23. **Nessuno studia.**

   _____

24. **Ne ho tanti.**

   _____

25. **Ognuno deve mangiare bene.**

   _____

26. **Non c'è niente di buono da mangiare.**

   _____

27. **Qualcosa è cambiato.**

   _____

28. **Alcuni non lavorano.**

   _____

29. **Ci sono vari da considerare.**

   _____

30. **Molti pensano di sì.**

   _____

Assigning Ownership with Possessive Adjectives and Pronouns

You use possessive adjectives and pronouns to show who owns what. Like all adjectives, possessive adjectives must agree in number and gender with the nouns they accompany. In English, possessive adjectives reflect the possessor (and don't have agreement issues beyond that). But in Italian, as with all adjectives, possessives have four endings: **-o** (masculine, singular), **-a** (feminine, singular), **-i** (masculine, plural), and **-e** (feminine, plural). And the possessive adjectives agree in number and gender with the thing possessed.

The multiple uses of ne

The little two-letter word **ne** means a multitude of things. When you use it with numbers or amounts, it means *of it* or *of them*. In English, you often don't express *of it* or *of them*. And in Italian, the **ne** is often redundant. You hear it all the time, however, and you sound more Italian by incorporating it into your language. For example:

Hai figli? Sì, ne ho tre. (*Do you have children? Yes, I have three [of them].*)

Vuoi del vino? Sì, ne vorrei un po'. (*Would you like some wine? Yes, I'd like a little [of it].*)

I bambini hanno paura dei fantasmi? Sì, ne hanno paura. (*Are the kids afraid of ghosts? Yes, they're afraid of them.*)

Ne also means *some* or *any,* often replacing an indefinite pronoun, as in these examples:

Ci sono medici qui? Sì, ce ne sono. (*Are there doctors here? Yes, there are some.*) (**Note:** When **ci** is used with **ne**, it becomes **ce.**)

Ci sono medici qui? Sì, ce ne sono molti. (*Are there doctors here? Yes, there are many.*)

Ci sono turisti a Siena? Sì, ce ne sono troppi. (*Are there tourists in Siena? Yes, there are too many.*)

Table 13-3 shows you the possessive adjectives and pronouns, which are the same, in each form. Notice that I include the definite articles (see Chapter 3), which you can think of as part of the adjective itself.

Table 13-3		Possessive Adjectives and Pronouns		
Masculine Singular	*Feminine Singular*	*Masculine Plural*	*Feminine Plural*	*English Translation (Adjective/Pronoun)*
il mio	**la mia**	**i miei**	**le mie**	*my/mine*
il tuo	**la tua**	**i tuoi**	**le tue**	*your/yours* (informal)
il suo	**la sua**	**i suoi**	**le sue**	*his, her, its, your* (formal)/*his, hers, its, yours*
il nostro	**la nostra**	**i nostri**	**le nostre**	*our/ours*
il vostro	**la vostra**	**i vostri**	**le vostre**	*your/yours* (informal)
il loro	**la loro**	**i loro**	**le loro**	*their, your* (formal)/*theirs, yours*

Note: **Loro** is the only form that remains the same for all genders and numbers.

Agreement in Italian is between the adjective or pronoun and the noun. For example, in English, *her book* tells you that the owner of the book is female. In Italian **il suo libro** can mean *his book, her book, its book, your* (formal) *book.* Sometimes, in the interests of clarity, you need to be more explicit; for example, **il libro di Chiara** (*Chiara's book*) leaves no doubt about whose book it is.

Context goes a long way toward establishing clarity. For example: **Andiamo con Luigi. La sua macchina è più comoda** (*We're going with Luigi. His car is more comfortable*). It's clear from the context that the car is Luigi's. And another example: **La professoressa ci dà in prestito i suoi libri** (*The teacher is lending us her books*). If the teacher is lending out books, it's safe to assume that they're probably hers.

You don't always need the article with the possessive. If you're talking about *one* family member, with no descriptive modifiers, you omit the article. But the minute you add an adjective or talk about more than one family member, the article returns. See the following examples:

No Article	*With Article*
mio fratello (*my brother*)	**il mio caro fratello** (*my dear brother*)
	i miei fratelli (*my brothers*)
tua sorella (*your sister*)	**la tua bella sorella** (*your beautiful sister*)
	le tue sorelle (*your sisters*)
suo padre (*his, her, your* [formal] *father*)	**il suo vecchio padre** (*his, her, your* [formal] *old father*)

No Article	*With Article*
nostro figlio (*our son*)	**il nostro caro figlio** (*our sweet son*)
	i nostri figli (*our sons, our children*)
	le nostre figlie (*our daughters*)
vostro zio (*your uncle*)	**il vostro zio malato** (*your sick uncle*)
	i vostri zii (*your uncles, your aunts and uncles*)
	le vostre zie (*your aunts*)

Loro, however, always uses the article. **Loro** itself is invariable, but the definite article you use with it agrees with the number and gender of the family member, as in **il loro padre** (*their father*) and **la loro madre** (*their mother*).

You consider certain names for family members as being already modified, and they need the article as well, such as **mamma** (*Mom*), **babbo** (*Daddy*), and **papà** (*Papa*). (Be sure to put the accent on **papà**; without it [**papa**], you're talking about the Pope.) Thus, you say **la mia mamma** (*my mom*) but **mia madre** (*my mother*).

In speech, you often omit the adjective altogether when using **mamma, babbo,** and **papà.** For example: **La mamma lavora troppo — anche il babbo** (*[My] mom works too much — [my] daddy, too*).

Translate the following phrases into Italian, using possessive adjectives. Use the article if necessary.

Q. *his house*

A. **la sua casa** _____

31. *my car* _____

32. *your* (familiar, singular) *brother* _____

33. *his sweet grandmother* _____

34. *her houses* _____

35. *my cousins* _____

36. *her mother* _____

37. *his daughters* _____

38. *our class* _____

39. *your* (familiar, plural) *city* _____

40. *their books* _____

Italian names for family members

Here's a quick list of the Italian names for various family members. (Note that pets aren't considered family members.)

✔ **padre** (*father*)

✔ **madre** (*mother*)

✔ **fratello** (*brother*)

✔ **sorella** (*sister*)

✔ **figlio/figlia** (*son/daughter*)

✔ **zio/zia** (*uncle/aunt*)

✔ **cugino/cugina** (*male cousin/female cousin*)

✔ **nonno/nonna** (*grandfather/grandmother*)

✔ **brother-in-law/sister-in-law** (*cognato/cognata*)

✔ **father-in-law/mother-in-law** (*suocero/suocera*)

Replacing Nouns with Possessive Pronouns

To form possessive pronouns, you use the possessive adjectives and simply omit a modified noun. These *are* pronouns after all, and they replace the noun. Generally, you keep the article, even with individual, unmodified relatives, when you use possessive pronouns. Here are some examples:

> **Io porto i miei occhiali da sole. Tu porti i tuoi?** (*I'm wearing my sunglasses. Are you wearing yours?*)

> **Mia madre viene alla festa. Viene la tua?** (*My mother is coming to the party. Is yours coming?*)

> **Luigi guida la sua macchina; io uso la mia.** (*Luigi is driving his car; I'm using mine.*)

> **Noi preferiamo la nostra scuola; voi preferite la vostra.** (*We prefer our school; you prefer yours.*)

> **Io parlo con la mia mamma e tu parli con la tua.** (*I'll talk to my mom and you talk to yours.*)

> **I loro figli sono maleducati, ma i nostri, no.** (*Their kids are rude, but ours aren't.*)

Often, after the verb **essere,** you omit the article altogether and use only the pronoun, as in **È mio** (*It's mine*).

And sometimes, when you don't have to state ownership or a relationship explicitly, you omit the possessive adjective entirely. This applies to close relatives (**la mamma** [*mom*], **il babbo** [*daddy*]), body parts (**il naso** [*nose*], **la bocca** [*mouth*]), and items of clothing (**il vestito** [*dress*], **i guanti** [*gloves*]). For example:

> **Il babbo è stanco oggi.** (*[My] daddy is tired today.*)

> **Non mangiare con la bocca aperta!** (*Don't eat with [your] mouth open!*)

> **Ho perso i guanti.** (*I've lost [my] gloves.*)

Use possessive pronouns to complete the following sentences and phrases, according to the English word in parentheses.

Q. Luigi legge il suo libro; io leggo _____ (*mine*).

A. il mio

41. Noi portiamo i nostri figli, voi portate _____ (*yours*).

42. I miei cugini, _____ (*his*).

43. le vostre macchine, _____ (*mine*).

44. le nostre case, _____ (*theirs*).

45. quel libro? È _____ (*hers*).

46. I nostri parenti, _____ (*yours* [singular, familiar]).

47. I tuoi gatti, _____ (*ours*).

48. la loro nonna, _____ (*his*).

49. il suo veterinario, _____ (*its*).

50. il mio dentista, _____ (*hers*).

Answer Key

1 quello

2 Quell'

3 Questa

4 Quella

5 quelle

6 Questo

7 Quegli

8 quelle

9 quelli

10 Questi

11 alcuni, parecchi

12 troppi

13 tanti

14 pochi

15 molto

16 ogni, qualsiasi, qualunque

17 vari, diversi

18 parecchie

19 altre

20 nessuna

21 *Few have come today.*

22 *I don't like so many.*

23 *No one studies.*

24 *I have so many.*

25 *Everyone must eat well.*

26 *There's nothing good to eat.*

27 *Something has changed.*

28 *Some don't work.*

29 *There are various [things] to consider.*

30 *Many think so.*

31 **la mia macchina**

32 **tuo fratello**

33 **la sua cara nonna**

34 **le sue case**

35 **i miei cugini**

36 **la loro madre**

37 **le sue figlie**

38 **la nostra classe**

39 **la vostra città**

40 **i loro libri**

41 **i vostri**

42 **i suoi**

43 le mie

44 le loro

45 suo

46 i tuoi

47 i nostri

48 la sua

49 il suo

50 il suo

Chapter 14

Making Transitions, Forming Connections, and Commenting

In This Chapter

▶ Forming compound sentences with coordinating conjunctions

▶ Linking clauses with subordinating conjunctions

▶ Using relative pronouns to join dependent and independent clauses

▶ Tying ideas together with transitional elements

▶ Expressing thoughts or emotions with interjections

*I*magine having to speak without the ability to join subjects or nouns: "I went to Italy. He went to Italy. We visited Rome. We visited Venice." Isn't it so much better — and faster — to be able to say, "He and I went to Italy and visited Rome and Venice"? *Conjunctions* are words that join words or phrases, sentences or clauses together to let you form compound and complex sentences. They add body and flow to your language and save you time.

Conjunctions let you produce more complex, descriptive thoughts rather than choppy, simple ones. Some conjunctions require specific verb forms (tenses and moods), which I discuss in detail in Chapters 19, 20, and 22.

The two main types of conjunctions in Italian are coordinating (which join two, grammatically equal parts of a sentence) and subordinating (which join a subordinate or dependent clause to a main or independent clause). They serve to tie thoughts and ideas together as do other transitional words like *for example, because of,* and *meanwhile.* Relative pronouns also clarify, explain, or elucidate who or what leads to one thing or another: *The boy who rented the house is a medical student. The car that I saw was speeding.*

You can easily get carried away in another language and get lost with so many clauses and transitions, so interjections come to the rescue. These words allow you to tie ideas together and to be very clear about your reactions. Often, just a single word or a short phrase, interjections give you a way to comment, briefly and to the point.

In this chapter, I emphasize conjunctions and transitions, but I also show you economic ways to comment so that you can be (and sound) in control of Italian.

Connecting Words or Sentences with Coordinating Conjunctions

Coordinating conjunctions link elements of equal value or stature. For example, in the sentence, "He and I went downtown," *and* joins two subjects together — *he* and *I*. In the sentence, "He went downtown, and I went home," *and* joins two clauses of equal value together — *he went downtown* and *I went home*. In both examples, *and* is a coordinating conjunction.

And is a positive coordinating conjunction because it combines more than one subject or idea together; negative conjunctions separate subjects or ideas (such as *neither . . . nor* constructs). For example: *Neither he nor I wanted to go to the movie.*

The most commonly used coordinating conjunctions are **e** (*and*) and **ma** (*but*). **Ma** fulfills the same function as **e** by joining two independent clauses of equal value. For example: **Lui ed io siamo amici** (*He and I are friends*); **Lei era triste, ma io ero felice** (*She was sad, but I was happy*). In both sentences, conjunctions link things of equality — subjects in the first and independent clauses in the second.

Here are a couple other facts about **e**:

✔ The conjunction **e** doesn't carry an accent as the word for *he/she/it is* or *you* (formal) *are* does (**è**).

> **La ragazza è italiana e ha una famiglia grande.** (*The girl is Italian and has a large family.*)

✔ You add the letter **d** to **e** when **e** precedes a vowel because it makes the word or flow of the sentence sound better. In fact, it's called the *euphonic e.*

> **Lui è italiano ed io sono americana.** (*He is Italian, and I am American.*)

Table 14-1 shows you the most commonly used Italian coordinating conjunctions.

Table 14-1	Coordinating Conjunctions
Italian	*English Translation*
e	and, instead
ma	but
o	or
però, tuttavia	however
anche	even
anzi	to the contrary, indeed
cioè	that is
perciò	for that reason, so, therefore
né . . . né	neither . . . nor (also, either . . . or)
sia . . . sia	be it . . . be it
non solo . . . ma anche	not only . . . but also

Like prepositions, conjunctions can have various meanings, depending on context.

> ✔ **E** can mean both *and* and *instead*. For example: **Credevo che lui dormisse e leggeva.** (*I thought he was sleeping; instead he was reading.*)

> ✔ **Anzi** means both *on the contrary* and *indeed*. For example: **Fa fresco, anzi fa freddo.** (*It's chilly; indeed it's cold.*)

> ✔ **O** can be *or* as a conjunction, and you can also use it as *or* to provide another definition or example, as in **Studia la zoologia, o il mondo degli animali** (*He is studying zoology, or the world of animals*).

Consider the joining of two equal elements in the following sentences.

> **Marco e Riccardo sono amici, ma le loro mogli sono sorelle.** (*Marco and Riccardo are friends, but their wives are sisters.*)

> **Lui è intelligente, anzi brillante.** (*He is smart, even brilliant.*)

> **È un medico, cioè un chirurgo.** (*He's a doctor, that is, a surgeon.*)

> **Non mi piace né carne né pesce.** (*I like neither meat nor fish.*)

> **Sia la madre sia il padre, sono molto simpatici.** (*Be it the mother or the father, they are both nice.*)

Fill in the blanks in the following sentences, using the coordinating conjunction in parentheses. Here's an example.

Q. Lui _____ (*and*) **lei cantano e ballano.**

A. e

1. **Noi andiamo alla spiaggia, _____** (*but*) **loro vanno in montagna.**

2. **I bambini sono giovani _____** (*and*) **simpatici.**

3. **È un lavoro molto difficile, _____** (*however*) **proverò a farlo.**

4. **Non è _____** (*either*) **carne _____** (*or*) **pesce.**

5. **Io vorrei studiare _____** (*not only*) **giapponese _____** (*but also*) **cinese.**

6. **La scuola è buona, _____** (*indeed*) **è perfetta.**

7. **Vado in ufficio, _____** (*so*) **non posso prendere un caffè.**

8. **Non è mica stupido, _____** (*on the contrary*) **è molto furbo.**

9. **Il mio computer è vecchio, _____** (*but*) **il suo è nuovo.**

10. **Il professore è di Firenze, _____** (*that is*) **è fiorentino.**

Connecting Clauses with Subordinating Conjunctions

Subordinating conjunctions reveal the relationship between a dependent clause and an independent one. They can complete, modify, explain, or clarify meaning, and they usually include words such as *although* (**sebbene**)*, because* (**perché**)*, and since* (**siccome**).

Subordinating conjunctions generally begin a sentence and introduce a clause that joins another clause (main or independent). For example:

> "Although he went downtown, I went home." *Although* clarifies what you and he did.

> "Although it was freezing, we went to the game." Here, *although* explains a situation.

Here's an example of an Italian subordinating conjunction:

> **Non ci vengo perché sono impegnatissima.** (*I'm not coming because I'm really swamped.*) **Perché sono impegnatissima** depends on **Non ci vengo** and explains the reason behind the independent clause.

You can use some subordinating conjunctions with the indicative mood (factual expressions). Table 14-2 lists the most common subordinating conjunctions. The guiding questions that these subordinating conjunctions answer are *why, how, to what degree,* and *when.* (See Chapter 11 for how to ask questions and use these forms interrogatively.)

Note: Other subordinating conjunctions require the subjunctive mood (a speculative verb form). I give these detailed treatment in Chapters 19, 20, and 22.

Table 14-2	Subordinating Conjunctions
Italian	*English Translation*
perché	because
siccome	since, because
come	as
così ... che	so ... that
a tal punto	so ... that
così ... come	as ... as
quando	when
per quanto	as far as
se (with the present or future indicative)	if
mentre	whereas

Consider the following sentences. The subjunctive conjunctions and the dependent clauses they introduce tend to stand out and allow you to be precise and clear in what you're communicating.

> **Perché lui non voleva andare alla festa, non siamo andati.** (*Because he didn't want to go to the party, we didn't go.*)

> **Siccome è presto, ho tempo per fare una passeggiata.** (*Because it's early, I have time to take a walk.*)

> **Ero così stanca che non potevo dormire.** (*I was so tired that I couldn't sleep.*)

> **Ero stanca a tal punto che non potevo dormire.** (*I was so tired that I couldn't sleep.*)

> **Francesca è così simpatico che tutti l'amano.** (*Francesca is so nice that everyone loves her.*)

> **Quando arriverò, ti chiamerò.** (*When I arrive, I'll call you.*)

> **Se pioverà, rimarrò a casa.** (*If it rains, I'll stay home.*)

> **Mentre dormivi, io studiavo.** (*While you were sleeping, I was studying.*)

Choose from the subordinating conjunctions in the word bank, and fill in the blanks in the following sentences. You may use some of the words twice. An example follows.

Perché	siccome	così . . . che	quando	mentre
Per quanto	se	così . . . come	a tal punto	come

Q. _____ verrà lui, verrai te?

A. Se

11. La nonna non è _____ vecchia _____ credevo.

12. _____ so io, le ragazze sono a scuola.

13. _____ nevica, le scuole non possono aprire.

14. Il signore era ricco _____ che i soldi non gli interessavano.

15. Io dormirò _____ i ragazzi saranno tornati.

16. Gli animali mangiano _____ hanno fame.

17. _____ non posso guidare, devo chiedere aiuto agli amici.

18. Tu incontri gli amici _____ io studio?

19. Non l'ho fatto _____ mi hai fatto vedere.

20. La professoresa era _____ intelligente _____ gli studenti la temevano.

Joining Clauses with Conjunctions

To join clauses that belong together, you use coordinating conjunctions; to join clauses that are dependent on one another, you use subordinating conjunctions. See the following examples and explanations:

- ✔ **Lui ha mangiato un primo e un secondo con contorni e due dolci perché aveva fame.** (*He ate a first course, a second course with side dishes, and two desserts because he was hungry.*) **E** links things of equal value (courses of a meal); **perché** explains why he ate all those things.

- ✔ **Non gli piacciono né cani né gatti perché soffre dalle allergie.** (*He doesn't like either dogs or cats because he suffers from allergies.*) **Né** and **né** equate things of equal value (dogs and cats); **perché** tells you why he doesn't like dogs and cats.

- ✔ **Tu preferisci restare con me oppure uscire?** (*Do you prefer to stay here with me or to go out?*) **Oppure** offers a choice between two equal things.

- ✔ **Non vogliamo studiare, però proviamo.** (*We don't want to study, however, we'll try.*) **Però** links the two verbs — things of equal worth.

Linking Independent Clauses to Dependent Clauses with Relative Pronouns

Just as you use subordinating conjunctions to join an independent clause to a dependent clause, you can use relative pronouns to accomplish the same thing — to clarify, to explain, to elucidate.

For example, in the sentence **Lo studente, che lavora molto, merita i voti buoni** (*The student who works hard deserves good grades*), the clause *who works hard* begins with a pronoun, *who,* and explains more about the student who gets good grades.

Table 14-3 shows you the relative pronouns and their English equivalents.

Table 14-3	Relative Pronouns
Italian	*English Translations*
che	*who, whom, that, which*
chi	*those who, one who*
cui	*that, which, whom,* and with a definite article, *whose*
il, la quale; i, le quali	used to replace **che** and **cui**

Keep these things in mind when linking clauses in Italian with relative pronouns:

✔ In Italian, **che** refers to both people and things; Italian has no distinction between *who* and *that*, as there is — or at least should be — in English.

> **Il libro che ho appena finito era meravigliosa.** (*The book that I just finished was marvelous.*)

✔ **Chi** is most often used generically, to refer to unspecified people, and it appears in many proverbs.

> **Chi dorme, non piglia pesci.** (Literally: *He who sleeps doesn't catch any fish.*) The English equivalent of this phrase is *The early bird catches the worm.*

> **Chi vince ha sempre ragione.** (*He who wins is always right.*) In English, you'd say, *Might is right.*

> **Chi cerca, trova.** (*Seek and you shall find.*)

✔ **Cui** is usually preceded by a preposition, as in these examples:

> **Le persone a cui ho telefonato non erano a casa.** (*The people whom I called weren't home.*)

> **Il gatto per cui ho comprato il cibo speciale, non lo mangia.** (*The cat for whom I bought the special food, won't eat it.*)

✔ If **cui** is preceded by a definite article (**il, la, i,** or **le**), which reflects the number and gender of the person or thing you're referring to, it means *whose*.

> **Ho appena comprato una nuova macchina, il cui colore è stupendo!** (*I just bought a new car whose color is terrific!*) **Colore** is masculine singular, so you use the article **il** with **cui.**

> **Hai visto la casa, la cui loggia è crollata?** (*Did you see the house whose upper story porch is falling down?*) **Loggia** is feminine singular, so you use **la.**

> **La signora Bartoli, le cui figlie sono ballerine, è proprio goffa.** (*Mrs. Bartoli, whose daughters are dancers, is really clumsy.*) **Ballerine** and the definite article **le** are both feminine plural.

> **L'insegnante, i cui figli sono proprio antipatici, è simpatico.** (*The teacher, whose kids are really not nice, is nice.*) **Figli** and **i** agree in number, plural, and gender (masculine).

✔ You can use **quale** instead of either **che** or **cui.** It must carry a definite article that agrees with the number and gender of what or who it refers to. It has, however, only one singular form (**quale**), which is both masculine and feminine. Likewise, it has only one plural form (**quali**).

> **Il ragazzo de cui ti ho parlato . . .** is the same as **Il ragazzo del (di + il) quale ti ho parlato.** (*The boy about whom I spoke to you . . .*)

> **Un'amica che abita a Boston . . .** is the same as **Un'amica la quale abita a Boston.** Both mean *a friend who lives in Boston.*

> **Io non ho visto il film di cui mi hai parlato** or **Io non ho visto il film del (di + il) quale mi hai parlato.** (*I didn't see the movie about which you told me.*)

When the definite article follows a preposition, it combines with that preposition to form one word. You can find more details in Chapter 12.

Translate the following phrases and sentences into Italian, using relative pronouns as necessary. Here's an example.

0. *the book that I bought*

A. **il libro che ho comprato**

21. *whose father* _____

22. *whose mother* _____

23. *whose books* _____

24. *whose cars* _____

25. *about which* _____

26. *the girl who* _____

27. *the boy who* _____

28. *the books in which* _____

29. *the house that* _____

30. *he who* _____

Using Other Transitional Elements

To keep your Italian flowing and to make it coherent, you need not only conjunctions and relative pronouns that connect words, phrases, or sentences but also transitional linguistic elements that tie larger thoughts or ideas together. Often, these elements include the conjunctions and relative pronouns that you find throughout this chapter.

To introduce or close an idea or train of thought, you may say *above all, in the end, before anything, on the other hand,* and so on. Table 14-4 lists common transitional elements that you use in daily conversation and writing.

Table 14-4	Common Transitional Elements
Italian	*English Translation*
riguardo a	*with regards to*
nel frattempo	*in the meanwhile*
per esempio	*for example*
cioè	*that is*
a causa di	*because of*
bisogna considerare	*one needs to consider*

Italian	English Translation
si deve avere in mente	one must keep in mind
si deve avere presente	one must keep in mind
malgrado che	despite
invece	instead
allo stesso tempo	at the same time
in fin dei conti	in the end
in ogni caso	in any case
da questo si deduce che	from this, one can conclude that
soprattutto	above all
da una parte	on the one hand
dall'altro lato	on the other hand
basterebbe fare un esempio	it's enough to give this example
è meglio dire	it's better to say
intendevo dire	I meant to say
chiaramente	clearly

This list could go on and on. Suffice it to say that these short phrases and single words can tie one paragraph or one thought to another, as in these examples:

> **Lui studiava; nel frattempo io preparavo da mangiare.** (*He was studying; in the meanwhile, I fixed something to eat.*) **Nel frattempo** ties the two events in the sentence together.

> **Ci sono quattro ragazzi in quel gruppo, cioè Marco, Antonio, Riccardo e Massimo.** (*There are four boys in that group, that is, Marco, Antonio, Riccardo, and Massimo.*) **Cioè** lists or elucidates just who the four boys in the group were.

Interjecting and Commenting with Interjections

Interjections often mimic imperatives. Interjections let you command and comment at the same time. They can be made up of all the other parts of speech (see Chapter 1), but how you use them is what makes them interjections (because you often interject such words or comments to express a thought or emotion). In this section, I divide interjections into types: greetings and goodbyes, toasts, expressions of dismay and surprise, and congratulations and compliments.

All interjections multitask, depending on your tone of voice. **Bello!** for example, can mean *Beautiful! Great! Terrific!* It can also mean just the opposite, if you change how you say it. For example, say that your computer decides to go on the fritz when you're in the middle of an urgent project. **Bello!** in this case means something like *Great. Isn't that just dandy!* (Note the sarcastic tone.)

Saying hello and goodbye

The most useful interjections as you make your way through the day are those that allow you to greet and say goodbye to others. They include the following:

- **A dopo, a più tardi, a presto** are ways of saying *see you after, later, soon.* **Ci vediamo** is a way to say *we'll see each other again,* with the *soon* implied.

- **Addio, arrivederci** (informal), and **arrivederLa** (formal) all mean *goodbye.*

- **Benarrivato, bentornato,** and **benvenuto** all are ways of saying *welcome* or *welcome back.*

- While **buon giorno** and **buona sera** can mean either *hello* or *goodbye* (Literally: *good day* and *good evening*), you use **buona notte** (*good night*) only when saying a final goodbye. You can say **buona notte** when you put children to bed and follow it with **sogni d'oro** (*sweet dreams*). In parts of Italy, you say **buondì** (*good day*) instead of **buon giorno.**

- **Ciao** is informal and means both *hello* and *bye* as well.

- **Salve,** imported directly from Latin, also means *hello* and is used with friends.

- **Pronto** is used to say *hello* on the telephone. It literally means *ready.*

Making toasts

The most famous toast in Italian is probably **cin cin** (*to your health*). You also say **alla salute** (*to your health*). Before eating, however, you normally say **buon appetito** (*good appetite*). Other phrases used as toasts include **buon compleanno** (*happy birthday*), **auguri** (*best wishes*), and **viva . . .** (*long live . . .*).

Expressing dismay or surprise

Because you can make almost any word an interjection, you're practically unlimited in using expressions of dismay and surprise. I include expressions of please and thanks here because they often reflect either dismay or surprise. You can say something as simple as **bene** (*good, well, well done*), which also can mean *okay, fine by me,* and so on. Some general interjections that you may find useful appear in the following list.

- **accipicchia, accidenti, ah, cavolo** (*darn*)

- **basta** (*enough*) and its synonym **uffa**

- **grazie** to mean *thanks,* **grazie infinite** (*infinite thanks*), and **molte grazie** (*many thanks*); or less formal expressions: **figurati** (*think nothing of it*) and **niente** (*it's nothing*)

- **ohimè** (*oh dear*)

- **per carità, per piacere, per favore** (*please*)

Giving congratulations and compliments

Always useful, you can use the following words of congratulations and compliments liberally:

- ✔ **Beato te, fortunate te** both mean *lucky you* and are used informally.

- ✔ **Bravo** has come into English to mean *well done,* or *you're really good.* In Italian, it means the same thing, but it has four forms: masculine singular (**bravo**), masculine plural (**bravi**), feminine singular (**brava**), and feminine plural (**brave**). These forms agree in number and gender with the person(s) you're complimenting.

- ✔ You can use **congratulazioni, complimenti,** and **felicitazioni** to say *congratulations.*

Answer Key

1. ma

2. e

3. però, tuttavia

4. né . . . né

5. non solo . . . ma anche

6. anzi

7. perciò

8. anzi

9. ma

10. cioè

11. così . . . come

12. per quanto

13. se

14. a tal punto

15. quando

16. perché

17. siccome

18. mentre

19. come

20. così che

`21` **il cui**

`22` **la cui**

`23` **i cui**

`24` **le cui**

`25` **di cui**

`26` **la ragazza che**

`27` **il ragazzo che**

`28` **i libri nei quali**

`29` **la casa che**

`30` **chi**

Chapter 15

Describing Actions with Adverbs

. . . .

In This Chapter

▶ Using adverbs to describe actions

▶ Breaking down adverbs by function

▶ Putting adverbs in their place

▶ Comparing equalities and inequalities

. . . .

*Y*ou use adverbs to describe how you're doing something, when you're doing it, and to what extent. Adverbs add color and meaning to sentences by letting others know in what manner an action was taken. For example, *I left regretfully* tells a different story than *I left eagerly.*

Curiosity, comparison, evaluation, and judgment account for the many adverbs you find in any language. Adverbs let you answer questions about how (*badly, cleverly*), when (*this morning, yesterday*), where (*over there, outside*), and how much (*a lot, a little*).

In Italian, adverbs are easy to form and use. They're not masculine or feminine, so they don't change to agree in number and gender with anything. They're invariable and dependable. In this chapter, I show you *how* and *when* to form and use different kinds of adverbs, *where* to place them in sentences, and *how much* they add descriptively to your Italian.

Getting Acquainted with Italian Adverbs

Adverbs come in two types, according to their roots: those that derive from adjectives and those that don't. Both kinds modify verbs (*he studies a lot*), adjectives (*very beautiful*), and even other adverbs (*very well*). The following sections give you details about forming adverbs from adjectives and using original adverbs.

Making an adverb from an adjective in English means adding *-ly,* for example, *brief* (adjective) becomes *briefly* (adverb), and *private* (adjective) changes to *privately* (adverb). Adverbs made from adjectives tend to talk about *how* you do something; original adverbs tend to talk about *when, where,* and *how much.*

Forming adverbs from adjectives

Adverbs that come from adjectives are easy to form. You take the feminine singular form of an adjective, such as **vera** (*true*) or **recente** (*recent*), and add **-mente** (the equivalent of the English *-ly*). That's it. **Vera** becomes **veramente** (*truly*), and **recente** becomes **recentemente** (*recently*). Other examples are **rapidamente** (*rapidly*), **lentamente** (*slowly*), **certamente** (*certainly*), and **chiaramente** (*clearly*).

Exceptions to this simple formation include adjectives that end in **-le** or **-re**, so long as these last two letters are preceded by a vowel. These adjectives drop the final **-e** and add **-mente.** Here are some examples: **speciale** (*special*), **specialmente** (*especially*); **generale** (*general*), **generalmente** (*generally*); **regolare** (*regular*), **regolarmente** (*regularly*); **popolare** (*popular*), **popolarmente** (*popularly*).

When using adverbs, you don't have to worry about gender or number agreement issues as you do with adjectives (see Chapters 5 and 13 for more on adjectives). With adverbs, all you have to do is use them.

Make the following adjectives into adverbs. I include the English meaning to make the change from adjective to adverb clear.

Q. **facile** (*easy*), _____ (*easily*)

A. **facilmente**

1. **precisa** (*precise*), _____ (*precisely*)

2. **triste** (*sad*), _____ (*sadly*)

3. **onesta** (*honest*), _____ (*honestly*)

4. **specifica** (*specific*), _____ (*specifically*)

5. **rara** (*rare*), _____ (*rarely*)

6. **intelligente** (*intelligent*), _____ (*intelligently*)

7. **singolare** (*singular*), _____ (*singularly*)

8. **estrema** (*extreme*), _____ (*extremely*)

9. **chiara** (*clear*), _____ (*clearly*)

10. **sensibile** (*sensitive*), _____ (*sensitively*)

Getting to know the original adverbs

Italian also has countless so-called *original adverbs,* which are those that don't derive from adjectives. No forming or altering is necessary with these adverbs; you can simply use them as is.

Here's a list of some of the more common original adverbs.

- **abbastanza** (*enough*)
- **allora** (*then*)
- **anche** (*also*)
- **ancora** (*still, yet, again*)
- **anzi** (*to the contrary, as a matter of fact*)
- **appena** (*as soon as, just now*)
- **assai** (*very*)
- **bene, male** (*well, not well or badly*)
- **ci** (*here, there*)
- **contro** (*against*)
- **così . . . come** (*as . . . as*)
- **dappertutto** (*everywhere*)
- **davvero** (*really, truly*)
- **di nuovo** (*again*)
- **domani** (*tomorrow*)
- **dopo** (*after*)
- **finora** (*until now*)
- **fra** (**tra**) **poco** (*in a little while*)
- **già** (*already*)
- **in fretta** (*hurriedly*)
- **inoltre** (*moreover*)
- **insieme** (*together*)
- **invece** (*instead*)
- **lì, là** (*there*)

- **lontano, vicino** (*far, near*)
- **mai** (*never, ever*)
- **meno** (*less*)
- **mica** (*not at all, not in the slightest*)
- **molto, poco** (*much, little*)
- **nel frattempo** (*in the meanwhile*)
- **oggi, oggigiorno** (*today, nowadays*)
- **oltre** (*besides*)
- **ormai** (*by now*)
- **per caso** (*by chance*)
- **più** (*more*)
- **piuttosto** (*rather*)
- **poi** (*then, after*)
- **presto, tardi** (*early, late*)
- **prima** (*first, before*)
- **purtroppo** (*unfortunately*)
- **quasi** (*almost*)
- **qui, qua** (*here*)
- **sempre, mai** (*always, never*)
- **solo** (*only*)
- **spesso** (*often*)
- **stamani, stasera** (*this morning, this evening*)
- **su, giù** (*up, down*)
- **subito** (*immediately, right away*)
- **tanto . . . quanto** (*as much . . . as*)

Here are a few examples of these adverbs in action:

Come stai? Bene, grazie. (*How are you? Well, thanks.*)

Ci incontriamo domani? (*Shall we meet up tomorrow?*)

Lui non è mica magro. (*He's not at all thin*).

Sorting Adverbs by Function

When trying to commit adverbs to memory and use them properly, you may find it easier to sort them by their jobs, or by which questions they answer. For example,

bene (*well*) tells how someone feels, as in **Come stai? Bene, grazie** (*How are you? Well, thanks*). **Domani** (*tomorrow*) tells you *when* you're meeting someone. **Su e giù, qua e là** (*up and down, here and there*) tells you *where* something is happening. **Mica** (*not at all*) tells *how much* or *to what* degree.

The following sections describe types of questions adverbs can answer and which adverbs are appropriate to use in which instance.

Telling how: Adverbs of manner

You use adverbs of manner to explain *how* something or someone acted or simply was (**Come ha parlato Marco? Ha parlato chiaramente** [*How did Marco speak? He spoke clearly*] or **Come si era vestita? Semplicemente** [*How was she dressed? Elegantly*]). You also use adverbs of manner to answer basic, daily questions, such as **Come stai? Bene, grazie** (*How are you? Well, thanks*) and **Come stanno i tuoi? Stanno tutti bene** (*How is your family? Everyone's well*).

Telling when: Adverbs of time

Adverbs of time describe when an action will take place. You use them to let others know what date and time something will happen (**Andiamo domani** [*Let's go tomorrow*]) or in what order of events something will occur (**Appena arriverò, ti chiamerò** [*As soon as I arrive, I'll call you*]). You can also use adverbs of time to explain whether something has ever happened (**I bambini non hanno mai mangiato tartufi** [*The kids have never eaten truffles*]).

Telling where: Adverbs of place

If you're placing people or events inside (**dentro**), outside (**fuori**), in front of (**davanti a**), behind (**dietro a**) — in short, in a physically identifiable location — you're using adverbs of place.

The most common adverb of place is **ci** (*here, there*). For example: **Ci sono studenti qui** (*There are students here*) and **C'è nessuno?** (*Is anyone here?*) Note that in Italian, you have to specify whether you're talking about something singular (**c'è** [*there is*]) or something plural (**ci sono** [*there are*]).

Sometimes **ci** is written as **vi**, but **vi** is an archaic use, not commonly found in modern Italian.

Telling how much: Adverbs of degree

These adverbs answer the questions *how much* or *to what degree?* I deal with these adverbs more extensively in the section "Making Comparisons with Adverbs." If you want to explain that something was especially good or bad or interesting, an adverb of degree allows you to do that: **Le ragazze sono specialmente interessanti** (*The girls are especially interesting*).

The most common adverb of degree is **molto** (*very*), as in **Riccardo è molto elegante** (*Riccardo is very elegant*). The opposite of **molto** is **poco** (*not very*): **Il libro è poco chiaro** (*The book isn't very clear*). Because **molto** and **poco** are also adjectives, meaning *many* and *few,* you can put **molto** the adverb (*very*) with **poco** the adjective (*few*) and say **molto poco** (*very few*).

Although **molto** is the most common form of *very,* adding the adverbial suffix **-issimo** is another way to say *very.* You attach **-issimo** to adjectives by dropping the final letter from the adjective and adding **-issimo,** for example, **bravo** (*good*) becomes **bravissimo** (*very good*). Because you add it to an adjective, **-issimo** changes its endings to reflect the gender and number of the adjective. For example, to make **un ragazzo bravissimo** (*a very good boy* [masculine, singular]) plural, you change the ending to **i,** like so: **due ragazzi bravissimi** (*two very good boys* [masculine, plural]); and **una ragazza bravissima** (*a very good girl* [feminine, singular]) changes to **due ragazze bravissime** (*two very good girls* [feminine, plural]).

Translate the following adverbs into Italian. Feel free to refer to the list of original adverbs; the more you look at these words, the more familiar they become. Some adverbs may have more than one answer.

Q. *then*

A. **allora, poi**

11. *in a little while* _____

12. *less* _____

13. *more* _____

14. *as soon as* _____

15. *very* _____

16. *unfortunately* _____

17. *often* _____

18. *only* _____

19. *by now* _____

20. *already* _____

Placing Adverbs in Sentences

You can choose, to some degree, where you place adverbs in a sentence. Generally, they follow verbs, precede adjectives, start a sentence if you're being particularly emphatic, and sometimes split up helping verbs and past participles (see Chapter 16 for details). Here, I outline where these adverbs fall within a sentence and provide examples of each:

✔ Adverbs that modify verbs, *follow* the verbs in a sentence.

> **Studiano regolarmente e molto.** (*They study regularly and a lot.*)
>
> **Mangiano fuori se fa bel tempo.** (*They eat outside if the weather is nice.*)
>
> **Mi dispiace tanto.** (*I'm so sorry.*)

✔ When adverbs modify adjectives, they *precede* the adjectives.

> **È una donna molto bella.** (*She is a very beautiful woman.*)
>
> **Lui è assai intelligente.** (*He is very intelligent.*)
>
> **Il medico non è completamente contento.** (*The doctor isn't completely happy.*)

✔ To be emphatic, you can *start a sentence* with an adverb.

> **Purtroppo, non è vero.** (*Unfortunately, it isn't true.*)
>
> **Generalmente, non si fa.** (*Generally, you don't do that.*)
>
> **Normalmente, non è un problema.** (*Normally, it's not a problem.*)

✔ A few adverbs can fall *between a helping verb* (**essere** [*to be*] or **avere** [*to have*]) *and a past participle:*

> **Non sono <u>ancora</u> arrivati.** (*They haven't <u>yet</u> arrived.*)
>
> **Lei ha <u>appena</u> finito i compiti.** (*She has <u>just now</u> finished the homework.*)
>
> **Ho <u>già</u> parlato con loro.** (*I have <u>already</u> spoken with them.*)
>
> **Il babbo ha <u>sempre</u> detto di no.** (*Daddy has <u>always</u> said no.*)
>
> **Gli insegnanti non hanno <u>mai</u> guadagnato molto.** (*Teachers have <u>never</u> earned much.*)

Making Comparisons with Adverbs

In general, you make three kinds of comparisons in Italian: those of equality (*as pretty as her mother*), inequality (*more rich than smart; less tall than his father*), and comparative and relative or absolute superlatives (*better, worse, the best, the very worst*). Each comparison uses specific adverbs and forms in its own idiosyncratic way. I explore these comparisons in the following sections.

Equalities

Comparisons of equality use adverbs to say that two (or more) things are equal. You use **così . . . come** (*as . . . as*) or **tanto . . . quanto** (*as much . . . as*) to make such comparisons.

✔ The **così . . . come** construction puts **così** before an adjective, as in these examples:

> **Quel ragazzo è così bello come suo padre.** (*That boy is as handsome as his father.*)

> **Questa nuova casa non è così comoda come quella vecchia.** (*This new house isn't as comfortable as that old one.*)

You often leave out **così**, because it's understood rather than voiced; for example: **Lei è [così] vecchia come mio nonno** (*She is as old as my grandfather*) and **Lui è [così] brutto come la fame** (*He is as ugly as hunger* [an Italian proverb]).

Other times, you follow **come** with a verb, as shown in these examples:

> **Il lavoro non è così facile come credevo.** (*The work isn't as easy as I thought.*)

> **La valigia non è così pesante come credevo.** (*The suitcase isn't as heavy as I thought.*)

✔ **Tanto**, from the **tanto . . . quanto** way of stating comparisons, also must precede an adjective:

> **Laura è tanto simpatica quanto sua sorella.** (*Laura is as nice as her sister.*)

You don't leave **tanto** out of the stated comparison, however. See these examples:

> **La nostra casa è tanto vecchia quanto la vostra.** (*Our house is as old as yours.*)

> **Il liceo è tanto famosa quanto l'università.** (*The high school is as famous as the university.*)

Inequalities

With comparisons of inequality, you say that something is more (**più**) or less (**meno**) big, small, numerous — whatever — than something else; for example: **più grande** (*more grand*), **meno simpatico** (*less nice*), **più case** (*more houses*), and **meno ponti** (*fewer bridges*).

In the sentences **Lei è più alta di suo fratello** (*She is taller than her brother*) and **Ci sono più bambini che adulti** (*There are more children than adults*), *than* is translated as **di** or **che,** depending on what you're comparing. Here, I explain when to use **di** and when to use **che:**

✔ If you're comparing two distinct things or people, you use **di.** Here are some examples:

> **Il gatto è più giovane del cane.** (*The cat is younger than the dog.*)

> **Le tue ricette sono più buone di quelle nel libro.** (*Your recipes are better than those in the book.*)

> **L'italiano è più bello dell'inglese.** (*Italian is prettier than English.*)

In each example, you're comparing two things (a cat and a dog, someone's recipes to a book's recipes, and Italian and English), so you use **di** to mean *than.*

✔ To comment on one thing and compare two characteristics or properties of that one thing, you use **che** or **di quel che** to mean *than,* as in these examples:

> **Firenze ha meno abitanti che turisti.** (*Florence has fewer inhabitants than tourists.*)

> **Lui è più bello che intelligente.** (*He is more handsome than [he is] smart.*)
>
> **Mi piace più leggere che guardare la televisione.** (*I like reading more than [I like] watching television.*)

All three sentences have single subjects: **Firenze** (*Florence*), **lui** (*he*), and **io** (*I*). In each case, you're discussing one thing or person and comparing things about that person or thing, so you use **che**.

If you want to say, for example, that Venice is cleaner than you thought, that is, following *than* with a conjugated verb (*I thought*), then you say **Venezia è più pulita di quel che credevo.** Here are a couple more examples where you use **di quel che**:

> **I gatti sono più simpatici di quel che mi hai detto.** (*The cats are nicer than you told me.*)
>
> **Il museo è meno vicino di quel che sembrava.** (*The museum is less near than it seemed.*)

Comparatives and relative and absolute superlatives

You can make comparatives and relative and absolute superlatives (all forms of adverbs that are stronger by degrees than a plain old adverb), by using one of the following adverbs.

Adverb	Comparative	Relative	Absolute
bene (*well*)	**meglio** (*better*)	**il meglio** (*best*)	**benissimo** (*very well*)
male (*badly*)	**peggio** (*worse*)	**il peggio** (*the worst*)	**malissimo** (*very badly*)
poco (*little*)	**meno** (*less*)	**il meno** (*the least*)	**pochissimo** (*very little*)
molto (*much*)	**più** (*more*)	**il più** (*the most*)	**moltissimo** (*very much*)

Adverbs modify verbs, adjectives, and other adverbs. The adverbial comparatives and the relative and absolute superlatives, then, must accompany only verbs, adjectives, and other adverbs. Here are some examples:

> **Sarebbe meglio non parlarne.** (*It would be better not to talk about it.*)
>
> **La situazione va di male in peggio.** (*The situation is going from bad to worse.*)
>
> **Questa poesia è scritta bene, ma quella è scritta meglio.** (*This poetry is written well, but that is written better.*)
>
> **Carlo mangia il più possibile e studia il meno possibile.** (*Carlo eats the most possible and studies the least possible.*) (In more idiomatic English, you say *Carlo eats as much as possible and studies as little as possible.*)

> **Si sente meglio? Sì, sto benissimo.** (*Are you feeling better? Yes, I'm very well.*)
>
> **Ti è piaciuto il film? Moltissimo.** (*Did you like the film? Very much.*)

Occasionally, the addition of **-issimo** is unexpected, as in **Dove sono? Dappertuttissimo!** (*Where are they? Very much everywhere* or *"everywhere-issimo."*) (See the earlier section "Telling how much: Adverbs of degree" for details on **-issimo**.)

Translate the following sentences into idiomatic English.

Q. **Maria si sente malissimo.**

A. *Maria is feeling very sick.*

21. **Marco è così buono come suo nonno.**

   _____

22. **L'insegnante è più intelligente di quel che credevo.**

   _____

23. **Sono tanto nervoso quanto contento.**

   _____

24. **Un ragazzo canta peggio dell'altro.**

   _____

25. **L'Italia ha più politici che preti.**

   _____

26. **Beatrice è più bella della sorella.**

   _____

27. **Io mangio il meno possibile.**

   _____

28. **È meglio non farlo.**

   _____

29. **L'attrice è più simpatica che ricca.**

   _____

30. **Ci è piaciuto pochissimo quel libro.**

   _____

Answer Key

1 precisamente

2 tristemente

3 onestamente

4 specificamente

5 raramente

6 intelligentemente

7 singolarmente

8 estremamente

9 chiaramente

10 sensibilmente

11 fra poco

12 meno

13 più

14 appena

15 molto, assai

16 purtroppo

17 spesso

18 solo

19 ormai

20 già

21   *Marco is as good as his grandfather.*

22   *The teacher is smarter than I thought.*

23   *I'm as nervous as I am happy.*

24   *One boy sings worse than the other.*

25   *Italy has more politicians than priests.*

26   *Beatrice is more beautiful than her sister.*

27   *I eat as little as possible.*

28   *It's better not to do it.*

29   *The actress is nicer than she is rich.*

30   *We liked that book very little.*

Part IV

Talking about the Past, Future, and Conditional

Questions That Determine Verb Tenses

Verb Tense	Questions
Present	**Cosa succede?** (What is going on?) **Cosa fai?** (What are you doing?) **Cosa succede?** (What's happening?)
Present perfect	**Cosa è successo?** (What happened?) **Cosa hai fatto?** (What did you do?)
Imperfect	**Cosa succedeva?** (What was going on?) **Com'era?** (What was something or someone like?) **Cosa facevi?** (What did you used to do?)
Future	**Cosa succederà?** (What will happen?) **Cosa farai?** (What will you do?)
Conditional	**Cosa succederebbe?** (What would happen?) **Cosa faresti?** (What would you do?)

web extras

Of the fourteen tenses in Italian, four are compound. Brush up on using compound tenses at
www.dummies.com/extras/italiangrammar.

In this part . . .

✔ Reflect on or share stories of events that happened in the past by conjugating the past tense of Italian verbs.

✔ Use reflexive verbs in the past tense to talk about your day or your life in general.

✔ Talk about what you'll do in the future — be it where you'll go for lunch or what you'll do when you retire — by understanding the future tense in Italian.

✔ Imagine what you could do "if only . . ." with the conditional mood.

Chapter 16

Been There, Done That: Talking in the Past Tense

- -

In This Chapter

▶ Using the present perfect tense

▶ Choosing your "helper" verb

▶ Comparing various forms of the past

▶ Adding nuance to verb meaning

- -

*N*o matter how much you live in the present, you spend a lot of time talking about the past. You tell people where you're from, where you've been, and how long you've been doing something. Whether something occurred in the last ten minutes or the last ten years, understanding how to express events in the past tense is key to communicating in any language.

The past tenses in English are easy to use, if often irregular in form. In Italian, the past tenses are also frequently irregular. But in Italian, it gets a little more complicated: Past tense constructions require a knowledge of *conditions* that English doesn't. For example, in English, you may say *The kids went to school in Chicago*. In Italian, the verb you use for *went* depends on when the kids went to school in Chicago. Did they always go there? Did they go for a summer program? More than once? Was it a hundred years ago?

In English, you supply this information with elaboration. *The kids went to school in Chicago during the 2012 to 2013 school year*. Or during their childhood. Or around the turn of the last century. Or for summer programs in general. Or for specific summer programs. In Italian, if this information isn't directly stated, you imply it by the tense of the verb you use.

In this chapter, I show you how to be this specific as you express events in the past tense. I also walk you through constructing the present perfect (**passato prossimo**, or the near past) and the imperfect (**imperfetto**, or the habitual, repeated, or ongoing past) and help you understand when to use each one.

Forming the Present Perfect Tense

The *present perfect* is a compound verb, so it takes two words. One is the past participle such as *looked* (**guardato**), *baked* (**cotto**), *bought* (**comprato**), *asked* (**domandato**) and *said* (**detto**); the other is a helping verb (**essere** or **avere**) conjugated in the present tense. (See Chapters 7 and 17 for conjugations of the helping verbs.)

To form the past participle, remove the characteristic **-are**, **-ere**, and **-ire** endings from infinitives (unconjugated verbs) and replace them with **-ato**, **-uto**, or **-ito**, as shown in Table 16-1.

Table 16-1	Forming the Regular Past Participle
Infinitive	*Past Participle*
mangiare (*to eat*)	**mangiato** (*eaten, ate*)
ricevere (*to receive*)	**ricevuto** (*received*)
dormire (*to sleep*)	**dormito** (*slept*)
capire (*to understand*)	**capito** (*understood*)
cercare (*to look for*)	**cercato** (*looked for*)
guardare (*to look at*)	**guardato** (*looked at*)
parlare (*to speak*)	**parlato** (*spoken*)
volere (*to want*)	**voluto** (*wanted*)
potere (*to be able*)	**potuto** (*to have been able*)
credere (*to believe, to think*)	**creduto** (*believed, thought*)

These participles correspond to their English counterparts, which often end in *-ed*, such as *looked*. However, many irregular English past participles don't end in *-ed*, such as *bought, saw,* and *read.* Italian, too, has many irregular past participles. Some verbs even have two forms to choose from, such as the ones in Table 16-2.

Table 16-2	Forming the Irregular Past Participle for verbs that conjugate with Avere
Infinitive	*Past Participle*
vedere (*to see*)	**veduto** or **visto** (*saw, seen*)
prendere (*to take*)	**preso** (*taken, took*)
leggere (*to read*)	**letto** (*read*)
scrivere (*to write*)	**scritto** (*written, wrote*)
rispondere (*to reply*)	**risposto** (*replied*)
aprire (*to open*)	**aperto** (*opened*)
chiudere (*to close*)	**chiuso** (*closed*)
venire (*to come*)	**venuto** (*came*)
fare (*to make, to do*)	**fatto** (*made, did*)
dire (*to tell*)	**detto** (*said*)
perdere (*to lose*)	**perduto, perso** (*lost*)
accendere (*to light; turn on*)	**accesso** (*light; turned on*)

chiedere (*to ask*)	**chiesto** (*asked*)
comporre (*to compose*)	**composto** (*composed*)
decidere (*to decide*)	**deciso** (*decided*)
mettere (*to put; to place*)	**messo** (*to put; placed*)
offrire (*to offer*)	**offerto** (*offered*)
spegnere (*to turn off*)	**spento** (*turn off*)
spendere (*to spend*)	**speso** (*spent*)
vincere (*to win*)	**vinto** (*won*)

Table 16-3 lists some irregular verbs that take **essere** in the past. For more on when to use which auxiliary, or helper, verb, see the following section.

Table 16-3	**Irregular Past Tense Verbs That Take Essere**
Infinitive	*Past Participle*
morire (*to die*)	**morto** (*died*)
nascere (*to be born*)	**nato** (*born*)
rimanere (*to remain*)	**rimasto** (*remained*)
scendere (*to come/go down*)	**sceso** (*fell*)
venire (*to come*)	**venuto** (*came*)
vivere (*to live*)	**vissuto** (*lived*)

You can also use past participles as adjectives, so long as they agree in number and gender with what they're describing. For example, **la casa preferita** (*the favorite house*) is feminine and singular, so **preferita** is as well.

Il libro preferito (*the favorite book*) is masculine and singular, so **preferito** reflects that. Speaking of an enthusiastic audience at a concert, the late Luciano Pavarotti urged the conductor to give an encore, and said **Sono proprio riscaldati** (*They're really warmed up*). **Riscaldati** (from **riscaldare** [*to warm up*]) refers to members of the audience and is masculine and plural.

Choosing Avere or Essere as Your Auxiliary Verb

To activate the participles, you need an auxiliary or helping verb, either **avere** (*to have*) or **essere** (*to be*) conjugated in the present tense. You use **avere** with *transitive verbs* — verbs that can (though don't always) take a direct object; they "transit" action from the subject to a direct object. You use **essere** with verbs that can't take a direct object, called *intransitive verbs,* which are frequently verbs of motion, of coming and going, of leaving and returning. I discuss how to use both helping verbs in the following sections.

Transiting action with avere

Direct objects answer the questions *who?* or *what?* **Ho trovato la chiave** (*I found the key*). What did I find? *The key.* **Lui ha scritto una lettera d'amore** (*He wrote a love letter*). What did he write? *A love letter.* **Ho visto gli studenti** (*I saw the students*). Who did I see? *The students.*

Think literally for a moment, and the conjugation with **avere** will make perfect sense. **Ho** = *I have;* **trovato** = *found; I have found.* What did I find? **La chiave.** **Lui ha** = *he has;* **scritto** = *written; he has written.* What has he written? **Una lettera d'amore.** Both verbs answer the question what, and direct the subjects' actions through the verbs to direct objects.

In the following table, I show you how to conjugate the past participle of **trovare** (*to find*) using the helping verb **avere.**

trovare (to find)	
io **ho trovato**	noi **abbiamo trovato**
tu **hai trovato**	voi **avete trovato**
lui, lei, Lei **ha trovato**	loro, Loro **hanno trovato**

Sometimes the direct object isn't stated but understood. In this case, you still use **avere** to form the present perfect. The most commonly used verbs with unstated direct objects are **parlare** (*to speak*) because you speak speech, **dormire** (*to sleep*) because you sleep sleep, **sognare** (*to dream*) because you dream dreams, and **camminare** (*to walk*) because you, well, walk the walk.

Verbs with built-in prepositions, such as **cercare** (*to look for*), **aspettare** (*to wait for*), and **pagare** (*to pay for*), take direct object pronouns in Italian (though in English they usually take indirect object pronouns).

Moving with essere

Verbs of motion (going, coming, arriving, leaving) or of stopping motion (staying) do not take direct objects. They conjugate with **essere** instead of with **avere**, and the subject and past participle agree in number and gender. Again, think literally for a moment. **Lui è** (*he is*) + **andato** (*gone*). *He is gone. He went.* Or **lei è** (*she is*) + **andata** (*gone*). *She is gone. She went.*

Also, as I explain in Chapter 17, *all* reflexive verbs conjugate in the present perfect with **essere.**

The following table shows a verb of motion, **andare** (*to go*), conjugated in the present perfect with **essere.**

andare (to go)	
io **sono andato/andata**	noi **siamo andati/andate**
tu **sei andato/andata**	voi **siete andati/andate**
lui, lei, Lei **è andato/andata**	loro, Loro **sono andati/andate**

Deciding between avere and essere

Some verbs "cross-conjugate," meaning they can use either **essere** or **avere** as a helper. Their meanings tell you which helper to use. For example, take **cambiare** (*to change*). It means one thing to say **ho cambiato casa** (*I changed houses*) (*I moved*) and quite another to say **sono cambiato** (Literally: *I am changed*) (*I have changed*).

Here's another example with **finire. Ho finito il libro** (*I finished/have finished the book*), but **la commedia è finita** (*the play is over*) or **lui è finito in prigione** (*he ended up in prison*). The helping verb changes the meaning and function of the verb's past tense.

You don't really want to say **sono finito** because it does not mean *I'm finished/I'm done in*. Instead, it means *there is no hope for me,* or, by extension, *I'm dead.*

Both **essere** and **avere** always conjugate with themselves to form the present perfect. Thus, **sono stato/sono stata** means *I was* (masculine and feminine speakers). **Ho avuto**, meanwhile, means *I have had/I had.* The following tables show these two verbs conjugated in their entirety .

essere (to be)	
io **sono stato/stata**	noi **siamo stati/state**
tu **sei stato/stata**	voi **siete stati/state**
lui, lei, Lei **è stato/stata**	loro, Loro **sono stati/state**

avere (to have)	
io **ho avuto**	noi **abbiamo avuto**
tu **hai avuto**	voi **avete avuto**
lui, lei, Lei **ha avuto**	loro, Loro **hanno avuto**

Give the past participle of the following infinitives. Be careful: Some are irregular. Here's an example.

Q. **cominciare**

A. **cominciato**

1. pagare _____

2. vedere _____

3. mangiare _____

4. finire _____

5. fare _____

6. prendere _____

7. capire _____

8. leggere _____

9. scrivere _____

10. ripetere _____

Conjugating with avere

Putting a verb into the past when the helper is **avere** involves three steps. First, form a past participle from the infinitive (for example, **mangiare** becomes **mangiato** and **preferire** becomes **preferito**). Second, conjugate **avere** so that it reflects the subject (**io ho, tu hai,** and so on). Third, combine the two forms, and you've arrived in the past.

To form the past with **avere,** conjugate **avere** in the present indicative tense and use the appropriate form of **avere** with past participles. As for the irregular past participles, those require some memorization. See the earlier section "Transiting action with avere" to review this process.

Here are some examples of the past tense using **avere:**

> **Io ho mangiato tutti i biscotti.** (*I ate all the cookies.*)
>
> **Lui ha letto due libri durante il fine settimana.** (*He read two books over the weekend.*)
>
> **Lei ha scritto molte lettere oggi.** (*She wrote many letters today.*)
>
> **Abbiamo ricevuto una bella lettera dalla zia.** (*We received a lovely letter from our aunt.*)
>
> **Avete capito?** (*Have you understood?*)
>
> **Hanno detto una bugia.** (*They told a lie.*)

Complete the following sentences by filling in the past tense of the specified verb. If you're unsure whether the past participle is regular or irregular, refer to the earlier section "Forming the present perfect tense." Remember that each answer has two words. Here's an example.

Q. I ragazzi _____ (mangiare) troppi dolci oggi.

A. hanno mangiato

11. Tu _____ (leggere) il libro?

12. Ieri loro _____ (vedere) un bel film.

13. Riccardo _____ (perdere) i documenti.

14. Tu ed io _____ (rispondere) alle domande.

15. I bambini _____ (guardare) la tivvù oggi?

16. Mario e Paolo _____ (chiudere) il negozio.

17. Voi _____ (prendere) un caffè bello caldo.

18. I genitori _____ (dire) di no.

19. Tu _____ (avere) una risposta da loro, vero?

20. Le ragazze non _____ (trovare) il gattino.

Avere verbs don't require you to make the participle agree with the subject. They do require agreement, however, if you use a direct object pronoun. (See Chapter 8 for a review of pronouns.) As with most pronouns, direct object pronouns precede the verb. They agree in number and gender with the noun they replace.

Fill in the direct object pronouns from this list that can replace the following nouns. See the example.

mi (*me*)   **ti** (*you*)   **lo** (*him/it*)   **la** (*her/it*)
ci (*us*)   **vi** (*you* [plural])   **li** (*them*)   **le** (*them*)

Q. I cani

A. li

21. le scuole _____

22. gli amici _____

23. il negozio _____

24. la macchina _____

25. Mario e Francesca _____

26. i fratelli _____

27. la verdura _____

28. le signorine _____

29. la madre ed il padre _____

30. tu, Luisa, e Giovanni _____

When direct object pronouns precede the conjugated **avere** verbs, they look like this.

> **Hanno visitato il museo. L'hanno visitato.** (*They visited the museum. They visited it.*) **Lo** (*it*) substitutes for **il museo,** but because it already agrees in number and gender with the participle, **visitato,** nothing changes. **Lo** does contract with **hanno,** in the interests of flow.

Now compare these sentences.

> **Hanno visitato la chiesa. L'hanno visitata.** (*They visited the church. They visited it.*) **La** (*it*) substitutes for **la chiesa,** so the past participle, **visitata,** takes on a feminine, singular ending.

Here are a few more examples:

> **Ho comprato le scarpe. Le ho comprate.** (*I bought the shoes. I bought them.*) **Scarpe** are feminine plural, so the pronoun and the participle's ending are also feminine plural.

> **Hai visto gli amici? Li hai visti?** (*Have you seen your friends? Have you seen them?*) **Gli amici**, masculine plural, requires the corresponding masculine plural ending on the participle.

> **Mario ha visto Laura. Mario l'ha vista.** (*Mario saw Laura. Mario saw her.*) This time, the ending agrees with a feminine singular pronoun.

The direct object pronouns **mi, ti, ci,** and **vi** don't require agreement between themselves and the past participle. Such agreement, still, does occur — **Lui ci ha chiamati** (*He called us*) — it's entirely optional, though.

Replace the direct object (underlined) in the following sentences with a direct object pronoun, making any necessary changes to the past participle as well, as the example does.

0. Franco ha trovato <u>i cuccioli</u> nella strada.

A. Franco li ha trovati nella strada.

31. La nonna ha mandato <u>baci</u> a noi.

_____

32. **Mirella ed io abbiamo ricevuto <u>le cartoline</u> ieri.**

_____

33. **Il babbo ha pagato <u>il conto</u>.**

_____

34. **Loro hanno studiato <u>la biologia</u>.**

_____

35. **Tu hai visitato <u>la chiesa ed il museo</u>, vero?**

_____

36. **Gli studenti hanno ordinato <u>vino ed acqua</u>.**

_____

37. **Lei ha portato <u>pantaloni corti</u>.**

_____

38. **Lei ha comprato <u>una macchina</u>.**

_____

39. **I bambini hanno frequentato <u>una scuola privata</u> l'anno scorso.**

_____

40. **I gattini hanno mangiato <u>le piante</u>.**

_____

Conjugating with essere

To conjugate a verb in the present perfect, using **essere** as its helper, you need to take three steps.

1. **Form a past participle.**

   For example, **andare** becomes **andato** and **partire** becomes **partito**.

2. **Conjugate essere in the present tense so that it reflects the subject.**

   For example, **io sono, tu sei, lei è,** and so on.

3. **Make the subject and the past participle agree in number and gender.**

Lui è andato but **lei è andata. Noi** (a mixed group, thus masculine plural) **siamo andati. Noi** (a group of women) **siamo andate.**

The conjugated form of **essere** reveals the subject and that determines the gender and number of the past participle. Here are some examples:

È stato a casa. (*He was at home.*)

È partita stamattina. (*She left this morning.*)

Siamo andate a teatro insieme. (*We went to the theater together.*)

Franco e Chiara sono arrivati tardi. (*Franco and Chiara arrived late.*)

The participles' endings tell you that the first subject was a man; the second was a woman; the third, all women; and the fourth, a mixed gender group. For this last example, remember that if you have a mixed group (even one man and 17 women, for example), you use the masculine.

Complete the following sentences by filling in the past tense of the specified verb. If you're unsure whether the past participle is regular or irregular, refer to the earlier section "Forming the Present Perfect Tense." Remember that each answer has two words. Here's an example:

Q. I ragazzi e le ragazze _____ (andare) in campagna.

A. sono andati

41. Il teatro _____ (chiudere).

42. I nonni _____ (partire) ieri.

43. Carla e Giovanni _____ (ritornare).

44. Tu, quando _____ (andare)?

45. Loro _____ (venire) alla festa.

46. Voi _____ (ritornare) a mezzanotte, vero?

47. Io (fem.) _____ (essere) a scuola.

48. Maria e Luisa _____ (arrivare) presto.

49. Tu, io e Giorgio _____ (essere) a casa.

50. Le studentesse _____ (partire) per l'Italia.

The Peculiarities of Essere and Avere

Both **essere** and **avere** have their own peculiarities. **Avere** wants agreement between participles and direct object pronouns. (If there were ever a reason to be specific, that would be it!) **Essere** wants agreements between participles and subjects. Something the two helping verbs share, however, is the ability to accept a word inserted between the helping verb and the past participle. This makes English speakers who were taught never to split an infinitive (such as *to already know*) nervous. For Italian speakers, the equivalent reaction is evoked when verbs are separated, generally (**non posso lo leggere**).

In this case, though, in a compound tense, you can insert several little words: **già** (*already*), **appena** (*just*), and **ancora** (*yet*). The following constructions, then, are both normal and acceptable in Italian.

La signora è già partita. (*The lady has already left.*)

Sono appena arrivati. (*They have already arrived.*)

Non hanno ancora parlato con il direttore. (*They haven't yet spoken with the director.*)

Over and Done with: The Past Absolute

You use the present perfect to talk about past (completed) actions. For example:

> **Giuseppe è arrivato.** (*Giuseppe has arrived.*)
>
> **Maria ha dato dei bei regali.** (*Maria gave some beautiful presents.*)
>
> **Non sono andati.** (*They didn't go.*)

You use the past absolute to discuss a completed action from long ago and far away.

> **Giuseppe arrivò negli Stati Uniti molti anni fa.** (*Giuseppe arrived in the United States many years ago.*)
>
> **Maria diede dei bei regali.** (*Maria gave beautiful presents.*)
>
> **Non andarono a scuola.** (*They didn't go to school.*)

As you see, the past absolute consists of just one conjugated verb. It conjugates by adding the appropriate endings to the verb stem (see Chapter 6). For the three types of infinitives, the endings are as follows:

-are verbs: parlare (*to speak*): **io parlai, tu parlasti, lui, lei, Lei parlò, noi parlammo, voi parlaste, loro parlarono**

-ere verbs: ripetere (*to repeat*): **io ripetei, tu ripetesti, lui, lei, Lei ripetè, noi ripetemmo, voi ripeteste, loro ripeterono**

-ire verbs: dormire (*to sleep*): **io dormii, tu dormisti, lui, lei, Lei dormì, noi dormimmo, voi dormiste, loro dormirono**

The past absolute (**il passato remoto**) stem is highly irregular. The following chart shows you some of the most common forms.

Verb	Stem
avere *(to have)*	ebb
essere *(to be)*	fu
conoscere *(to know)*	conobb
sapere *(to know)*	sepp
vivere *(to live)*	viss
vedere *(to see)*	vid
stare *(to stay)*	stett
dare *(to give)*	died
dire *(to say)*	diss
fare *(to make, to do)*	fec
nascere *(to be born)*	nacqu
piacere *(to like)*	piacqu
venire *(to come)*	venn
volere *(to want)*	voll *(the meaning changes in the past absolute from wants to insists)*
scrivere *(to write)*	scriss
rompere *(to break)*	rupp

If you want to see these forms in action, I recommend looking at the titles of operatic arie: **"donna non vidi mai"** (*I never saw such a woman*), **"vissi d'arte"** (*I lived for art*), and **"nacqui all'affanno"** (*I was born to worry*). Or take a look at a biography: **Rossini nacque il 29 febbraio nel 1792** (Rossini was born February 29, 1792); **morì nel 1868** (*He died in 1868*). Remember that the past absolute is the literary past, and you are going to find it useful to recognize, if not produce. As for use in everyday speech, the past absolute does get used in parts of Tuscany and the south of Italy often to refer to the not so distant past.

Once Upon a Time: The Imperfect Tense

The imperfect tense is just that — imperfect. In other words, the actions of imperfect verbs aren't perfected, not finished. The imperfect tense sets the stage for what's to come and frequently answers questions like, "What was something or someone like? What did you used to do (habitually, regularly)? What was happening?"

The imperfect tense allows you to use verbs to describe physical and mental states. If someone was rich, poor, hungry, thirsty, sleepy, sad, happy, in love, out of love, then you use the imperfect tense to express these conditions.

The imperfect also tells you about things that used to be or that used to happen. For example: *I used to cut school every day. It was a beautiful time. The weather was glorious. Every Sunday they came to dinner. Every Monday we had leftovers.*

You can combine the imperfect with the present perfect, which I describe in the earlier section "Forming the Present Perfect Tense," to indicate that while one thing was going on (in the imperfect tense), something else happened (in the present perfect). *While I was eating* (imperfect), *the phone rang* (present perfect).

Other uses of the imperfect include telling what time it was (*it was 3:00 in the morning*), discussing weather conditions (*it was a dark and stormy night*), and reporting indirect discourse (what someone said). *My friend told me* (present perfect) *that he was* (imperfect) *unhappy*.

Forming the imperfect

The imperfect tense is the most regular of any of the Italian verb tenses. To form it, you drop only the final two letters (**-re**) from any infinitive, leaving the stem to which you attach subject-specific endings.

Here's the good news: The endings are the same for all the different conjugations. Nothing in Italian could (or ever will be) simpler. The examples in Table 16-4 show you what I mean.

Table 16-4	Conjugations in the Imperfect Tense	
-are Verbs	*-ere Verbs*	*-ire (including isc) Verbs*
parlare (*to talk*)	**scrivere** (*to write*)	**dormire** (*to sleep*)
io parla**vo**	scrive**vo**	dormi**vo**
tu parla**vi**	scrive**vi**	dormi**vi**
lui, lei, Lei parla**va**	scrive**va**	dormi**va**
noi parla**vamo**	scrive**vamo**	dormi**vamo**
voi parla**vate**	scrive**vate**	dormi**vate**
loro, Loro parla**vano**	scrive**vano**	dormi**vano**

You can also translate these forms as, for example, *I used to sleep,* or simply, *I slept.*

Fill in conjugated forms of the verbs in parentheses, according to subject, as shown in the example.

Q. Io _____ (leggere)

A. leggevo

51. Tu _____ (mangiare)

52. Lui _____ (parlare)

53. Loro _____ **(scrivere)**

54. I bimbi _____ **(dormire)**

55. Tu e Laura _____ **(ripetere)**

56. Io _____ **(andare)**

57. Noi _____ **(preferire)**

58. Gli amici _____ **(venire)**

59. Voi _____ **(giocare)**

60. La donna _____ **(finire)**

Of all Italian verbs, only three come to mind that are irregular in the imperfect tense. **Essere** is irregular because it's always irregular. Irregularity is in its nature and, no doubt, part of its charm. (**Avere** is regular, for a change.) The following table shows you how **essere** conjugates in the imperfect.

essere (to be)	
io ero	noi eravamo
tu eri	voi eravate
lui, lei, Lei era	loro, Loro erano

All the physical and emotional states of being introduced with **essere** and **avere** in Chapter 7 are likely to appear in the imperfect tense (as opposed to the present perfect).

The other two verbs that are irregular in the imperfect are **dire** (_to tell, to say_) and **fare** (_to make, to do_). Their Latin roots show, and their stems respectively are **dice** and **face** (from the Latin verbs **dicere** and **facere**). See the following tables for these verb conjugations.

dire (to tell, to say)	
io dicevo	noi dicevamo
tu dicevi	voi dicevate
lui, lei, Lei diceva	loro, Loro dicevano

fare (to make, to do)	
io facevo	noi facevamo
tu facevi	voi facevate
lui, lei, Lei faceva	loro, Loro facevano

Translate the following phrases from English into Italian, using the imperfect form. Here's an example.

0. *I was waiting.*

A. **Aspettavo**

61. *We were eating.* _____

62. *I used to go.* _____

63. *They studied.* _____

64. *He was happy.* _____

65. *She was hungry.* _____

66. *Lorenzo was working.* _____

67. *They were poor.* _____

68. *It was midnight.* _____

69. *I was cold.* _____

70. *She was packing the suitcases.* _____

Perfecting the use of the imperfect

Certain clues tell you to use the imperfect tense, which I explain here. Adverbial expressions (saying when or how often something happened) include the following:

- ✔ **a volte** (*sometimes*)
- ✔ **di quando in quando** (*sometimes, from time to time*)
- ✔ **ogni giorno** (*every day*)

    (**ogni** [anything]) (*every* [anything])
- ✔ **mentre** (*while*)
- ✔ **senza sosta** (*without stopping*)
- ✔ **spesso** (*often*)
- ✔ **di solito** (*usually*)

Here are a few sample sentences:

Lui lavorava senza sosta. (*He worked without stopping.*)

Ogni giorno leggevo un po'. (*Every day I read a little bit.*)

Mentre mangiavamo, ascoltavamo l'opera. (*While we were eating, we were listening to the opera.*)

Certain verbs, if you think about their meaning (Did you feel a certain way? What were you thinking, fearing, loving?), also predominantly use the imperfect in the past. They all indicate an ongoing state of mind. A few of these follow.

- ✔ **pensare** (*to think*)
- ✔ **amare** (*to love*)
- ✔ **credere** (*to believe, to think*)
- ✔ **desiderare** (*to want*)
- ✔ **odiare** (*to hate*)
- ✔ **temare** (*to fear*)
- ✔ **volere** (*to want*)

Keep in mind that your meaning determines the tense. If, for example, you say that someone *gave a party,* or in a fairy tale, *gave a ball,* **lui ha dato un ballo.** But, if he *was giving a party* for some purpose, then **lui dava un ballo.**

Adding Nuance to Meaning with Verb Tense

La sfumatura (*nuance*) is an art historical term that refers to shading. Choice of verb tenses allows you to add nuance to your Italian. Not all verbs undergo changes in meaning, but those that do can lend precision to your language.

Pensare (*to think*) doesn't change meaning. **Ho pensato** (*I had a thought*) and **pensavo** (*I was thinking*) essentially mean the same thing, though **ho pensato** leaves you open to the questions, *just one? Was it lonely?*

The prepositions that follow **pensare,** however, do modify the meaning to some degree. **Pensare a** means *to think about,* and you can express it as **ci penso** (*I'm thinking about it*); this phrase can be useful when confronted with an overzealous store clerk. **Pensare di,** on the other hand, means *to intend to.* **Non pensavo di interrompere** (*I didn't intend to interrupt*).

Five other verbs have more definite changes in meaning, depending on the tense you use, including **conoscere** (*to know a person or place, to be acquainted with*), **sapere** (*to know [how to]*), **dovere** (*to have to*), **potere** (*to be able to*), and **volere** (*to want*). See Table 16-5 for these verbs' subtleties of meaning.

Table 16-5	Verbal Nuance with Tenses		
Infinitive	*Present Indicative*	*Imperfect*	*Present Perfect*
conoscere (*to know*)	**conosco** (*I know*)	**conoscevo** (*I knew*)	**ho conosciuto** (*I met [someone]*)
sapere (*to know*)	**so** (*I know*)	**sapevo** (*I knew [how to]*)	**ho saputo** (*I found out*)
dovere (*to have to*)	**devo** (*I have to*)	**dovevo** (*I was supposed to*)	**ho dovuto** (*I had to*)
potere (*to be able to*)	**posso** (*I can*)	**potevo** (*I was able to*)	**ho potuto** (*I managed*)
volere (*to want*)	**voglio/vorrei** (*I want/would like*)	**volevo** (*I wanted*)	**ho voluto** (*I wanted [and more or less insisted]*)

Some of these changes are slight, but they allow you to achieve a certain specificity of language. Probably the most important changes are in **conoscere**, **sapere**, and **dovere**.

> **La madre di Marco? Non la conoscevo ma l'ho conosciuta ieri.** (*Marco's mother? I didn't know her but met her yesterday.*)

> **Dovevo studiare, ma non ne avevo voglia.** (*I was supposed to study, but I didn't feel like it.*) Compare this with **Ho dovuto studiare per l'esame.** (*I had to study for the exam.*)

A side effect of using the imperfect involves manners. It's simply more polite to say that you wanted to see someone (**volevo vedere il dottore**) than to say that you want to see someone. Consider the English counterparts. *I want to see the doctor. I wanted to see the doctor.* The second sentence is less brusque. The same holds true for the Italian.

Answer Key

1 pagato

2 veduto, visto

3 mangiato

4 finito

5 fatto

6 preso

7 capito

8 letto

9 scritto

10 ripetuto

11 hai letto

12 hanno visto

13 ha perso

14 abbiamo risposto

15 hanno guardato

16 hanno chiuso

17 avete preso

18 hanno detto

19 hai avuto

20 hanno trovato

21 le

22 li

23 lo

24 la

25 li

26 li

27 la

28 le

29 li

30 vi

31 li ha mandati

32 le abbiamo ricevute

33 l'ha pagato

34 l'hanno studiata

35 li hai visitati

36 li hanno ordinati

37 li ha portati

38 l'ha comprata

39 l'hanno frequentata

40 le hanno mangiate

41 è chiuso

42 **sono partiti**

43 **sono ritornati**

44 **sei andato/andata**

45 **sono venuti**

46 **siete ritornati**

47 **sono stata**

48 **sono arrivate**

49 **siamo stati**

50 **sono partite**

51 **mangiavi**

52 **parlava**

53 **scrivevano**

54 **dormivano**

55 **ripetevano**

56 **andavo**

57 **preferivamo**

58 **venivano**

59 **giocavi**

60 **finiva**

61 **mangiavamo**

62 **andavo**

63 **studiavano**

64 **era contento**

65 **aveva fame**

66 **Lorenzo lavorava**

67 **Erano poveri**

68 **Era mezzanotte**

69 **Avevo freddo**

70 **Faceva le valigie**

Chapter 17

Reflexive Verbs in the Past

....

....

You use reflexive verbs in Italian throughout the day, from when you wake to when you fall asleep. Reflexive verbs often express personal actions, such as ways you care for yourself. For example, to say that you brushed your teeth, you use the verb **lavarsi i denti.** You also use reflexive verbs to communicate ways you interact with others, for example, **innamorarsi** (*to fall in love*).

The reflexive part of a reflexive verb refers to the pronouns that you use to accompany them. For example, you say **mi chiamo** to indicate *my name is* (Literally: *I call myself* because **mi** indicates where you directed the action of **chiamo** [*I call*]). **Si innamorano** means *they fall in love with each other;* **innamorano** means *they fall in love* and the pronoun **si** means *with each other.*

The reflexive infinitive is a variation of the **-are, -ere,** and **-ire** infinitives. It drops the **-e** from all three and replaces it with **-si.** This conjugation tells you that the verb reflects action back onto the subject through an added pronoun, called, appropriately enough, the *reflexive pronoun.*

You can find an overview of all pronouns in Chapter 8 and a survey of reflexive verbs in the present tense in Chapter 9. You may want to review both chapters before continuing.

In this chapter, I introduce you to common Italian reflexive verbs, show you how reflexive and reciprocal verbs work in the present perfect tense, and walk you through using these verbs in the imperfect tense.

Looking at Commonly Used Reflexive Verbs

The most common reflexive verbs are the ones that carry you through the day, meaning they express common, everyday actions. Here are the most frequently used reflexive verbs in Italian.

- **accorgersi (di)** (*to realize*)
- **addormentarsi** (*to go to sleep*)
- **affrettarsi** (*to hurry*)
- **alzarsi** (*to get up*)
- **arrabbiarsi** (*to get angry*)
- **avvicinarsi** (*to get near*)
- **chiamarsi** (*to be named*)
- **coprirsi** (*to cover up*)
- **dedicarsi (a)** (*to work at, to dedicate oneself to*)
- **divertirsi** (*to have a good time*)
- **divorziarsi** (*to get divorced*)
- **domandarsi** (*to wonder*)
- **farsi il bagno, la doccia** (*to take a bath, shower*)
- **fermarsi** (*to stop*)
- **innamorarsi** (*to fall in love*)

- **lamentarsi** (*to complain*)
- **laurearsi** (*to graduate*)
- **lavarsi** (*to wash up*)
- **lavarsi i denti** (*to brush your teeth*)
- **mettersi** (*to get dressed, to wear*)
- **muoversi** (*to move [bodily]*)
- **pettinarsi** (*to comb your hair*)
- **preoccuparsi** (*to worry*)
- **prepararsi** (*to prepare*)
- **radersi** (*to shave*)
- **ricordarsi (di)** (*to remember*)
- **spogliarsi** (*to undress*)
- **sposarsi** (*to get married*)
- **svegliarsi** (*to wake up*)
- **trasferirsi (isc)** (*to move [from one city to another, for example]*)
- **vestirsi** (*to get dressed*)

One other reflexive verb is extremely important: **trovarsi.** It's a synonym for both **essere** and **stare,** another way to say *to be.* Here are a few examples:

Mi trovo molto bene. (*I'm very well.*)

Dove ti trovi? (*Where are you?*)

Si trovano in Italia. (*They are in Italy.*)

The following section explains how to use these verbs with reflexive pronouns.

Forming the Present Perfect of Reflexive Verbs

The present perfect lets you talk about the past in specific terms. It answers the question *What happened?* or *What did you do?* It refers to a completed past action or event.

The present perfect is a compound tense, consisting of a past participle (such as *saw, went, bought, looked,* or *asked*) and a conjugated helping verb — in this case, **essere.** All reflexive verbs conjugate with **essere.** Always. Without exception.

To discuss the past with a reflexive verb, you need three words:

- **The reflexive pronoun:** This pronoun reflects the action of the verb back onto the subject: **mi** (*myself*), **ti** (*yourself*), **si** (*himself, herself, itself, yourself* [formal]), **ci** (*ourselves*), **vi** (*yourselves*), and **si** (*themselves, yourselves* [formal]).

- **The helping verb:** This is the conjugated form of **essere** that's appropriate to the subject.

- **The past participle of the verb you're using:** For example: **Mi sono svegliato/svegliata** (*I woke [myself] up*). In English you don't usually state the *self* being addressed by the verb. The past participle reflects the gender and number of both the giver and the receiver of the action. If you're a woman, you say **svegliata,** ending the past participle with the feminine singular **-a.** A man says **svegliato,** using the masculine singular ending, **-o.**

To review the formation of past participles in general, see Chapter 16.

Table 17-1 shows you how these three words fit together and how the pronoun and participle reflect the subject. The table demonstrates these concepts using the verb **alzarsi** (*to get [oneself] up*).

Table 17-1   Conjugation of the Reflexive Verb Alzarsi in the Present Perfect Tense

[Subject] and Reflexive Pronoun	Helping Verb Essere	Past Participle
[io] mi	sono	**alzato** ([masculine, singular] *I got up*)
[io] mi	sono	**alzata** ([feminine, singular] *I got up*)
[tu] ti	sei	**alzato** ([masculine, singular] *you got up*)
[tu] ti	sei	**alzata** ([feminine, singular] *you got up*)
[lui] si	è	**alzato** (*he got up*)
[lei] si	è	**alzata** (*she got up*)
[Lei] si	è	**alzato/alzata** ([formal, masculine/feminine, singular] *you got up*)
[noi] ci	siamo	**alzati** ([masculine, plural or mixed group] *we got up*)
[noi] ci	siamo	**alzate** ([feminine, plural] *we got up*)
[voi] vi	siete	**alzati** ([masculine, plural or mixed group] *you got up*)
[voi] vi	siete	**alzate** ([feminine, plural] *you got up*)
[loro] si	sono	**alzati** ([masculine, plural or mixed group] *they got up*)
[loro] si	sono	**alzate** ([feminine, plural] *they got up*)
[Loro] si	sono	**alzati/alzate** ([formal, masculine/feminine, plural] *you got up*)

Consider this use of reflexive verbs in your (imaginary and admittedly extravagantly full) day, for example:

Mi sono svegliato/svegliata alle 5.00. (*I woke up at 5:00.*)

Mi sono alzato/alzata immediatamente. (*I got up immediately.*)

Mi sono lavato/lavata i denti. (*I brushed my teeth.*)

Mi sono fatto/fatta la doccia. (*I took a shower.*)

Mi sono pettinato/pettinata. (*I did my hair.*)

In ufficio, mi sono arrabbiato/arrabbiata perché i clienti si sono lamentati. (*In the office, I got angry because the clients complained.*)

Mi sono ricordato/ricordata di un appuntamento all'università. (*I remembered an appointment at the university.*)

Mi sono laureato/laureato. (*I graduated.*)

Mi sono divertito/divertita con degli amici. (*I had fun with some friends.*)

Mi sono innamorato/innamorata. (*I fell in love.*)

Mi sono sposato/sposata. (*I got married.*)

Mi sono domandato/domandata: è possibile tutto questo? (*I asked myself: Is all this possible?*)

A casa, finalmente, ci siamo addormentati. (*At home, finally, we went to sleep.*)

Using the reflexive present perfect, fill in the sentences with the conjugated forms of the verbs in parentheses. Here's an example:

0. I bambini _____ (svegliarsi) molto presto.

A. si sono svegliati

1. La famiglia _____ (trasferirsi [isc]) in Italia.

2. Lui _____ (mettersi) una cravatta oggi.

3. Noi _____ (divertirsi) tantissimo ieri sera.

4. Io _____ (prepararsi).

5. Paolo e Francesca _____ (innamorarsi) subito.

6. Ieri gli studenti _____ (laurearsi).

7. Lei _____ (affrettarsi).

8. Voi _____ (alzarsi) tardi.

9. Loro _____ (divorziarsi).

10. Tu _____ (lamentarsi).

Using Reciprocal Verbs in the Present Perfect

Reciprocal verbs in the present perfect show how people interacted, as in these examples:

> **Si sono parlati.** (*They talked to each other.*)
>
> **Si sono visti.** (*They saw each other.*)
>
> **Si sono incontrati.** (*They met each other for dinner or coffee.*)

Obviously, it takes more than one person to do these things, so you use only plural verb forms.

To use the reciprocal reflexive in the present perfect, you need the following three components:

- ✔ **A reflexive pronoun to indicate interaction:** You have only three to choose from: **ci** (*we interact*), **vi** (*you* [plural] *interact*), and **si** (*they interact*).

- ✔ **The conjugated helping verb (essere):** For example, **ci siamo, vi siete,** or **si sono.**

- ✔ **A past participle:** For example, **alzati/alzate** or **parlati/parlate,** in either the masculine plural or the feminine plural form.

Here are some example sentences:

> **Ci siamo conosciuti a scuola.** (*We met [each other] at school.*)
>
> **Vi siete ricordate?** (*Did you remember each other?*)
>
> **Dove si sono conosciuti i genitori?** (*Where did your parents meet [each other]?*)

You can make almost any verb a reciprocal reflexive. All you need to remember is that the action of the verb goes between two or more people. **Parlare** (*to speak*), for example, isn't normally a reflexive verb. If you want to say *We spoke to each other on the phone,* however, you can turn it into a reciprocal reflexive: **Ci siamo parlati al telefono.**

Just as you can make almost any verb reciprocal by adding pronouns that change its meaning to include a reference to "each other," you can also make any reflexive verb nonreflexive.

Consider the changes in the following sentences. In the present perfect tense, you say **Mi sono divertita** (*I had a good time*) (*I amused myself*). But to make this verb nonreflexive, you say **Ho divertito i bambini** (*I amused the children*). To carry this example a step further, the verb can become reciprocal in meaning (as well as a regular present perfect) if you change it to **Ci siamo divertiti** (*We had a good time*) (*We amused each other*).

You can see this same progression of meanings in this set of examples:

Mi sono svegliata. (*I woke [myself] up.*)

Ho svegiato i bambini. (*I woke the kids.*)

Ci siamo svegliati. (*We woke each other up.*)

Forming the Imperfect of Reflexive Verbs

The imperfect is the simplest of all verb tenses in Italian. Most conjugations are regular, and the endings are the same for **-are, -ere,** and **-ire** (including **isc**) verbs. See Chapter 16 for the conjugation in the imperfect tense.

The imperfect tense answers these questions: *What was going on? What did you used to do?* (In English, this question is sometimes rendered as *What would you do in those days?*) *What was something or someone like?* You use the imperfect to

- **Describe physical, mental, and emotional states of being:** *I was happy* (or *sad, tall, short, poor, rich,* or whatever the case may be).

- **Talk about time and weather:** *It was midnight* or *It was freezing,* for example.

- **Reminisce:** *Remember when we used to. . . .*

With reflexive verbs, you often use the imperfect to describe habits and customs. Here are a couple of examples:

Il gatto si lamentava quando aveva fame. (*The cat complained when it was hungry.*)

Lui si metteva una cravata ogni giorno. (*He put on a tie every day.*)

Certain verbal clues tell you to use the imperfect. To review those, see Chapter 16. Keep in mind that you're not under time constraints with the imperfect. You're not talking about something that happened just once, between, say, 2:00 and 2:30 in the afternoon, when it was raining. You're talking about things that were habitual and ongoing.

The key phrase in English that triggers the imperfect is *used to,* as in *I used to go to the museum every Thursday afternoon. We used to eat fish all the time. She used to shop early in the day.*

The following tables show you just how regular reflexive verbs are conjugated in the imperfect tense. *Note:* I provide the translations only for **alzarsi,** but **mettersi** and **divertirsi** follow the same pattern.

alzarsi (to get up)	
Io mi alzavo (*[I] used to get up*)	**noi ci alzavamo** (*[we] used to get up*)
Tu ti alzavi (*[you] used to get up*)	**voi vi alzavate** (*[you] used to get up*)
lui, lei, Lei si alzava (*[he, she, it, you* (formal)*] used to get up*)	**loro, Loro si alzavano** (*[they, you* (formal)*] used to get up*)

mettersi (to wear, to put on)	
io **mi mettevo**	noi **ci mettevamo**
Tu **ti mettevi**	voi **vi mettevate**
Lui, lei, Lei **si metteva**	loro, Loro **si mettevano**

divertirsi (to have a good time)	
io **mi divertivo**	noi **ci divertivamo**
Tu **ti divertivi**	voi **vi divertivate**
Lui, lei, Lei **si divertiva**	loro, Loro **si divertivano**

Checking Out Reciprocal Forms in the Imperfect

As I mention earlier in this chapter, you can make almost all verbs reciprocal. Consider these examples:

> **Si parlavano ogni giorno.** (*They talked to each other every day.*)

> **Vi vedevate spesso.** (*You saw each other often.*)

> **Ci visitavamo ogni estate.** (*We visited each other every summer.*)

In the imperfect, reciprocal reflexives are not just descriptive; they have an almost gossipy quality.

> **Si amavano tanto.** (*They loved each other so much.*)

> **Si vedevano ogni giorno.** (*They saw each other every day.*)

The easiest way to remember whether to use the present perfect of the imperfect is to keep in mind clues dealing with time and emotional or physical states.

Present perfect clues that tell you that you're talking about a completed past action include

- ✔ **ieri** (*yesterday*)
- ✔ **ieri sera** (*yesterday evening, last night*)
- ✔ **la settimana scorsa** (*last week*)
- ✔ **lunedì, martedì, . . .** (*Monday, Tuesday, . . .*)

Here are some example sentences:

Ieri ci siamo divertiti moltissimo. (*Yesterday, we had a great time.*)

La settimana scorsa vi siete sposati, vero? (*Last week, you got married, right?*)

Lunedì mi sono trasferita. (*Monday, I moved.*)

Clues that you should use the imperfect, on the other hand, indicate emotional or physical states of being, or habitual or ongoing actions or events, and are often accompanied by these words or phrases:

- ✔ **ogni . . .** (*every . . .*)
- ✔ **ogni giorno, ogni anno, ogni inverno** (*every day, every year, every winter*)
- ✔ **qualche volta** (*sometimes*)
- ✔ **frequentemente** (*frequently, often*)
- ✔ **mentre** (*while*)
- ✔ **sempre** (*always*)
- ✔ **da bambino/da bambina** (*as a child*)

Thus, you may say some of the following expressions:

Ogni giorno ci divertivamo. (*Every day, we had fun.*)

Il lunedì si parlavano. (*Every Monday, they talked to each other.*)

Si pensavano sempre. (*They thought about each other all the time.*)

Verbs that lend themselves to the imperfect (though they can also appear in the present perfect) include those listed here. Remember that they can be reflexives, reciprocal reflexives, or not reflexives at all.

- ✔ **amare** (*to love*)
- ✔ **odiare** (*to hate*)
- ✔ **desiderare** (*to desire, to want*)
- ✔ **volere** (*to want, to love*)
- ✔ **pensare** (*to think*)

Here are some examples of these verbs in action:

> **Si amavano tanto.** (*They loved each other so much.*)
>
> **Ci odiavamo.** (*We hated each other.*)
>
> **Si volevano bene.** (*They loved each other well.*)
>
> **Si pensavano.** (*They were thinking about each other.*)

Keeping in mind the clues that help you distinguish between use of the present perfect and the imperfect, complete the following sentences with the reflexive or reciprocal reflexive form of the verb in parentheses, using one of the past tenses. Here's an example:

Q. **Da bambini, loro _____ (volersi) bene.**

A. **si volevano**

11. **La domenica, lei ed i bambini _____ (divertirsi).**

12. **Io _____ (preoccuparsi) sempre.**

13. **Ieri noi _____ (vedersi).**

14. **Ogni giorno gli amici _____ (vedersi).**

15. **Domenica, loro _____ (laurearsi).**

16. **Ieri sera, io _____ (addormentarsi) presto.**

17. **Mentre loro _____ (parlarsi), io leggevo un libro.**

18. **Io _____ (trovarsi) molto bene a Venezia.**

19. **Da bambino, tu _____ (lamentarsi) spesso.**

20. **Mentre parlavano con il poeta, Paolo e Francesca _____ (ricordarsi) del tempo felice.**

Answer Key

1 si è trasferita

2 si è messo

3 ci siamo divertiti

4 mi sono preparato/preparata

5 si sono innamorati

6 si sono laureati

7 si è affrettata

8 vi siete alzati/alzate

9 si sono divorziati

10 ti sei lamentato/lamentata

11 si divertivano

12 mi preoccupavo

13 ci siamo visti

14 si vedevano

15 si sono laureati

16 mi sono addormentato/addormentata

17 si parlavano

18 mi trovavo

19 ti lamentavi

20 si sono ricordati

Chapter 18

Future Tense and Conditional Mood

*T*alking about things you plan to do (what you're going to have for dinner, where you're going on your vacation) or might do (what you'd do if you won the lottery) requires that you understand the future tense and conditional mood. The key English word that tells you to use the future tense is *will: I will go* is a simple future construction. *He will have left; they will have eaten by now* are both in the future perfect tense.

The key English word that tells you to use the conditional is *would: I would go. He would have gone. They would travel if possible.* You can create the conditional mood in the present and the past tenses: *I would go, but I have no free time* is in the present conditional; *they would have studied, but they didn't feel like it* is a past conditional.

Of all the Italian tenses and moods, the future and the conditional have the most irregular forms. They don't follow general rules of formation (where you drop the **-are, -ere, -ire** from the infinitives to get stems, such that **parlare** becomes **parl-**) only because the stem is so frequently modified. Instead, they attach endings to the stem to reveal the subject.

In this chapter, I explain the differences between tense (present, past, and future) and mood (indicative, subjunctive, imperative, and conditional) and how tense and mood interact. A mood, such as the conditional, has tenses: the present conditional (*I would go*) and the past conditional (*I would have gone*). And all tenses appear in any one of the four moods.

I present the future and conditional together in this chapter because they share the same irregularities of formation. You save time and energy by studying them at the same time. After reading this chapter, you'll feel comfortable with both of these verb conjugations, and you'll be able to use them to make your Italian more sophisticated.

Understanding Tense and Mood

Verb tenses are variations on a theme, and that theme is time. Past, present, and future determine how you conjugate verbs by making specific changes to the "raw" form of the verb, or the infinitive, that reveal the time frame you're talking about.

An infinitive by itself (**parlare** [*to speak*], **scrivere** [*to write*], **dormire** [*to sleep*]) is inert. It doesn't show any action. You need to remove the infinitive's ending (**-are, -ere,** or **-ire**) to produce a stem (**parl-, scriv-, dorm-**). To that stem, you add endings that reveal the subject that carries out actions and brings a verb to life. (See Chapters 6 and 7 to review this process.)

Verb endings tell you not only who or what carries out an action but also when that action takes place. In English, you say *I eat* (present), *I ate* (past), *I will eat* (future) — forms of the infinitive *to eat*. Italian does the same thing, and I explain the endings for tenses in Chapters 6, 7, 9, 10, 16, 17, 19, 20, 21, and 22.

When using verbs, you also need to consider the verb's mood. Moods include the indicative (factual), subjunctive (subjective), imperative (commanding), and conditional (which is dependent on conditions or a "what if" frame of mind). You use different endings for each mood. (See Chapters 19, 20, 21, and 22 for details.)

In the next section I show you how to build the future conjugations. In the later section "Testing the Conditions: The Conditional Mood," I give you details about using the conditional. The future and the conditional share the characteristics that make them irregular. You can both master and differentiate them at the same time.

Forming the Future Tense

To talk about the future, you need to keep the word *will* in your mind. *I <u>will</u> do this . . .* (some time in the future); *I <u>will</u> have done this . . .* (some time in the future after something else has happened or by a certain time).

I have good news. The future tense endings for all conjugations (that is, for **-are, -ere,** and **-ire** verbs) are the same (**-ò, -ai, -à, -emo, -ete,** and **-anno**). Also on the positive side, you attach the endings to stems formed when you drop *only* the final **-e** from the infinitive (the exception to this form are the **-are** verbs, which I discuss in the next section).

You can see how this works with the future tense verb conjugation of **scrivere** in the following table.

scrivere (to write)	
scriverò (*I will write*)	**scriveremo** (*we will write*)
scriverai (*you will write*)	**scriverete** (*you all will write*)
scriverà (*he, she, it, you* [formal] *will write*)	**scriveranno** (*they, you* [formal] *will write*)

The accents on the first and third person singular (**io** and **lui, lei, Lei**) endings tell you to stress the final syllable.

Compare the conjugation of **scrivere** to those for **dormire** and **finire**, shown in the following tables.

dormire (to sleep)	
dormirò	dormiremo
dormirai	dormirete
dormirà	dormiranno

finire (to finish)	
finirò	finiremo
finirai	finirete
finirà	finiranno

As you see, the endings are the same for **-ere** and **-ire** verbs. The **-ire** (**isc**) verbs also use these endings. See Chapter 6 for details about **-ire** (**isc**) verbs.

In the following sections, I explore some exceptions to these conjugations with **-are** verbs and also show you how to work with irregular roots in the future tense.

Spelling out -are exceptions with the future tense

The **-are** verbs make one more change to the endings for future tense, unique to their conjugation: The characteristic **a** of the infinitive (**parlare** [*to speak*], **imparare** [*to learn*], **comprare** [*to buy*], and so on) changes to **e**. So, for example, **parlare** becomes **parlerò** (*I will speak*) rather than **parlarò**. The flow from **e** to **rò** is much more fluid than from **a** to **rò.**

Take a look at the following conjugation of **parlare** to see how this spelling change affects **-are** future tense conjugations.

parlare (to speak)	
parlerò (*I will speak*)	**parleremo** (*we will speak*)
parlerai (*you will speak*)	**parlerete** (*you all will speak*)
parlerà (*he, she, it, you* [formal] *will speak*)	**parleranno** (*they, you* [formal] *will speak*)

Other **-are** verbs that require you to make spelling changes to the stem take place because of the change from **a** to **e.** I outline these changes in the following sections. To review general pronunciation and spelling rules, see Chapter 2.

Figuring out -gare and -care verb conjugations

Keep in mind that **-are** verbs always maintain the sound of the infinitive. So if the infinitive ends in **-gare** or **-care,** you need to add an **h** to the stem in the future tense. Only by adding **h** before the replacement letter of **e** can you maintain the original hard sound that **a** produces.

For example, the stem for **pagare** (*to pay for*) becomes **pagher-,** and the stem for **cercare** (*to look for*) becomes **cercher-.** They conjugate as follows.

pagare (to pay for)	
pagherò	pagheremo
pagherai	pagherete
pagherà	pagheranno

cercare (to look for)	
cercherò	cercheremo
cercherai	cercherete
cercherà	cercheranno

Making exceptions with -giare, -ciare, and other -iare verbs

For the **-are** verbs that end in **-giare** and **-ciare,** you remove the letter **i** before adding the future tense endings because you no longer need to soften the **g** or the **c** when it precedes the letter **e.** Here are example conjugations for **mangiare** and **cominciare.**

mangiare (to eat)	
mangerò	mangeremo
mangerai	mangerete
mangerà	mangeranno

cominciare (to begin)	
comincerò	cominceremo
comincerai	comincerete
comincerà	cominceranno

The exception to this rule involves those verbs, like **inviare** (*to send*), that stress the **i** before the endings in the present tense (see Chapter 6). When you stress the **i** — that is, when you separate its sound from the **a** that follows instead of using it as a diphthong (with in-vi-a-re, for example, you pronounce each syllable; with co-min-cia-re, you use the **i** to soften the **c** and produce the sound heard in the English *ch*) — you don't need to keep the **i** in the future tense conjugation. See the following conjugations.

inviare (to send)	
invierò	invieremo
invierai	invierete
invierà	invieranno

cominciare (to begin)	
comincerò	cominceremo
comincerai	comincerete
comincerà	cominceranno

Fill in the future form of the verbs in parentheses, according to the subject. Here's an example.

O. Riccardo e Lorenzo _____ (cominciare) il lavoro domani.

A. cominceranno

1. Io gliene _____ (parlare) domani.

2. Tu _____ (mangiare) quello?

3. La signora _____ (imparare) l'italiano prima di andare.

4. Noi _____ (leggere) il libro per il corso.

5. Voi _____ (dormire) tardi.

6. Paolo _____ (pagare) il conto.

7. Loro _____ (cercare) biglietti per il viaggio.

8. Tu ed io [noi] _____ (viaggiare) insieme.

9. Io non gli _____ (scrivere).

10. Le ragazze _____ (comprare) delle belle scarpe per il ballo.

Working with irregular roots in the future tense

A number of verbs have irregular stems in the future tense — that is, stems where you don't simply drop the final **e** from the infinitive. Irregular stems sometimes reflect an adjustment to sound or make language more fluid (compare **anderò** with **andrò**, for example; the latter is easier to say and sounds less clumsy, more smooth). At other times, irregular stems seem to have no logic to them. You simply must commit them to memory as you encounter them.

For example, **essere** (*to be*) and **avere** (*to have*) are irregular in the future tense but only in the stem. Both verbs take the same future tense endings you use for regular verb stems. (See the earlier section "Forming the Future Tense" to review the future tense endings.)

Essere's stem becomes **sar-**; **avere**'s stem becomes **avr-.** The following tables show you their conjugations in the future tense.

essere (to be)	
sarò	saremo
sarai	sarete
sarà	saranno

avere (to have)	
avrò	avremo
avrai	avrete
avrà	avranno

Other verbs share the irregularities of these stems. I outline their characteristics in the following sections.

Verbs that drop the a or e

Some verbs drop the characteristic **a** or **e** from their infinitives, thus forming irregular stems, before adding the future tense endings, as you can see in the following tables.

andare (to go)	
andrò	andremo
andrai	andrete
andrà	andranno
Lui andrà in Italia quest'estate. (*He will go to Italy this summer.*)	

sapere (to know)	
saprò	sapremo
saprai	saprete
saprà	sapranno
Nessuno saprà. (*No one will know.*)	

vedere (to see)	
vedrò	vedremo
vedrai	vedrete
vedrà	vedranno
Loro vedranno il film a New York. (*They will see the movie in New York.*)	

Other verbs that work the same way include **dovere** (**dovrò** [*I will have to*]), **potere** (**potrò** [*I will be able to*]), and **vivere** (**vivrò** [*I will live*]).

Verbs that keep the a

Some verbs retain the characteristic **a** from their **-are** infinitives, including the following.

dare (to give)	
darò	daremo
darai	darete
darà	daranno
Daremo tutti i soldi agli animali. (*We'll give all the money to animals.*)	

fare (to do, to make)	
farò	faremo
farai	farete
farà	faranno
Tu non farai niente. (*You won't do anything.*)	

stare (to stay, to be)	
starò	staremo
starai	starete
starà	staranno
Lui starà all'albergo in centro. (*He will stay in the hotel downtown.*)	

Verbs that double the r

Two verbs in particular — **volere** (*to want*) and **venire** (*to come*) — create brand new stems, **vorr-** and **verr-**, respectively. These verbs are examples of ones you simply need to memorize. There's no logic to the formation of their stems.

volere (to want)	
vorrò	vorremo
vorrai	vorrete
vorrà	vorranno
Io vorrò un caffè bello caldo. (*I will want a boiling hot cup of coffee.*)	

venire (to come)	
verrò	verremo
verrai	verrete
verrà	verranno
Loro verranno fra due settimane. (*They'll come within two weeks.*)	

Other verbs that insert an **rr** into the future stem include **bere** (*to drink*), which becomes **berr-**; **tenere** (*to keep*), which becomes **terr-**; **valere** (*to be worth*), which becomes **varr-**; and **rimanere** (*to remain*), which becomes **rimarr-**. Here are some example sentences with these verbs:

> **Berrò un bicchiere di vino.** (*I will drink a glass of wine.*)
>
> **Terrà la chiave.** (*He'll keep the key.*)
>
> **Non ne varrà la pena.** (*It won't be worth it.*)
>
> **Rimarranno a casa.** (*They'll stay home.*)

Using the verbs in parentheses, complete the sentences with the future tense. If the subject isn't clear, I add it in parentheses.

Q. Paola, dove _____ (tu, andare)?

A. andrai

11. Mi _____ (tu, fare) un favore?

12. La mamma _____ (sapere).

13. Io non lo _____ (fare).

14. Voi ci _____ (essere)?

15. Loro _____ (vivere) con gli amici.

16. Domani Marco _____ (avere) un po' di tempo libero.

17. Noi _____ (studiare) stasera.

18. Voi _____ (vedere) il nuovo film?

19. I bambini _____ (leggere) molto durante l'estate.

20. Chiara e Laura _____ (visitare) noi?

Talking about the Future

Knowing how to conjugate future tense verbs is a great start (see the earlier sections of this chapter), but when and where do you use the future tense? Here are some possibilities:

✔ To talk about what's fairly certain to occur, sooner or later:

Andrò a scuola. (*I will go to school.*)

Parlerà con gli studenti. (*He will talk to the students.*)

Andremo al mare in aprile. (*We will go to the seaside in April.*)

Verranno per le nozze di Marisa. (*They will come for Marisa's wedding.*)

✔ To talk about probability, often a way to be subtle or polite:

Dove sarà? (*Where can it be?*)

Lui avrà 90 anni. (*He's probably 90 years old.*)

Le ragazze saranno americane. (*The girls are probably American.*)

Costerà un patrimonio. (*It probably costs a fortune.*)

✔ To make clear that you expect something to happen (in other words, as a kind of command):

Giulia e Francesco, mangerete la verdura. (*Giulia and Francesco, you <u>will</u> eat the vegetables.*)

Often, the future tense gives way to the present tense, if it's not too distant or is absolutely certain. For example: **Domani vado a scuola** (*Tomorrow, I'm going to school*). It's really a matter of personal choice whether you want to use the future tense or the present tense in some cases.

Translate the following sentences into English from Italian. Follow the example.

Q. **I ragazzi saranno italiani.**

A. *The boys are probably Italian.*

21. **Io avrò molto lavoro domani.**

_____

22. **Bambini, farete i compiti** [*homework*] **dopo scuola.**

_____

23. **Costerà molto molto.**

   _____

24. **Loro, dove saranno?**

   _____

25. **Voi saprete studiare.**

   _____

Forming the future perfect tense

You often call the future perfect tense the future past tense because it refers to something you _will have_ done by a specified time: _I will have finished by tomorrow. They will have left by then._

The future perfect tense is a compound tense. You use one of the helping verbs (**essere** [_to be_] or **avere** [_to have_]) in front of a past participle (**parlato** [_spoken_], **scritto** [_written_], **andato** [_gone_], for example) as the following examples show. (To review formation of past participles, and to see which ones aren't regular, see Chapter 16.)

> **Prima di domani, io sarò andata via.** (_Before tomorrow, I'll have gone away._)
>
> **Prima di domani, avrò finito il libro.** (_Before tomorrow, I'll have finished the book._)

When forming the future perfect tense, you conjugate _only_ the helping verb, in the simple future, according to the subject of your sentence.

You use **essere** with verbs of motion — **andare** (_to go_), **venire** (_to come_), **tornare** (_to return_), for example — and with _all_ reflexive verbs — **alzarsi** (_to get up_), **informarsi** (_to find out_). It also conjugates with itself.

> **Paolo sarà tornato ma sua moglie non sarà tornata.** (_Paul will have returned, but his wife won't have [returned]._)
>
> **Saranno arrivati.** (_They will have arrived._)
>
> **Le ragazze si saranno incontrate.** (_The girls will have met each other._)
>
> **Mi sarò informata.** (_I will have found out._)

You use **avere** with verbs that can take direct objects, or verbs that answer the questions who or what (**vedere** [_to see_]; **comprare** [_to buy_]). When using **avere**, you conjugate it in the future tense, but the past participle remains unchanged, not agreeing with the subject.

> **Lui avrà comprato una macchina.** (_He will have bought a car._)
>
> **Loro avranno visto il film.** (_They will have seen the film._)
>
> **Noi avremo mangiato da Carlo.** (_We will have eaten at Carlo's._)
>
> **Voi avrete parlato con lui.** (_You all will have talked with him._)

Complete the following sentences, using the future perfect tense of the verbs in parentheses. I include the helping verbs along with the main verbs so you can focus on the form and not whether to use **avere** or **essere.** Here's an example:

Q. Noi _____ (essere tornare).

A. saremo tornati

26. Lorenzo _____ (avere mangiare) tutti i biscotti.

27. Voi _____ (avere vedere) i ragazzi a Firenze.

28. Io _____ (avere leggere) il nuovo libro.

29. Lei _____ (essere venire) alla festa.

30. Tu _____ (essere informarsi)?

Talking about the hypothetical future

Among its other peculiarities, the future tense doubles up when you use it to discuss possibilities. In English, you say *If I do this, then I will do that as well.* You use a present tense verb and follow it with a future tense verb. You use the present in a dependent clause and the future in the independent one.

In Italian, you use the future tense in both parts of the sentence. For example:

> **Se arriverò presto, ti chiamerò.** (*If I [will] arrive early, I'll call you.*)

Three words in particular trigger this double future construction: **se** (*if*), **appena** (*as soon as*), and **quando** (*when*).

> **Se andrò, ti farò sapere.** (*If I go, I'll let you know.*)

> **Quando arriveremo, visiteremo i musei.** (*When we arrive, we'll visit the museums.*)

> **Appena arriverò, ti chiamerò.** (*As soon as I arrive, I'll call you.*)

Other ways of talking about the hypothetical future involve using the subjunctive mood, which I explain in detail in Chapters 19 and 20.

Translate the following sentences from Italian into English, being as idiomatic as possible. Here's an example:

Q. Se Luigi studierà, vedrà i risultati.

A. *If Luigi studies, he'll see results.*

31. Appena sapranno, ci diranno.

_____

32. **Quando arriverete, noi mangeremo.**

   _____

33. **Se Mario non andrà, non vedrà gli amici.**

   _____

34. **Appena riceverò una lettera, ti farò sapere.**

   _____

35. **Se avranno un momento libero, verranno a trovarci.**

   _____

Testing the Conditions: The Conditional Mood

The four moods in Italian let you separate fact from opinion and conjecture. By using them, you can impart subtlety and sophistication linguistically.

- ✔ The **indicative** is factual and straightforward: _He is Italian._ (See Chapters 6 and 7 for a discussion of the indicative.)

- ✔ The **imperative** exerts a certain control: _Do that._ (See Chapter 9.)

- ✔ The **subjunctive** is subjective; it allows you to inject hope, doubt, fear, and uncertainty into your Italian. You use it to state things contrary to fact: _If I were president. . . ._ (Chapters 19, 20, 21, and 22 give you details about the subjunctive.)

- ✔ The **conditional** is dependent on conditions: _I would do this, but I'm too tired._ You know you're in conditional territory when you see the word _would._ I explore the conditional mood in the following sections.

Forming the present conditional

The present conditional expresses what you would do if only you could. _I would go, but I don't have the time. They would like the book. He would live in the center of the city, but he can't afford it._

The conditional endings for all conjugations (**-are**, **-ere**, and **-ire** verbs in the present conditional and the past conditional) are the same (**ei, -esti, -ebbe, -emmo, -este,** and **-ebbero**). The endings attach to stems formed when you drop _only_ the final **e** from the infinitive. And most important of all, as you see in the next sections, "Spelling out **-are** exceptions with the conditional mood" and "Working with irregular roots in the conditional mood," conditional stems are identical to those used in the future tense (see the earlier sections of this chapter on the future tense).

This conjugation of **scrivere** (*to write*) shows you what I mean.

scrivere (to write)	
scriverei (*I would write*)	**scriveremmo** (*we would write*)
scriveresti (*you would write*)	**scrivereste** (*you all would write*)
scriverebbe (*he, she, it, you* [formal] *would write*)	**scriverebbero** (*they, you* [formal] *would write*)

Compare the conjugation of **scrivere** (*to write*) to **dormire** (*to sleep*) and **finire** (*to finish*).

dormire (to sleep)	
dormirei	dormiremmo
dormiresti	dormireste
dormirebbe	dormirebbero

finire (to finish)	
finirei	finiremmo
finiresti	finireste
finirebbe	finirebbero

As you can see, the endings are the same for **-ere** and **-ire** verbs. The **-ire** (**isc**) verbs also use these endings. See Chapter 6 for details about **-ire** (**isc**) verbs.

Spelling out -are exceptions with the conditional mood

The **-are** verbs make one more change in the conditional mood, unique to their conjugation. The characteristic **a** of the infinitive (**parlare** [*to speak*], **imparare** [*to learn*], **comprare** [*to buy*], and so on) changes to **e**. So **parlare** becomes **parlerei** (*I would speak*). The flow from **e** to **rei** is much more fluid than if you were to keep the **a** and say **parlarei**.

Take a look at the following conjugation of **parlare** to see how this spelling change affects **-are** conditional conjugations.

parlare (to speak)	
parlerei (*I would speak*)	**parleremmo** (*we would speak*)
parleresti (*you would speak*)	**parlereste** (*you all would speak*)
parlerebbe (*he, she, it, you* [formal] *would speak*)	**parlerebbero** (*they, you* [formal] *would speak*)

Other **-are** verbs that require you to make spelling changes to the stem take place because of the change from **a** to **e**, as I explain in the following sections. To review general pronunciation and spelling rules, see Chapter 2.

Figuring out -gare and -care conjugations

Remember that **-are** verbs always maintain the sound of the infinitive. So if the infinitive ends in **-gare** or **-care**, you need to add an **h** to the stem in the conditional mood. Only by adding **h** before the replacement letter of **e** can you maintain the original hard sound that **a** produces.

For example, the stem for **pagare** (*to pay for*) becomes **pagher-,** and the stem for **cercare** (*to look for*) becomes **cercher-**. See their conjugations in the following tables.

pagare (to pay for)	
pagherei	pagheremmo
pagheresti	paghereste
pagherebbe	pagherebbero

cercare (to look for)	
cercherei	cercheremmo
cercheresti	cerchereste
cercherebbe	cercherebbero

Making exceptions with -giare, -ciare, and other -iare verbs

For the **-are** verbs that end in **-giare** and **-ciare,** you remove the letter **i** before adding the conditional endings because you no longer need to soften the **g** or the **c** when it precedes the letter **e.** Here are example conjugations of **mangiare** and **cominciare** in the conditional mood.

mangiare (to eat)	
mangerei	mangeremmo
mangeresti	mangereste
mangerebbe	mangerebbero

cominciare *(to begin)*	
comincerei	cominceremmo
cominceresti	comincereste
comincerebbe	comincerebbero

The exception to this rule involves those verbs, like **inviare** *(to send)*, that stress the **i** before the endings in the present tense, or at least separate the **i** from the following vowel, **a** (see Chapter 6). When you stress the **i**, — that is, when you separate its sound from the **a** that follows instead of using it as a diphthong, you keep it in the conditional mood conjugation, as the following table shows.

inviare *(to send)*	
invierei	invieremmo
invieresti	inviereste
invierebbe	invierebbero

Fill in the conditional form of the verbs in parentheses, according to the subject. Here's an example.

0. Riccardo e Lorenzo _____ (cominciare) il lavoro domani.

A. comincerebbero

36. Io gliene _____ (parlare) domani.

37. Tu _____ (mangiare) quello?

38. La signora _____ (imparare) l'italiano ma non vuole studiare.

39. Noi _____ (leggere) il libro per il corso.

40. Voi _____ (dormire) tardi.

41. Paolo _____ (pagare) il conto.

42. Loro _____ (cercare) biglietti per il viaggio.

43. Tu ed io [noi] _____ (viaggiare) bene insieme.

44. Io non gli _____ (scrivere).

45. Le ragazze _____ (comprare) delle belle scarpe per il ballo, ma non hanno soldi.

Working with irregular roots in the conditional mood

A number of verbs have irregular stems in the conditional — that is, stems where you don't simply drop the final **e** from the infinitive. These same verbs have irregular stems in the future (see the earlier section "Working with irregular roots in the future tense"). Irregular stems sometimes reflect an adjustment to sound or make language more fluid (compare **anderei** with **andrei,** for example; the latter is easier to say and sounds less clumsy, more smooth). At other times, irregular stems seem to have no logic to them. You simply need to commit them to memory as you encounter them.

For example, **essere** (*to be*) and **avere** (*to have*) are irregular in the conditional but only in the stem. The conditional endings are the same as for regular stems. (See the earlier section in this chapter "Forming the Present Conditional" to review the conditional endings.)

Essere's stem becomes **sar-; avere**'s stem becomes **avr-.** The following tables show you their conjugations in the conditional.

essere (to be)	
sarei	saremmo
saresti	sareste
sarebbe	sarebbero

avere (to have)	
avrei	avremmo
avresti	avreste
avrebbe	avrebbero

Other verbs share the irregularities of these stems. I explain their characteristics in the following sections.

Verbs that drop the a or e

Some verbs drop the characteristic **a** or **e** from their infinitives, thus forming irregular stems, before adding the conditional endings, as you can see in the following tables.

andare (to go)	
andrei	andremmo
andresti	andreste
andrebbe	andrebbero
Lui andrebbe in Italia quest'estate. (*He would go to Italy this summer.*)	

sapere (to know)	
saprei	sapremmo
sapresti	sapreste
saprebbe	saprebbero
Nessuno saprebbe. (*No one would know.*)	

vedere (to see)	
vedrei	vedremmo
vedresti	vedreste
vedrebbe	vedrebbero
Loro vedrebbero il film a New York. (*They would see the movie in New York.*)	

Other verbs that work the same way include **dovere** (*to have to*), **potere** (*to be able to*), and **vivere** (*to live*). **Dovere** and **potere,** however, change their meanings slightly in the conditional: **Dovere** changes from *to have to* and means *should or ought to,* such as **Dovrei studiare** (*I should study*); **potere** changes from *to be able to* into *might or could,* such as **Potrei studiare** (*I might study*). See the section "Speaking with the Conditional" for more info.

Verbs that keep the a

Some verbs retain the characteristic **a** from their **-are** infinitives, including the following.

dare (to give)	
darei	daremmo
daresti	dareste
darebbe	darebbero
Noi daremmo tutti i soldi agli animali. (*We would give all the money to animals.*)	

fare (to do, to make)	
farei	faremmo
faresti	fareste
farebbe	farebbero
Tu non faresti niente. (*You wouldn't do anything.*)	

stare (to stay, to be)	
starei	staremmo
staresti	stareste
starebbe	starebbero
Lui starebbe all'albergo in centro. (*He would stay in the hotel downtown.*)	

Verbs that double the r

Two verbs in particular — **volere** (*to want*) and **venire** (*to come*) — create brand new stems, **vorr-** and **verr-**, respectively. Because there's no particular logic to their formation, you'll simply have to memorize them.

volere (to want)	
vorrei	vorremmo
vorresti	vorreste
vorrebbe	vorrebbero
Io vorrei un caffè bello caldo. (*I would want a boiling hot cup of coffee.*)	

venire (to come)	
verrei	verremmo
verresti	verreste
verrebbe	verrebbero
Loro verrebbero fra due settimane. (*They would come within two weeks.*)	

Other verbs that insert an **rr** into the conditional stem include **bere** (*to drink*), which becomes **berr-**; **tenere** (*to keep*), which becomes **terr-**; **valere** (*to be worth*), which becomes **varr-**; and **rimanere** (*to remain*), which becomes **rimarr-**. Here are some example sentences with these verbs:

Berrei un bicchiere di vino. (*I would drink a glass of wine.*)

Terrebbe la chiave. (*He'd keep the key.*)

Non ne varrebbe la pena. (*It wouldn't be worth it.*)

Rimarrebbero a casa. (*They'd stay home.*)

Using the verbs in parentheses, complete the sentences with the conditional. If the subject isn't clear, I add it in parentheses.

Q. Paola, dove _____ (tu, andare)?

A. andresti

46. Mi _____ (tu, fare) un favore?

47. La mamma _____ (sapere).

48. Io non lo _____ (fare).

49. Voi ci _____ (essere)?

50. Loro _____ (vivere) con gli amici.

51. Domani Marco _____ (avere) un po' di tempo libero.

52. Noi _____ (studiare) stasera.

53. Voi _____ (vedere) il nuovo film?

54. I bambini _____ (leggere) molto durante l'estate.

55. Chiara e Laura _____ (visitare) noi?

Speaking with the conditional

You use the conditional to talk about what would happen or what you would do —
but other conditions enter in: *I would go, but I don't have tickets.*

Frequently, the conditional occurs in one of two clauses in a sentence. *They would
study, but they don't have school until next week. We would gladly go to Italy, but the
tickets are horribly expensive right now.* Just as often, the conditional requires use of
the subjunctive. *I would buy that house <u>if I were rich</u>.* The conditional (*would buy*) is
followed by an imperfect subjunctive (*I were*). (See Chapters 19, 20, 21, and 22 for an
overview of the use of the subjunctive with the conditional.)

The conditionals of **potere** (*to be able to*) and **dovere** (*to have to*), unlike other conditionals, change their fundamental meanings in this mood. **Potere** in the conditional
carries the sense of *could* or *might*. Instead of **posso venire** (*I am able to come*) (*I can
come*), **potrei venire** means *I might come, I could come (but there are no guarantees!).*
For example:

> **Lui potrebbe aiutarci.** (*He could help us [but will he?].*)

> **Noi potremmo farlo**. (*We might do it [if we feel like it].*)

Dovere changes from a duty, something that has to be done, to *should* or *ought to*.
Again, there are no guarantees.

> **Dovrebbe studiare ma non ne ha voglia.** (*He should study but doesn't feel like it.*)

> **Gli studenti devono — no, dovrebbero — studiare le lingue.** (*Students have to —
> no, should — study languages.*)

You can find more information about how to form these essentially snarky comments
in Chapter 21.

Forming the conditional perfect

You often call the conditional perfect the conditional past because it refers to something you would have done by a specified time. *I would have finished by tomorrow, but I got sidetracked. They would have left by then if the weather had cooperated.*

The conditional perfect is a compound tense. You use one of the helping verbs (**essere** or **avere**) in front of a past participle (**parlato** [*spoken*], **scritto** [*written*], **andato** [*gone*], for example). (To review formation of past participles, and to see which ones aren't regular, see Chapter 16.)

> **Prima di domani, io sarei andata via, ma . . .** (*Before tomorrow, I'd have gone away, but . . .*)

> **Prima di domani, avrei finito il libro, ma dovevo lavorare.** (*Before tomorrow, I'd have finished the book, but I had to work.*)

When forming the conditional perfect, you conjugate *only* the helping verb in the conditional, according to the subject of your sentence.

You use **essere** with verbs of motion — **andare** (*to go*), **venire** (*to come*), **tornare** (*to return*), for example — and with *all* reflexive verbs — **alzarsi** (*to get up*), **informarsi** (*to find out*). It also conjugates with itself.

> **Paolo sarebbe tornato ma sua moglie non sarebbe tornata.** (*Paul would have returned, but his wife wouldn't have [returned].*)

> **Sarebbero arrivati, ma c'è stato uno sciopero.** (*They would have arrived, but there was a strike.*)

> **Le ragazze si sarebbero incontrate a scuola.** (*The girls would have met each other at school.*)

> **Mi sarei informata, ma non ho avuto un momento libero.** (*I would have found out, but I didn't have a free moment.*)

You use **avere** with verbs that can take direct objects, or verbs that answer the questions who or what (**vedere** [*to see*]; **comprare** [*to buy*]). When using **avere,** you conjugate it in the conditional, but the past participle remains unchanged, not agreeing with the subject. Here are some examples:

> **Lui avrebbe comprato la macchina, ma era troppo cara.** (*He would have bought the car, but it was too expensive.*)

> **Loro avrebbero visto il film.** (*They would have seen the film.*)

> **Noi avremmo mangiato da Carlo, ma lui è stato fuori città.** (*We would have eaten at Carlo's, but he was out of town.*)

> **Voi avreste parlato con Vicenzo, ma lui non rispondeva al telefono.** (*You all would have talked with Vicenzo, but he wasn't answering the phone.*)

Complete the following sentences, using the conditional perfect of the verbs in parentheses. I include the helping verbs along with the main verbs so you can focus on the form and not whether to use **avere** or **essere.** Here's an example:

Q. Noi _____ (essere tornare).

A. saremmo tornati

56. Lorenzo _____ (avere mangiare) tutti i biscotti.

57. Voi _____ (avere vedere) i ragazzi a Firenze.

58. Io _____ (avere leggere) il nuovo libro.

59. Lei _____ (essere venire) alla festa.

60. Tu _____ (essere informarsi)?

Answer Key

1. parlerò

2. mangerai

3. imparerà

4. leggeremo

5. dormirete

6. pagherà

7. cercheranno

8. viaggeremo

9. scriverò

10. compreranno

11. farai

12. saprà

13. farò

14. sarete

15. vivranno

16. avrà

17. studieremo

18. vedrete

19. leggeranno

20. visiteranno

21 *I will have lots of work tomorrow.*

22 *Kids, you will do your homework after school.*

23 *It probably costs a lot.*

24 *Where can they be?*

25 *You all will study.*

26 **avrà mangiato**

27 **avrete visto**

28 **avrò letto**

29 **sarà venuta**

30 **ti sarai informata**

31 *As soon as they know, they'll tell us.*

32 *When they arrive, we'll eat.*

33 *If Mario doesn't go, he won't see his friends.*

34 *As soon as I receive a letter, I'll let you know.*

35 *If they have a free moment, they'll come find us.*

36 **parlerei**

37 **mangeresti**

38 **imparerebbe**

39 **leggeremmo**

40 **dormireste**

41 **pagherebbe**

42 cercheranno

43 viaggeremmo

44 scriverei

45 comprerebbero

46 faresti

47 saprebbe

48 farei

49 sareste

50 vivrebbero

51 avrebbe

52 studieremmo

53 vedreste

54 leggerebbero

55 visiterebbero

56 avrebbe mangiato

57 avreste visto

58 avrei letto

59 sarebbe venuta

60 ti saresti informato

Part V
Expressing Subjectivity and Giving Orders

Five Reason to Learn Italian

✔ To understand and improve your English by getting a deeper understanding of how language forms: Most people learn to speak their native language very young by imitation and paying attention to what's being said around them. Learning a new language as you get older requires you to think of a system of rules and patterns, which can help you see the same types of patterns in your native language. Learning a second language helps you see how any language builds, with parts of speech, verb tenses, and even intonation.

✔ To exercise your memory and stave off mental decay: Studies show that exercising the brain by learning a second (or third or fourth) language keeps you alert, and, although not a guarantee against eventual brain degeneration, it postpones the normal effects of aging on the brain.

✔ To increase your marketability and earning potential: Many businesses want people with language skills. In the increasingly global economy, knowing another language makes doing business easier with your foreign counterparts. On average, salaries for multilingual people are 20 to 30 percent higher than for monolinguals.

✔ To travel more confidently and off the beaten track: Speaking another language lets you get away from the often crowded standard tourist spots. It allows you to roam about and participate in a culture rather than viewing it from the outside.

✔ To broaden your culinary, literary, and other cultural experiences: When you speak Italian, you open your world to culinary specialties beyond the tourist menu, and you give yourself the gift of Italian literature and opera in its original form, without anything getting lost in translation.

Pick up some phrases that will help you get by in Italian effectively and politely at www.dummies.com/extras/italiangrammar.

In this part . . .

✔ Talk about what might happen based on particular conditions being met with "if . . . then" phrases in Italian. Brush up on conditional clauses to express what will likely happen, what might happen, and what could be in a parallel universe.

✔ Express ideas that aren't rooted in reality as much as in desire, wish, hope, and expectation. Use the subjunctive mood to share what you'll do or feel at a point of time in the future if something occurs and to politely give orders.

✔ Discover how to form the past conditional to talk about what you would have, could have, or should have done.

Chapter 19

Dealing with Conditions Beyond Our Control: "If" Clauses and Passive Actions

- -

In This Chapter

▶ Expressing nearly certain, possible, and impossible conditions with **se**

▶ Getting personal and active with the impersonal and passive forms

- -

Two-letter words often prove to be the most complex, demanding, and ultimately the most useful in Italian. **Se** (*if*) is no exception. In a classic monolingual Italian dictionary, with tissue-paper thin pages and blindingly small type, **se** takes up almost an entire page.

"If" clauses — that is, clauses that begin with **se** — are hypothetical, but to differing degrees. In this chapter, I show you how to use **se** as an introduction to language that talks about reality, hypotheticals (possibility and probability), and things contrary to fact.

Think of these clauses as "if . . ., then . . ." clauses. "If" clauses introduce a conjecture and are followed by a clause giving a result. For example, **Se vinco i soldi, li do alla scuola dove insegno.** (*If I win the money, [then] I'm giving it to the school where I teach.*)

For each **se . . . poi** condition, you follow very specific rules about the verbs you use. Conditions of reality, those that are hypothetical, and those that are contrary to fact or completely subjective, each use different verb forms. I show you in individual tables just how each of these conditions is expressed.

Expressing Types of Conditionals

Hypothetical constructions consist of three kinds: those that deal with reality or certainty, those that express possibility, and those that allow you to discuss the impossible or the truly hypothetical. This section looks at all three.

Conditions within the realm of reality

You use **se** to introduce events that are almost certain to take place if certain conditions are met. For example, **Se piove, non mangiamo in giardino.** (*If it rains, we won't be eating in the garden.*) Or, **Se vogliono, possiamo andare al cinema.** (*If they want, we can go to the movies.*)

The verbs in these two sample sentences (**piove, mangiamo, vogliono, possiamo**) are in the present tense. The use of **se** requires you to follow one kind of verb with another specified verb. Generally, for example, a present tense verb — what is happening now or in the near (and certain) future in the **se** (*if*) clause — is followed by the same tense in the **poi** (*then*) clause.

Table 19-1 shows examples of the various possibilities of verb sequencing (which kinds of verbs you can use in **se . . . poi** constructions). All these examples express a reality — possibly a future reality — but one that's pretty certain.

Table 19-1	Se and Poi Clauses That Show Reality
"Se" (If) Clause	*"Poi" (Then) Clause*
Present: **se vuoi** (*if you want*)	Present: **lo facciamo** (*we'll do it*)
	Future: **lo faremo** (*we'll do it*)
	Imperative: **fammi sapere** (*let me know*)
Future: **se andrò** (*if I go*)	Present: **ti faccio sapere** (*I'll let you know*)
	Future: **ti farò sapere** (*I'll let you know*)
Imperfect: **se non volevano andare** (*if they didn't want to go*)	Imperfect: **mi potevano dire** (*they could have told me*)
Present perfect (past): **se non è arrivato** (*if he didn't arrive*)	Present: **arriva fra poco** (*he'll arrive soon*)
	Future: **arriverà fra poco** (*he'll arrive soon*)
Present perfect: **se non è arrivato** (*if he didn't arrive [on that train]*)	Imperfect indicative: **arrivava** (*he was arriving*)

For details on verb tenses and moods in general, see Chapters 6 and 7 for the present, Chapters 9 and 10 for special verbs in the present and other tenses, and Chapter 18 for the future and conditionals that generally do **not** use an "if" clause.

Choose the verb tense and conjugation that completes the **se** clause in the following sentences. Some questions may have more than one answer. Here's an example.

Q. Se tu _____ (desiderare), lo facciamo.

A. desideri, desidererai

1. Se tu _____ (avere) il tempo libero, ci andremo domani.

2. Se loro non _____ (volere), me ne potevano parlare.

3. Se lui _____ (arrivare), mangeremo insieme.

4. Se lei non _____ (studiare), non riceverà buoni voti.

5. Se Angelo e Guido _____ (andare), andrò anch'io.

6. Se tu _____ (preferire), resta qui.

7. Se io _____ (trovare) biglietti, verrai con me?

8. Se _____ (succedere) un'altra volta, griderò!

9. Se tu _____ (volere) sapere, gli ho telefonato.

10. Se loro _____ (partire), partiranno fra poco.

Navigating hypothetical constructions of probability (and possibility)

If a **se** clause is followed by a **poi** clause that refers to a possible, even probable, action that isn't at all certain, then you use different verb formations than you do in cases of **se . . . poi** clauses that deal with reality. **Se volessi, gliene parlerei.** (*If you wanted, I would talk to him about it.*)

In this case, the **se** clause uses the imperfect subjunctive (the subjective mood that expresses doubt, emotions, hopes, possibilities and even probabilities), and the **poi** clause verb goes into the present conditional (the mood that expresses what would take place), or, occasionally, the past conditional (to express what would have taken place). For details about the conditional, see Chapters 18 and 21.

Table 19-2 shows examples of sequencing **se** and **poi** clauses to indicate possibility or probability.

Table 19-2	Se and Poi Clauses That Show Possibility
"Se" (If) Clause	*"Poi" (Then) Clause*
Imperfect subjunctive: **se avesse il tempo** (*if he had the time*)	Present conditional: **ci potrebbe aiutare** (*he could help us*)

As you can see, the choices are limited. When indicating possibility or probability, the **se** clause appears in only one tense and mood (imperfect subjunctive), and the **poi** clause gives you only one choice (present conditional).

Using the imperfect subjunctive, complete the **se** clauses in the exercises. You may have to look at the **poi,** or second, clause to determine the subject of the **se** clause.

Q. Se _____ (avere) il tempo, lo farei volentieri.

A. avessi

11. Se _____ (ascoltare), sapreste ciò che è successo.

12. Se _____ (incontrare) Giorgio, cosa gli diresti?

13. Se Giulia _____ (comprare) le scarpe, sarebbe molto contenta.

14. Se _____ (ritornare) presto, potremmo studiare.

15. Se loro _____ (visitare), ci saremmo divertiti.

16. Se tu ed io _____ (parlarsi), ci capiremmo.

17. Se io _____ (essere) in te, non andrei con loro.

18. Se tu _____ (spiegare) bene, capirei.

19. Se _____ (vendere) la casa, dove andreste?

20. Se lui _____ (mentire), come sapresti?

Considering the impossible

Another use of the **se-poi** clauses involves reflecting on what's actually impossible, subjective, or contrary to fact. Again, the verb tenses and moods in both clauses reflect this turn of events. For example:

> **Se fossero arrivati ieri, avrebbero visto i loro zii.** (*If they had arrived last night, they would have seen their aunt and uncle.*) Had arrived (**fossero arrivati**) is a pluperfect subjunctive. This means you use the word *had* to indicate something that might or could have happened; *would have seen* (**avrebbero visto**) is a past conditional, indicating what would have come to pass if the conditions indicated in the **se** clause had happened.

In this case, the **se** clause adopts the pluperfect subjunctive, and the **poi** clause, the past conditional. Occasionally, the **poi** clause can use the present conditional as well, as in the following example:

> **Se non avessi mangiato tanto, no ti sentiresti male.** (*If you hadn't eaten so much, you wouldn't feel bad.*) Here *hadn't eaten* expresses the condition that could have happened; *wouldn't feel* shows the (im)possible result.

For more on the pluperfect subjunctive, see Chapter 22. Keep in mind it's a compound tense and thus uses a helping verb (**essere** or **avere**, conjugated) and a past participle (the -ed form of a verb, like *talked*, *walked*, and so on). Table 19-3 shows an example of properly sequencing a **se** clause to indicate impossibility.

Table 19-3	Se and Poi Clauses That Show Impossibility
"Se" Clause	*"Poi" Clause*
Pluperfect subjunctive: **se avessero letto il libro** (*if they had read the book*)	Present conditional: **capirebbero** (*they would understand*)
	Past conditional: **avrebbero capito** (*they would have understood*)

Notice the slight difference of meaning in the two sentences from Table 19-3.

> **Se avessero letto il libro, capirebbero.** (*If they had read the book, they would understand.*)

> **Se avessero letto il libro, avrebbero capito.** (*If they had read the book, they would have understood.*)

Fill in the appropriate form of the pluperfect subjunctive to complete the **se** phrase (*if this had happened*). Remember that the pluperfect is a compound verb tense and requires two verbs. Here is an example.

0. Se _____ (avere/sapere), gli avrei telefonato.

A. **avessi saputo**

21. Se _____ (avere/dormire), non avrebbero avuto sonno.

22. Se _____ (avere/leggere) il libro, capiresti.

23. Se _____ (essere/partire) in orario, il treno sarebbe arrivato in orario.

24. Se tu _____ (avere/prendere) thè, avresti potuto dormire.

25. Se voi mi _____ (avere/chiedere), vi avrei detto di sì.

26. Se _____ (avere/ricevere) la tua lettera, ti avremmo risposto.

27. Se _____ (essere/stare), ti avrei visto.

28. Se Fausta _____ (essere/alzarsi) presto, avrebbe visto l'aurora.

29. Se _____ (avere/chiudere) la finestra, non avresti avuto tanto freddo.

30. Se Antonietta _____ (essere/correre), non avrebbe perso il treno.

The what-if nature of this form of expression allows you to distinguish between fact and opinion, reality and fantasy. You can use your imagination, or you can stay firmly grounded in reality. Compare the following sentences, whose what-if structures are the same, but whose verb forms absolutely determine meaning.

✔ Certainty:

> **Se non arriva oggi, arriva domani.** (*If he doesn't arrive today, he'll arrive tomorrow.*)
>
> **Se non è arrivato, arriverà domani.** (*If he didn't arrive today, he'll arrive tomorrow.*)
>
> **Se non arriverà oggi, arriverà domani.** (*If he won't arrive today, he will tomorrow.*)

✔ Speculation or impossibility:

> **Se non fosse arrivato oggi, sarebbe arrivato domani.** (*If he hadn't arrived today, he would have arrived tomorrow.*)
>
> **Ti avrei telefonato se avessi saputo.** (*I would have called you if I had known.*)

The following phrases express certainty, possibility, and impossibility. Translate them into idiomatic English. See the example.

Q. **se desideravi**

A. **if you wanted**

31. **se fossi in te**

_____

32. **se avessi la voglia**

_____

33. **se lo avessi saputo**

_____

34. **se vuole**

_____

35. **se per caso lo incontri**

_____

36. **se mai sapessi qualcosa**

_____

37. **se fosse vero**

_____

38. **se non sbaglio**

_____

39. se potessi

_____

40. se non è vero?

_____

Putting a Personal Touch on the Impersonal and the Passive

Using the impersonal and passive forms of verbs is one way to avoid taking responsibility for actions. Saying "they say" or "one supposes" is much easier than taking direct responsibility for something. How many children have you heard use these forms with sentences like, "It was broken"?

In this section, I explore the impersonal (and the very similar **si passivante**) and show you how to distinguish them from the passive, often an equal abdication of responsibility.

Forming the impersonal in the present

The impersonal voice is neither active nor passive but a little of both. You may well have someone driving the action, but that someone can be shadowy or vague, at best. In English, you use the impersonal by referring to *one, they, it,* or *people.* You distance yourself.

One never knows what to expect.

They say he is looking for a new position.

It is said that a red sky in the morning means bad weather is coming.

In Italian, to make an impersonal statement, you simply attach the reflexive pronoun **si** to the third-person singular verb conjugation.

Si parla inglese. (*One speaks English* or *English spoken here.*)

Non si fa. (*One doesn't do that.*)

Si mangia bene in Italia. (*You eat well in Italy.*)

Non si sa mai. (*One never knows.*)

The Italian **si** does the same job that *you* or *one* does in English. To use the impersonal voice in other tenses and moods, you place the pronoun **si** before whichever conjugation you're using.

Non si parlava in chiesa. (*One didn't talk in church.*)

Si è arrivato puntualmente. (*One arrived punctually.*)

Un giorno, non si farà. (*One day, people won't do that.*)

The **si passivante** differs from the impersonal in that it can be used with both singular and plural forms of the third-person conjugation, according to the number of the direct object or subject, depending on your point of view.

> **Si mangiano biscotti per la merenda.** (*One eats cookies for snack.*)

Forming and using the passive voice

To form a passive voiced verb, you need the helping verb **essere.** The conjugated **essere** agrees in gender with the past participle accompanying it. For example:

> **I classici sono letti.** (*The classics are read.*)

To explain who is doing the reading, you use **da** to introduce that person:

> **da tutti gli studenti** (*by all the students*)

You don't use the passive voice extensively in spoken Italian, and it's more useful for recognition purposes (especially in written Italian) than for spoken. Why would you say, for example, **La camicia è lavata da Maria** (*The shirt is washed by Maria*) when you can say **Maria lava la camicia** (*Maria is washing the shirt*)?

Still, if you plan to use the passive, you need to know that you form it (**essere** and a past participle) in the same way for all verb tenses and moods. Consider the shirt washed by Maria.

- ✔ In the present: **La camicia è lavata da Maria.** (*The shirt is washed by Maria.*)

- ✔ In the past: **La camicia è stata lavata da Maria.** (*The shirt was washed by Maria.*)

- ✔ In the future: **La camicia sarà lavata da Maria.** (*The shirt will be washed by Maria.*)

Such a clean shirt!

If you still want to use the passive but tire of using **essere,** try substituting **andare** or **venire.**

> **La camicia viene lavata da Maria.** (*The shirt is [comes to be] washed by Maria.*)

> **La camicia va lavata da Maria.** (*The shirt is washed by Maria.*)

I recommend that you use the active voice in your Italian because it's more straight-forward and easier to understand than the passive.

Answer Key

1. hai, avrai

2. volevano

3. arriva, arriverà

4. studia, studierà

5. vanno, andranno

6. preferisci

7. trovo, troverò

8. succeed, succederà

9. vuoi

10. partono, partiranno

11. ascoltaste

12. incontrassi

13. comprasse

14. ritornassimo

15. visitassero

16. ci parlassimo

17. fossi

18. spiegassi

19. vendeste

20. mentisse

21   **avessero dormito**

22   **avessi letto**

23   **fosse partito**

24   **avessi preso**

25   **aveste chiesto**

26   **avessimo ricevuto**

27   **fossi stato**

28   **si fosse alzata**

29   **avessi chiuso**

30   **fosse corsa**

31   *if I were you*

32   *if you felt like it*

33   *if I had known*

34   *if you wish*

35   *if by chance you run into him*

36   *if you ever find out something*

37   *if it were true*

38   *if I'm not mistaken*

39   *if I could*

40   *if it's not true?*

Chapter 20

Getting into the Subjunctive Mood

● ●

In This Chapter

▶ Understanding when to use the subjunctive mood

▶ Composing the subjunctive in the present tense

▶ Using the subjunctive in the imperfect tense

● ●

*T*he subjunctive mood allows you to express emotions, desires, doubts, probabilities, possibilities, inevitabilities, fears, and nuances. It lets you make indirect (and very polite) commands.

The subjunctive is the logical counterpart to the indicative (see Chapter 6). While the indicative expresses facts and realities (*When I am president; I made the right decision*), the subjunctive is subjective and allusive (*If I were president; may you be happy; it's important that he make the right decision*).

I were? You be? He make? In English, the subjunctive can sound dreadfully wrong, taken out of context. In Italian, the use of the subjunctive mood is frequent. When in doubt, as they say, use the subjunctive.

Italian uses the subjunctive to add color, emotion, and nuance to the language. Although it's used less frequently than it used to be, having been replaced with indicative forms, the subjunctive is still eminently useful and obviously ubiquitous.

The very nature of the subjunctive makes it one of your most valuable linguistic tools. To be expressive, vague, or emotional, you need the subjunctive. To show nuance or to give your point of view, you need the subjunctive. The subjunctive mood is a linguistic tool that you will (or at least should) use often.

In this chapter, you take a tour of the present, present perfect, and imperfect subjunctive forms. By the time you finish, you'll probably wonder how you ever communicated without the subjunctive mood.

Identifying When to Use the Subjunctive

The subjunctive usually follows specific verbal triggers found in independent clauses that make very clear the necessity of using it. Because use of the subjunctive is conditional on other, usually indicative, elements of language, being able to identify the subjunctive's primary triggers, or so-called clue verbs, helps you understand its vast linguistic range. For example, **Penso** (clue verb in the present indicative, *I think*) + **che** (connector, *that*) + **sia** (present subjunctive of **essere**, *he is*) **content** (*happy*).

The tense of the clue verb determines the tense of the subjunctive. For example, a present indicative can be followed only by the present or present perfect subjunctive. So you can say *I doubt [that] he has gone,* but you can't say *I doubt [that] he had gone.*

Here are more example constructions of this relationship between indicative and subjunctive:

Present indicative tense + **che** + present subjunctive: **Credo** (*I believe*) + **che** + **lui vada** (*he's going*).

Future tense + **che** + present subjunctive: **Crederò** (*I will believe*) + **che** + **lui vada** (*he's going*).

Imperative mood + **che** + present perfect subjunctive: **Dimmi** (*Tell me*) + **che** + **lui sia andato** (*he left*).

Imperfect tense + **che** + imperfect subjunctive: **Credevo** (*I thought*) + **che** + **sapessi** (*you knew*).

Imperfect tense + **che** + pluperfect subjunctive: **Credevo** (*I thought*) + **che** + **fossi andato** (*you had gone*).

Conditional mood + **che** + imperfect subjunctive: **Vorrei** (*I would like*) + **che** + **tu venissi** (*you to come*).

Conditional mood + **che** + pluperfect subjunctive: **Vorrei** (*I would like*) + **che** + **tu fossi venuto** (*you to have come*).

The two clauses, or parts of the sentence that come before and after **che,** must have different subjects. If they have the same subject, you won't use the subjunctive but rather the infinitive, as in this example: **Spero andare** (*I hope to go*) (*I hope I may go*).

One exception to having two subjects involves using **se** (*if*) and **magari** (*if only, don't I wish*). For example: **Magari fossi ricca** (*Don't I wish I were rich*) and **se avessi il tempo libero, lo farei** (*If I had the free time, I'd do it*). The other exception to the two-subjects rule involves indirect commands: **che sia contento** (*may you be happy*).

Table 20-1 shows commonly used verbs that require the subjunctive. When these verbs appear in an independent clause, they connect to dependent (frequently subjunctive) clauses with the relative pronoun **che** (*that*). For example: **Insisto che tu faccia il lavoro** (*I insist that you do the work*); **ho paura che non sappiano guidare** (*I'm afraid that they don't know how to drive*).

Table 20-1	Verbs That Require the Subjunctive		
Italian Verb	*English Translation*	*Italian Verb*	*English Translation*
arrabbiarsi	*to be angry*	**lasciare**	*to let*
avere paura	*to be afraid*	**ordinare**	*to order*
comandare	*to command*	**pensare**	*to think*
consentire	*to agree to*	**permettere**	*to allow, permit*
credere	*to believe, to think*	**preferire (isc)**	*to prefer*
desiderare	*to want*	**pretendere**	*to aspire to*

Italian Verb	English Translation	Italian Verb	English Translation
dispiacere	to be sorry, displease	proibire (isc)	to forbid
dubitare	to doubt	richiedere	to request
esigere	to demand	sperare	to hope
essere contento/ triste	to be happy/sad	suggerire (isc)	to suggest
essere sorpreso	to be surprised	temere	to be afraid
insistere	to insist	volere	to want

Other clues that tell you when to use the subjunctive include impersonal expressions, certain conjunctions, and the occasional random phrase or word. Table 20-2 contains some of these.

Table 20-2	Other Triggers for the Subjunctive	
Impersonal Expressions	**Conjunctions**	**Miscellaneous Phrases**
basta che (*it's enough that*)	a meno che non (*unless*)	chiunque (*whoever*)
bisogna che (*it's necessary*)	affinché (*to the end that*)	dovunque (*wherever*)
conviene che (*it's convenient*)	benché (*although*)	qualunque (*whatever, whichever*)
è bene/meglio che (*it's good/better that*)	dato che (*given that*)	quantunque (*although*)
è essenziale che (*it's essential that*)	dopo che (*after*)	unico (*only*)
è facile/difficile che (*it's easy/difficult*)	finché non (*until*)	solo (*only*)
è importante che (*it's important that*)	in modo che (*so that*)	primo (*first*)
è necessario che (*it's necessary that*)	malgrado (*despite*)	ultimo (*last*)
è normale che (*it's normal that*)	nonostante che (*notwithstanding*)	se (*if*)
è peggio che (*it's worse that*)	poiché (*since*)	margari (*if only/ don't I wish*)
è possibile/impossibile che (*it's possible/impossible that*)	prima che (*before*)	
è probabile che (*it's probable that*)	purché (*so long as, provided that*)	
è raro che (*it's rare that*)	sebbene (*although*)	
pare che (*it seems that*)	senza che (*without*)	
peccato che (*too bad that*)	supposto che (*supposing that*)	

(continued)

Table 20-2 *(continued)*		
Impersonal Expressions	*Conjunctions*	*Miscellaneous Phrases*
può darsi che (*it's possible that*)		
sembra che (*it seems that*)		
si dubita che (*it is doubtful that*)		
sorprende che (*it is surprising that*)		

Forming the Present Subjunctive

To form the present subjunctive, you add characteristic verb endings (**-o, -i, -a, -iamo, -ate, -ano,** for example) that reveal the subject. The most significant change, however, involves switching the characteristic vowels around. For example, **-are** verbs change the characteristic **a** to **i** in the subjunctive conjugation; and **-ere, -ire,** and **-ire** (**isc**) verbs change their **e** and **i** to **a**. I show these changes in vowels in the following tables.

Note how each conjugation changes the indicative verb into a subjunctive. As you can see, the conjugation for the singular form in the subjunctive is the same for first person, second person, and third person, which is why you often include the subject pronouns when using the subjunctive. **Parli,** for example, can have the subject **io** (*I*), **tu** (*you*), or **lui, lei, Lei** (*he, she, you* [formal]).

parlare (to speak)	
io **parli**	noi **parliamo**
tu **parli**	voi **parliate**
lui, lei, Lei **parli**	loro, Loro **parlino**

scrivere (to write)	
io **scriva**	noi **scriviamo**
tu **scriva**	voi **scriviate**
lui, lei, Lei **scriva**	loro, Loro **scrivano**

dormire (to sleep)	
io **dorma**	noi **dormiamo**
tu **dorma**	voi **dormiate**
lui, lei, Lei **dorma**	loro, Loro **dormano**

capire (to understand)	
io **capisca**	noi **capiamo**
tu **capisca**	voi **capiate**
lui, lei, Lei **capisca**	loro, Loro **capiscano**

The singular forms are all the same after changing their vowels. The plural forms vary: **Noi** remains faithful to its indicative form, **voi** adds an **i,** and **loro** also changes its characteristic vowel.

Subjunctive verbs take on a meaning only somewhat different from the indicative form when combined with a subjunctive prompt. For example: **Lui dorme** (*He is sleeping*) and **Credo che lui dorma** (*I think he is sleeping*). This difference doesn't generally show up in English.

Fill in the subjunctive form of the regular verbs in the following sentences, as per the example.

Q. **Credi che lui ci _____ (scrivere)?**

A. **scriva**

1. **Suggeriamo che lui _____ (pagare) il conto.**

2. **Il medico vuole che tu _____ (restare) a casa.**

3. **È necessario che voi _____ (parlare).**

4. **Mi dispiace che loro mi _____ (dubitare).**

5. **Spero che tu _____ (scrivere) molte cartoline a noi.**

6. **Insistono che voi _____ (arrivare) presto.**

7. **Voglio che loro _____ (capire).**

8. **Ha paura che tu _____ (partire).**

9. **Può darsi che loro _____ (cantare).**

10. **Penso che lui _____ (leggere) poco.**

Taking a Closer Look at the Present Subjunctive

In Italian, **-are** verbs maintain the sound of their infinitives when they're conjugated. So to keep the hard sounds of the infinitives with verbs ending in **-care** and **-gare,** you add the letter **h** between their stems and the endings. Thus, you conjugate **cercare** (*to look for*) and **pagare** (*to pay for*) in the present subjunctive as the following tables show.

cercare (to look for)	
io **cerchi**	noi **cerchiamo**
tu **cerchi**	voi **cerchiate**
lui, lei, Lei **cerchi**	loro, Loro **cerchino**

pagare (to pay for)	
io **paghi**	noi **paghiamo**
tu **paghi**	voi **paghiate**
lui, lei, Lei **paghi**	loro, Loro **paghino**

Those **-are** verbs that end in **-giare** and **-ciare**, however, don't double the **i** that's already part of the stem. See the following conjugations.

mangiare (to eat)	
io **mangi**	noi **mangiamo**
tu **mangi**	voi **mangiate**
lui, lei, Lei **mangi**	loro, Loro **mangino**

cominciare (to become)	
io **cominci**	noi **cominciamo**
tu **cominci**	voi **cominciate**
lui, lei, Lei **cominci**	loro, Loro **comincino**

You use a double **i** only in verbs where you stress the **i**, like **inviare**.

inviare (to send)	
io **invii**	noi **inviamo**
tu **invii**	voi **inviate**
lui, lei, Lei **invii**	loro, Loro **inviino**

Irregular verbs in the indicative are generally irregular in the subjunctive. For a more extensive sampling of irregular verbs, see Chapter 7.

A general rule for figuring out how to put irregular verbs into the present subjunctive is to look at the first person singular form of the indicative conjugation. For example: **Dire** (*to say, tell*) is irregular in the indicative; its first person singular form is **dico**. The subjunctive stem takes its form from that and becomes **dic**. Table 20-3 shows some of the most common irregular verbs in the present subjunctive.

Table 20-3	Irregular Verbs in the Present Subjunctive	
Infinitive	*First Person Singular Indicative*	*Subjunctive Form Conjugations*
andare (*to go*)	**vado**	**io vada, tu vada, lui, lei, Lei vada, noi andiamo, voi andiate, loro, Loro vadano**
bere (*to drink*)	**bevo**	**io beva, tu beva, lui, lei, Lei beva, noi beviamo, voi beviate, loro, Loro bevano**
dire (*to say, tell*)	**dico**	**io dica, tu dica, lui, lei, Lei dica, noi diciamo, voi diciate, loro, Loro dicano**
dovere (*to have to*)	**devo**	**io deva, tu deva, lui, lei, Lei deva, noi dobbiamo, voi dobbiate, loro, Loro devano**
fare (*to make, do*)	**faccio**	**io faccia, tu faccia, lui, lei, Lei faccia, noi facciamo, voi facciate, loro, Loro facciano**
potere (*to be able to*)	**posso**	**io possa, tu possa, lui, lei, Lei possa, noi possiamo, voi possiate, loro, Loro possano**
rimanere (*to stay*)	**rimango**	**io rimanga, tu rimanga, lui, lei, Lei rimanga, noi rimaniamo, voi rimaniate, loro, Loro rimangano**
uscire (*to go out*)	**esco**	**io esca, tu esca, lui, lei, Lei esca, noi usciamo, voi usciate, loro, Loro escano**
venire (*to come*)	**vengo**	**io venga, tu venga, lui, lei, Lei venga, noi veniamo, voi veniate, loro, Loro vengano**
volere (*to want*)	**voglio**	**io voglia, tu voglia, lui, lei, Lei voglia, noi vogliamo, voi vogliate, loro, Loro vogliano**

Once again, the **noi** and **voi** use their regular indicative present forms. (See Chapter 7.)

Essere (*to be*) and **avere** (*to have*) are irregular in the subjunctive, as they are everywhere. Because you can use these two verbs in compound tenses (present perfect and pluperfect), they need some attention. See the following conjugations in the present subjunctive.

essere (to be)	
io **sia**	noi **siamo**
tu **sia**	voi **siate**
lui, lei, Lei **sia**	loro, Loro **siano**

avere (to have)	
io **abbia**	noi **abbiamo**
tu **abbia**	voi **abbiate**
lui, lei, Lei **abbia**	loro, Loro **abbiano**

Consider the present and present perfect uses in the following sentences.

Present	*Present Perfect*
Credo che lui ci sia. (*I think he's here.*)	**Credo che lui ci sia stato.** (*I think he was here.*)
Non credo che abbiamo abbastanza. (*I don't think we have enough.*)	**Non credo che abbiamo avuto abbastanza.** (*I don't think we had enough.*)
È importante che siate alla festa. (*It's important that you are at the party.*)	**È importante che siate stati alla festa.** (*It's important that you were at the party.*)
Dubito che lei abbia il tempo libero. (*I doubt she has the free time.*)	**Dubito che lei abbia avuto il tempo libero.** (*I doubt she had the free time.*)

Fill in the appropriately conjugated forms of the verbs in parentheses in the following sentences. Refer back to the subjunctive clues and forms presented in this chapter as needed. Here's an example:

Q. **Non lo faccio prima che tu lo _____ (fare).**

A. faccia

11. **È importante che loro _____ (imparare) la verità.**

12. **Credi che lei _____ (essere) disponibile?**

13. **La professoressa vuole che voi _____ (aprire) i libri.**

14. **Spero che tu _____ (pagare) perché io non ho soldi.**

15. **Che voi _____ (essere) molto lieti!**

16. **È necessario che i bambini _____ (mangiare) la verdura.**

17. **Dubito che lui _____ già _____ (essere arrivata).**

18. **Il medico suggerisce che tu _____ (perdere) qualche chilo.**

19. **Temo che gli studenti non _____ (essere) seri.**

20. **Hai cercato le chiavi? È possibile che _____ (essere) nella macchina?**

Fill in the sentences with the appropriate subjunctive conjugation. I include the verbs to use in parentheses. Be careful, though, because not all these sentences need the subjunctive. Hint: If the word **che** isn't visible, you probably don't need the subjunctive, though that isn't always the case.

Q. **È importante che loro _____ (mangiare).**

A. mangino

21. **Dimmi che _____ (essere) vero.**

22. **Lo faremo sebbene non ci _____ (piacere).**

23. È necessario che voi _____ (capire) bene.

24. Dubito che si _____ (essere parlati).

25. Luigi non vuole che loro lo _____ (fare).

26. Io penso a _____ (andare).

27. Chiunque _____ (essere), non ci sono!

28. Credo che voi _____ (essere usciti).

29. Gli piace _____ (leggere) un bel libro.

30. È un bell'uomo sebbene _____ (fumare).

Forming the Imperfect Subjunctive

If you look at the list of verbs and other triggers that prompt you to use the subjunctive (discussed earlier in the section "Identifying When to Use the Subjunctive") and consider which of those triggers express wishing, doubting, or feeling, you'll find that they all do just that. Is it even possible to express what you wanted, felt, or doubted without the imperfect subjunctive? If you're talking about your own feelings, not directing them toward others, then the answer is yes. Consider these examples:

Volevo visitare i nonni. (*I wanted to visit my grandparents.*)

Avevo paura di viaggiare in aereo. (*I was afraid to travel by plane.*)

What's missing in these examples is a second subject and there's no **che** to link your feelings to another's actions. Compare the following sentences to the first examples.

Volevo che tu visitassi i nonni. (*I wanted you to visit your grandparents.*)

Avevo paura che viaggiassero in aereo. (*I was afraid of their traveling by plane.*)

You can, of course, keep yourself the subject in two related parts of the same sentence. You just won't connect those two parts with **che**. Mimi, an operatic heroine, says to her love **Vorrei dir ma non oso, se venissi con voi?** (*I'd like to say, but don't dare, if I were to come with you?*)

The imperfect subjunctive lets you be passionate about things and people and even yourself. It's used extensively in opera, in all those musical pieces about love, hope, death, jealousy, and betrayal. That tells you something.

The imperfect subjunctive and the present subjunctive are the most commonly used forms of this mood. The imperfect can follow only the indicatives in the past tenses, the conditional mood, or **se** (*if*) and **magari** (*if only, I wish*). For example:

Magari fossi ricca! (*If only I were rich!*)

Lo farei, se avessi il tempo libero. (*I would do it if I had the free time.*)

Credevo che lo sapessi. (*I thought you knew.*)

The imperfect subjunctive speaks to events that happened in the same past as that of the introductory clause or phrase. It's a simultaneous past, if you will. It follows the same rules and responds to the same triggers as the present subjunctive, discussed in the section "Forming the Present Subjunctive," earlier in this chapter.

To form the imperfect subjunctive, you add characteristic, subject-dependent endings (**-assi, -asse, -assimo, -aste, -assero; -essi, -esse, -essimo, -este, -essero; -issi, -isse, -issimo, -iste,** and **-issero**) to verb stems. The conjugations in this tense of the subjunctive, however, use the characteristic vowels of the infinitive. See the following conjugations.

parlare (to speak)	
io **parlassi**	noi **parlassimo**
tu **parlassi**	voi **parlaste**
lui, lei, Lei **parlasse**	loro, Loro **parlassero**

ripetere (to repeat)	
io **ripetessi**	noi **ripetessimo**
tu **ripetessi**	voi **ripeteste**
lui, lei, Lei **ripetesse**	loro, Loro **ripetessero**

dormire (dormire)	
io **dormissi**	noi **dormissimo**
tu **dormissi**	voi **dormiste**
lui, lei, Lei **dormisse**	loro, Loro **dormissero**

Some irregular imperfect subjunctives, including **dire** (*to say, to tell*), **fare** (*to make, to do*), and **essere** (*to be*), use the same verb endings, though their stems are irregular. Check out their conjugations in the following tables.

dire (to tell, to say)	
io **dicessi**	noi **dicessimo**
tu **dicessi**	voi **diceste**
lui, lei, Lei **dicesse**	loro, Loro **dicessero**

fare (to do, to make)	
io **facessi**	noi **facessimo**
tu **facessi**	voi **faceste**
lui, lei, Lei **facesse**	loro, Loro **facessero**

essere (to be)	
io **fossi**	noi **fossimo**
tu **fossi**	voi **foste**
lui, lei, Lei **fosse**	loro, Loro **fossero**

Translate the following phrases into Italian. Because these phrases require imperfect tense subjunctives, they can only follow past tense indicative verbs, **se** (*if*), and **magari** (*if only, I wish*). Don't forget the connecting **che** (*that*) if it's needed. Here's an example:

Q. *I thought you* (**tu**) *knew.*

A. **Credevo che lo sapessi.**

31. *if you* (**tu**) *wanted*

_____

32. *She wanted him to write.*

_____

33. *I feared that he would be.*

_____

34. *if they were eating*

_____

35. *would that I could*

_____

36. *If you* (**voi**) *had the money*

_____

37. *He thought we were sleeping.*

_____

38. *that they knew*

_____

39. *that they had*

_____

40. *I believed that he was old.*

_____

Answer Key

1. paghi

2. resti

3. parliate

4. dubitino

5. scriva

6. arriviate

7. capiscano

8. parta

9. cantino

10. legga

11. imparino

12. sia

13. apriate

14. paghi

15. siate

16. mangino

17. sia arrivata

18. perda

19. siano

20. ci siano

21 sia

22 piaccia

23 capiate

24 siano parlati

25 facciano

26 andare

27 sia

28 siate usciti

29 leggere

30 fumi

31 se volessi

32 Lei voleva che lui scrivesse.

33 Avevo paura che lui fosse.

34 se mangiassero

35 magari potessi

36 se voi aveste i soldi

37 Credeva che dormissimo.

38 che sapessero

39 che avessero

40 Credevo che lui fosse vecchio.

Chapter 21

Second-Guessing Your Actions with the Past Conditional

In This Chapter

▶ Composing the past conditional

▶ Understanding the nuances in **potere** and **dovere**

▶ Talking about times when you would've, could've, should've

*I*f you're someone who likes to look back and think about what could have been, then this chapter is for you. The so-called conditional isn't a verb tense — you don't use it to indicate that something has happened but rather to express your mood or frame of mind about the past and to express your emotions and dreams.

For example, maybe you want to say that you would have moved to Italy right after college, but you were too busy pursuing a musical career. You can express thoughts like these with the past conditional.

The conditional mood in its various tenses allows you to speculate. Instead of saying you will definitely do something, you can use the past conditional to say that you would have done something. But you don't have to commit.

You can use the past conditional to explain your reasons for not doing something, like showing up at a party, by saying **Sarei andato/andata ma . . .** (*I would have gone, but . . .*). To express a conditional mood in the future tense, see Chapter 18.

In this chapter, I show you how to form the past conditional with helping verbs and how to use the past conditional to express what might have been or what may yet happen, depending on conditions being fulfilled.

Forming the Past Conditional

To form the past conditional, you combine a helping verb (**essere** [*to be*] or **avere** [*to have*]) conjugated in the present conditional with a past participle. (See Chapter 16 for details on using helping verbs and past participles.) You choose **essere** or **avere** depending on the verb it accompanies.

  ✔ Verbs that can take direct objects or that answer the questions *who* or *what* are conjugated with **avere.** For example, **trovare** (*to find*) can answer the question

> *what: What did you find?* So it conjugates with **avere** in the compound tense. So does **vedere** (*to see*): *Who did you see?*
>
> ✔ Verbs of motion (or cessation of motion) or verbs that can't take direct objects are conjugated with **essere.** For example, **andare** (*to go*) doesn't answer the question *who* or *what;* it addresses the question *where: Where did you go?* **Restare** (*to stay*) works the same way: *Where did you stay?*

Thus, you say **avrei** (*I would have*) **trovato** (*found*) **le chiavi** (*the keys*). What would you have found? *The keys.* The helping verb is **avere.** But **sarei** (*I would be*) **andato/ andata** (*gone*).

All reflexive verbs (see Chapter 17) are conjugated with **essere.** For example:

Mi sarei alzato/alzata presto . . . (*I would have gotten up early . . .*)

And **piacere** (*to like*) also always conjugates with **essere:**

Ti sarebbe piaciuto il film. (*You would have liked the film.*)

Vi sarebbero piaciuti i libri. (*You all would have liked the books.*)

The past participle of verbs conjugated with **essere** agrees in number and gender with the subject.

You form the past participle by removing the characteristic **-are, -ere,** and **-ire** endings from the infinitives and replacing them with **-ato, -uto,** and **-ito. Parlare** becomes **parlato,** for example, and **ripetere** becomes **ripetuto. Dormire** changes into **dormito.** Several **-ere** verbs have irregular past participles. To review these, along with the usage of both helping verbs, see Chapter 16.

The following tables show the conjugations of the present conditional of **essere** and **avere.**

essere (to be)	
sarei (*I would be*)	**saremmo** (*we would be*)
saresti (*you would be*)	**sareste** (*you would be*)
sarebbe (*he, she, it, you* [formal] *would be*)	**sarebbero** (*they, you* [formal] *would be*)

avere (to have)	
avrei (*I would have*)	**avremmo** (*we would have*)
avresti (*you would have*)	**avreste** (*you would have*)
avrebbe (*he, she, it, you* [formal] *would have*)	**avrebbero** (*they, you* [formal] *would have*)

The past conditional doesn't exist in a vacuum. It frequently makes up just half of a sentence:

Saremmo andati, ma eravamo al verde. (*We would have gone, but we were broke.*)

> **Avrebbe mangiato, ma non aveva fame.** (*She would have eaten, but she wasn't hungry.*)
>
> **Avrebbero trovato le chiavi, ma i bambini le avevano nascoste.** (*They would have found the keys, but the kids had hidden them.*)

If you break down the conditional components as follows, you see that they display a logic, or a certain sense:

> **Saremmo** (*we would have*) **andati** (*gone*). . . .
>
> **Avrebbe** (*she would have*) **mangiato** (*eaten*). . . .
>
> **Avrebbero** (*they would have*) **trovato** (*found*). . . .

Fill in the past conditional forms of the verbs (in parentheses) in the following phrases and sentences. The first five sentences use the helping verb **avere;** the second five sentences use **essere.** Here is an example:

Q. Io _____ (mangiare).

A. avrei mangiato

1. Tu _____ (leggere) il libro.

2. Marco e Laura _____ (scrivere).

3. Noi _____ (imparare) l'italiano.

4. Voi _____ (usare) la macchina.

5. Loro _____ (comprare) la macchina.

6. Io _____ (arrivare).

7. Lui _____ (partire).

8. Tu e Chiara _____ (stare).

9. I signori _____ (venire).

10. Noi _____ (andare).

Expressing What Might Have Been and What May Yet Be

Although the conditional generally translates into English as *would* (*I would work, they would go*), and the past conditional becomes *would have* (*I would have worked, they would have gone*), the semi-auxiliary verbs **potere** (*to be able*) and **dovere** (*to have to*) change meaning in all their conditional tenses. Compare the tense- and mood-determined meanings of **dovere** and **potere** shown in Table 21-1.

Table 21-1	Potere and Dovere in the Conditional Mood	
Present Indicative	*Present Conditional*	*Past Conditional*
Potere		
posso (*I can, am able to*)	**potrei** (*I could, might*)	**avrei potuto** (*I could have, might have*)
puoi (*you can, are able to*)	**potresti** (*you could, might*)	**avresti potuto** (*you could have, might have*)
può (*he/she/it, you* [formal] *can, he/she/it is able to, you* [formal] *are able to*)	**potrebbe** (*he/she/it, you* [formal] *could, might*)	**avrebbe potuto** (*he/she/it, you* [formal] *could have, might have*)
possiamo (*we can, are able to*)	**potremmo** (*we could, might*)	**avremmo potuto** (*we could have, might have*)
potete (*you all can, are able to*)	**potreste** (*you all could, might*)	**avreste potuto** (*you all could have, might have*)
possono (*they, you* [formal] *can, are able to*)	**potrebbero** (*they, you* [formal] *could, might*)	**avrebbero potuto** (*they, you* [formal] *could have, might have*)
Dovere		
devo (*I have to*)	**dovrei** (*I should*)	**avrei dovuto** (*I should have*)
devi (*you have to*)	**dovresti** (*you should*)	**avresti dovuto** (*you should have*)
deve (*he/she/it has to, you* [formal] *have to*)	**dovrebbe** (*he/she/it, you* [formal] *should*)	**avrebbe dovuto** (*he/she/it, you* [formal] *should have*)
dobbiamo (*we have to*)	**dovremmo** (*we should*)	**avremmo dovuto** (*we should have*)
dovete (*you all have to*)	**dovreste** (*you all should*)	**avreste dovuto** (*you all should have*)
devono (*they, you* [formal] *have to*)	**dovrebbero** (*they, you* [formal] *should*)	**avrebbero dovuto** (*they, you* [formal] *should have*)

The present conditional meaning of **potere**, used as a question, is polite: **Potrei chiedere un favore?** (*Could I ask a favor?*) It's the closest you can come in Italian to differentiating between the English *can* and *may*. In the present indicative **Posso chiedere un favore?** you're saying *Can I ask a favor?*

In general, however, the changes in meaning for **potere** and **dovere** result in a sort of hedging. The word *but* implies that although something might or could or even should happen, that won't necessarily be the case: **Mi puoi portare alla stazione? Potrei, ma . . .** (*Can you take me to the station? I could . . . but I might be busy or simply not feel like doing so.*) The implications are clear. Consider the following examples in which the first phrase states a fact while the second phrase is conditional:

> **Devo lavorare; dovrei lavorare.** (*I have to work; I should work.*) In short, *I have to work* is being compared to *I should work, but I really don't feel like it.*

Posso nuotare; potrei nuotare. (*I can swim; I might swim.*) In other words, *I can/I know how to swim,* but *I might . . . or might not.*

Gli studenti devono imparare tre lingue moderne; gli studenti dovrebbero imparare tre lingue moderne. (*The students have to learn three modern languages; the students should learn three modern languages.*) The first part of the sentence explains an obligation; the second expresses an opinion.

I turisti devono comportarsi bene; i turisti dovrebbero comportarsi bene. (*Tourists have to behave well; tourists should behave themselves.*) The two sentences have very different meanings. In the first, the tourists may be guests of the government or in a country that notes improper behavior and assigns penalties to it. The second expresses an opinion.

Other verbs, along with **dovere** and **potere,** allow you to construct sentences and express feelings and ideas through nuance. They definitely make you sound Italian!

Translate the following sentences and phrases into Italian, being careful to note the differences between *can* and *could/might* and between *have to* and *should.* Here's an example:

0. *Mario should*

A. **Mario dovrebbe**

11. *I can eat.*

   _____

12. *I could eat.*

   _____

13. *He has to sleep.*

   _____

14. *He should sleep.*

   _____

15. *We can go.*

   _____

16. *We might go.*

   _____

17. *They can sing.*

   _____

18. *They might sing.*

   _____

19. *You all have to dance.*

_____

20. *You all should dance.*

_____

Saying What You Would've, Could've, Should've Done

Would've, could've, and *should've* rarely stand alone. Usually, they make up only the first part of a sentence or phrase. In English, you can use the first part without explicitly adding a second: *He could have. They should have.* What's understood in English is precisely what he or they could have or should have done, depending on the context of the exchange.

Italian is more specific, as in **Avrebbe potuto scrivere** (*He could have written*) or **Sarebbero dovuti andare** (*They should have gone*).

To construct *could have* and *should have* sentences in Italian, you need the semi-auxiliary verbs (or verbs that differ from the true helping verbs **essere** and **avere**), **potere** (*to be able*) and **dovere** (*"ought," ought to*).

Of the many things you need to remember here, first you have to differentiate the past conditional that forms *without* the semi-auxiliary **dovere** or **potere**. What are you actually trying to say? **Sarei andato/andata** (*I would have gone*) or **sarei dovuto/dovuta andare** (*I should have gone*)? **Avrebbe scritto** (*he would have written*) or **avrebbe potuto scrivere** (*he could have written*)?

Carefully compare the following examples of **potere** and **dovere** in the conditional.

Potere (to be able)

Potrei andare. (*I might/could go*)

Potreste studiare. (*You all might/ could study.*)

Sarebbero potuti restare. (*They could have stayed.*)

Sarebbe potuto/potuta venire. (*He/she could have come.*)

Avrebbero potuto trovare i soldi. (*They could have found the money.*)

Avrebbe potuto scrivere. (*She could have written.*)

Dovere (to "ought," ought to)

Dovrei andare. (*I should go.*)

Dovreste studiare. (*You all should study.*)

Sarei dovuto/dovuta andare. (*I should have gone.*)

Saresti dovuto/dovuta venire. (*You should have come.*)

Avrei dovuto leggere il libro. (*I should have read the book.*)

Avresti dovuto comprare i biglietti. (*You should have bought the tickets.*)

Notice that the verb of motion, **andare,** takes the helping verb **essere;** and the verb that can take a direct object, **scrivere,** uses the helping verb **avere.**

Second, if you're using anything other than plain old *would have,* you need to use the semi-auxiliaries. And here's the tricky part. The semi-auxiliaries are accompanied by the true auxiliary or helping verbs **essere** and **avere.**

What you're actually doing is putting **potere** and **dovere** into the past conditional (**sarei dovuto/dovuta** [*I should have*]; **avrei potuto** [*I could have*]) and then adding the verb that tells what you should or could have done. You have to determine which true helping verb to use by looking at the infinitive that replaces the past participle and follows the helping and semi-auxiliary verbs. The only way to understand that process is to see it in action:

> **Sarei dovuto/dovuta andare.** (*I should have gone.*)
>
> **Avrei potuto scrivere.** (*I could have written.*)

The first example takes **essere** as its helping verb because **andare** is a verb of motion and can't take a direct object. The second example uses **avere** because **scrivere** can take a direct object, and in compound tenses, conjugates with **avere.**

As if all of this weren't enough, you need to keep one more thing in mind. When you use **essere** as your helping verb, the past participle of the semi-auxiliary (**potere, dovere**) has to agree in number and gender with the subject of the sentence, as in these examples.

> **Sarei dovuto/dovuta andare** (*I should have gone*). **Dovuto** tells you the subject is masculine singular; **dovuta** tells you the subject is feminine singular.
>
> **Saremmo dovuti/dovute andare** (*we should have gone*). **Dovuti** tells you that the subject is either a mixed gender group or all men and is masculine plural; **dovute** tells you that *we* refers to all women and is feminine plural.

The best way to grasp how these rather convoluted verb tense and mood combinations work is to see them in action. The following examples help to clarify the use of the past conditional, with and without additional (semi-auxiliary) verbs.

Saying *would have* requires only two verbs, as do all *compound tenses* — those tenses that form with **essere** or **avere** and a past participle.

> **Avrei letto ma avevo sonno.** (*I would have read, but I was sleepy.*)
>
> **Sarei andata ma non mi sentivo bene.** (*I would have gone, but I didn't feel good.*)
>
> **Voi avreste comprato la macchina se aveste il denaro?** (*Would you have bought the car if you had had the money?*)
>
> **I nonni sarebbero venuti ma non volevano viaggiare in aereo.** (*The grandparents would have come, but they didn't want to travel by plane.*)

You need three verbs to get the meaning of *could have* across.

> **Avrei potuto leggere ma avevo sonno.** (*I could have read, but I was sleepy.*)
>
> **Sarei potuto/potuta andare ma non mi sentivo bene.** (*I could have gone, but I didn't feel good.*)
>
> **Voi avreste potuto comprare la macchina se aveste il denaro.** (*You all could have bought the car if you had the money.*)
>
> **I nonni sarebbero potuti venire ma non volevano viaggiare in aereo.** (*The grandparents could have come, but they didn't want to travel by plane.*)

Should have also requires three verbs to get its meaning across.

> **Avrei dovuto leggere ma avevo sonno.** (*I should have read, but I was sleepy.*)
>
> **Sarei dovuto/dovuta andare ma non mi sentivo bene.** (*I should have gone, but I didn't feel good.*)
>
> **Voi avreste dovuto compare la macchina se aveste il denaro.** (*You all should have bought the car if you had the money.*)
>
> **I nonni sarebbero dovuti venire ma non volevano viaggiare in aereo.** (*The grandparents should have come, but they didn't want to travel by plane.*)

Keeping in mind the differences among *would have*, *could have*, and *should have*, translate the following phrases into Italian. Here's an example:

0. *I would have studied.*

A. **Avrei studiato.**

21. *He would have stayed.*

_____

22. *She would have left.*

_____

23. *We would have read.*

_____

24. *They would have given.*

_____

25. *He should have stayed.*

_____

26. *She should have left.*

_____

27. *They should have given.*

_____

28. *He could have stayed.*

_____

29. *She could have left.*

_____

30. *They could have given.*

_____

Answer Key

1. avresti letto

2. avrebbero scritto

3. avremmo imparato

4. avreste usato

5. avrebbero comprato

6. sarei arrivato/arrivata

7. sarebbe partito

8. sareste stati

9. sarebbero venuti

10. saremmo andati/andate

11. posso mangiare

12. potrei mangiare

13. deve dormire

14. dovrebbe dormire

15. possiamo andare

16. potremmo andare

17. possono cantare

18. potrebbero cantare

19. dovete ballare

20. dovreste ballare

21 **sarebbe restato**

22 **sarebbe partita**

23 **avremmo letto**

24 **avrebbero dato**

25 **sarebbe dovuto restare**

26 **sarebbe dovuta partire**

27 **avrebbero dovuto dare**

28 **sarebbe potuto restare**

29 **sarebbe potuta partire**

30 **avrebbero potuto dare**

Chapter 22

I Hope That You've Had Fun! The Past Subjunctive

In This Chapter

▶ Recognizing triggers for the subjunctive

▶ Implementing the different forms of the past subjunctive

▶ Putting tenses in their proper sequence

*W*ho doesn't want to show feelings, emotions, hopes, doubts, fears, and conjectures when using language? To express more than just the facts, you need what's called the *subjunctive mood*. The subjunctive is one of the most useful and ubiquitous verb moods in the Italian language — you can't avoid using it.

With the past subjective, you can express desires, dreams, emotions, probabilities, possibilities, fears, and doubts; for example, "I hope you had a nice vacation in Sicily." You distinguish fact from opinion by using the indicative or the subjunctive. For example, "I know he has arrived" states a fact, but "I hope he has arrived" shows a desire. The second sentence requires the subjunctive in Italian.

Unlike the indicative mood with its 14 tenses, the subjunctive has only 4: present, present perfect (or past), imperfect, and pluperfect. In this chapter, I show you how to use the present perfect or past (*I went*) and the pluperfect (*I had gone*) subjunctives. For an overview of the present and imperfect subjunctives, see Chapter 20.

In this chapter, I also explain how to form subjunctives, using helper verbs (mostly **essere** [*to be*] or **avere** [*to have*]), usually accompanied by a so-called trigger verb (*hope, want,* or any word that indicates desire or belief rather than fact).

Forming the Subjunctive with Triggers

A *trigger verb* implies that what's being expressed isn't a fact but rather a hope or desire. You can find examples of trigger verbs in Chapter 20.

The present perfect subjunctive usually follows a trigger verb in the present indicative tense, though occasionally it follows the indicative present perfect. The present perfect subjunctive can also follow an impersonal expression (also in the present indicative tense), some conjunctions, and a few set expressions.

Keep in mind that these triggers often appear in one of two clauses within the same sentence. For example: *I wish* (clause one) *that he had met the family* (clause two). *Wish* is the trigger because it expresses a desire instead of stating a fact. Each clause, separated by the word *that,* has its own subject (*I* in clause one; *he* in clause two).

For details on the subjunctive's verbal triggers or clues, check out Chapter 20.

Here are some examples of everyday phrases, using the present perfect subjunctive:

- ✔ **Credo che lui sia andato.** (*I think he has gone.*)
- ✔ **Dubito che lui sia andato.** (*I doubt that he has gone.*)
- ✔ **Penso che lui sia andato.** (*I think he has gone.*)
- ✔ **Spero che lui sia andato.** (*I hope he has gone.*)
- ✔ **Sono sorpresa che lui sia andato.** (*I'm surprised he has gone.*)
- ✔ **Basta che lui sia andato.** (*It's enough that he went [has gone].*)
- ✔ **È possibile che lui sia andato.** (*It's possible that he has gone.*)
- ✔ **Può darsi che lui sia andato.** (*It could be that he has gone.*)
- ✔ **Chiunque sia andato, non è lui.** (*Whoever has gone, it's not him.*)

Each present perfect subjunctive uses a helping verb (in the subjunctive conjugation) and a past participle. See the next section, "Piecing Together the Present Perfect Subjunctive," for details.

The subjunctive can be a personal, subjective form. For example, "I wish he had called" expresses a personal desire. But it can also be impersonal or brought on by *impersonal triggers* — the clues that tell you that you need to use a subjunctive form.

In fact, most impersonal phrases want the subjunctive, assuming a second clause with a different subject is also present. The following are examples:

Era importante che lo avessero letto. (*It was important that they had read it.*)

Peccato che lo avessi fatto. (*Too bad you did that.*)

Sometimes conjunctions, such as **benchè** (*although*) or **purché'** (*so long as*) require the subjunctive to follow (see Chapter 14).

Benchè sia tardi, io non sono stanca. (*Although it's late, I'm not tired.*)

Ci vado purché' lui non ci sia. (*I'm going so long as he's not there.*)

Although some single-word triggers for the subjunctive don't require two clauses, they're relatively rare. **Se** (*if*) and **magari** (*if only, don't I wish*) are perhaps the two most common of the independent verbal clues.

Se fossi stata ricca, avrei viaggiato spesso. (*If I had been rich, I'd have traveled often.*)

Magari avessi avuto il tempo! (*If only you had had the time!*)

Piecing Together the Present Perfect Subjunctive

Because the present perfect subjunctive is a compound verb, you have to conjugate only the helping verb, either **essere** (*to be*) or **avere** (*to have*). Here's some good news: Conjugating the helping verb then attaching it to past participles gives you either the present perfect or the pluperfect tense. So you can focus more on the verbal triggers than on memorizing a bunch of regular or irregular conjugations of main verbs.

In the following conjugations of **essere** and **avere** in the present perfect subjunctive, I use examples of past participles (**andato** [*gone*] and **mangiato** [*eaten*]). **Andato** uses **essere** as its helping verb because it doesn't take a direct object; **mangiato** uses **avere** because it can take a direct object. (See Chapter 16 to review which helping verb to use in compound tenses.)

Singular	*Plural*	*+ Past Participle*
io **sia**	noi **siamo**	**andato, andata** (singular)
tu **sia**	voi **siate**	**andati, andate** (plural)
lui, lei, Lei **sia**	loro, Loro **siano**	

Singular	*Plural*	*+Past Participle*
io **abbia**	noi **abbiamo**	mangiato
tu **abbia**	voi **abbiate**	
lui, lei, Lei **abbia**	loro, Loro **abbiano**	

To form past participles, remove the characteristic endings (**-are, -ere,** and **-ire**) and replace them with **-ato, -uto,** and **-ito.** When using **essere** as your helping verb, the past participle agrees in number and gender with the subject (for example, **andato, andata, andati,** and **andate**). So the phrase **Noi siamo andati** (*We went*) uses the masculine, plural ending on the participle **andati. Lei sia andata** (*She went*) uses the feminine, singular ending on the participle **andata.** (See Chapter 16 for more on past participles.)

When using **avere** as your helping verb, the past participle agrees with the direct object pronouns (**mi, ti, lo, la, ci, vi, li,** and **le**), which precede the verb, not the subject. If the helping verb is **essere,** then the past participle agrees in number and gender with the subject.

Fill in the present perfect subjunctive forms in the following sentences. Keep in mind that the helping verb conjugates, and the main verb assumes its past participle form. I include the helping verb so you can focus on formation rather than whether to use **essere** or **avere.** Here's an example:

Q. **Credo che Marco _____ (essere/partire).**

A. **sia partito**

1. **Dubito che loro _____ (avere/capire).**

2. Penso che i bambini _____ (avere/mangiare).

3. Può darsi che la signora _____ (essere/stare) a casa.

4. Chiunque _____ (essere/essere), era molto furbo.

5. È probabile che voi _____ (essere/arrivare) presto.

6. Siamo sorpresi che loro _____ (essere/venire).

7. Sembra che la festa _____ (avere/avere) molti invitati.

8. Dubito che tu _____ (avere/trovare) i biglietti.

9. Credo che Francesca _____ (avere/fare) quella foto.

10. È necessario che lei _____ (essere/andare).

Constructing the Past Perfect (Pluperfect) Subjunctive

Like the present perfect subjunctive, the pluperfect is a compound tense. So to create it, you need one of the helping verbs (**essere** [*to be*] or **avere** [*to have*]) conjugated in the imperfect subjunctive and the past participle of the main verb, such as in these examples:

Credevo che loro lo avessero già finito. (*I thought they had already finished it.*)

Pensava che tu fossi partito. (*He thought you had left.*)

The following conjugation of **essere** shows you how to construct the pluperfect subjunctive. I use the past participles **andato** (*gone*) and **mangiato** (*eaten*) because they require different helping verbs.

Singular	*Plural*	*+ Past Participle*
io **fossi**	noi **fossimo**	**andato, andata** (singular)
tu **fossi**	voi **foste**	**andati, andate** (plural)
lui, lei, Lei **fosse**	loro, Loro **fossero**	

Here's a similar conjugation of **avere** in the pluperfect subjunctive.

Singular	*Plural*	*+ Past Participle*
Io **avessi**	Noi **avessimo**	mangiato
Tu **avessi**	Voi **aveste**	
Lui, lei, Lei **avesse**	loro, Loro **avessero**	

Note that the pluperfect subjunctive, which is used after verbal triggers, is also used after **se** (*if*) and **magari** (*if only, I wish*), as is the imperfect subjunctive. For example:

Se avessi saputo, non sarei andata. (*If I had known, I wouldn't have gone.*)

Magari fossero venuti! (*I wish they had come!*)

To form the pluperfect subjunctive, you need a helping verb and a past participle, and it must follow a trigger verb in one of the indicative past tenses or in the conditional mood. (I explain the sequencing of tenses in the later section "Sequencing Tenses in the Subjunctive.") Here are some examples and explanations.

✔ **Vorrei che i bambini avessero imparato a parlare italiano.** (*I wish the children had learned to speak Italian.*)

Vorrei, in the conditional is followed by **avessero imparato,** the pluperfect subjunctive.

✔ **Ti avrei chiamato se avessi saputo.** (*I would have called had I known.*)

Avrei chiamato, a past conditional, is followed by **avessi saputo,** a pluperfect subjunctive.

✔ **Lui pensava che io l'avessi fatto.** (*He thought I had done it.*)

Pensava, an indicative imperfect, is followed by **avessi fatto,** the pluperfect subjunctive.

✔ **Temevo che i politici avessero speso troppi soldi.** (*I was afraid that the politicians had spent too much money.*)

Temevo, the imperfect indicative again, requires **avessero speso**, the pluperfect subjunctive.

Use the pluperfect subjunctive to fill in the blanks in the following sentences. I include the appropriate helping verb so you don't have to figure out which one to use. Here's an example.

Q. Era necessario che gli studenti _____ (essere/essere).

A. fossero stati

11. Lui voleva che noi _____ (essere/arrivare) presto.

12. Avevo paura che Riccardo non _____ (avere/mandare) l'assegno.

13. Dubitavano che lui _____ (essere/finire) bene.

14. Magari gli insegnanti _____ (avere/guadagnare) abbastanza.

15. Sembrava che loro _____ (avere/studiare).

16. Il ragazzo era triste che a lei non _____ (essere/piacere) il regalo.

17. Se lui _____ (avere/dire) di sì, ci sarei andata.

18. Vi avrei visitato se mi _____ (avere/dare) l'indirizzo.

19. Conveniva che noi _____ (essere/stare).

20. Lui insisteva che io gli _____ (avere/scrivere).

Sequencing Tenses in the Subjunctive

Following one tense with another that doesn't use the correct sequence is like listening to **canzoni stonate** (*out of tune songs*). Consider these examples in English.

> *I thought he is coming.*
>
> *He was unhappy that she doesn't like the present.*

They jar the ear, don't they? In Italian, the sequencing of tenses (and moods) is practically carved in stone. Specific indicative tenses require use of specific subjunctive tenses. You may find it helpful to compose exemplary sentences that show sequencing. Here's a formula with examples to help:

- ✔ Indicative tense (present, future) + **che** + subjunctive tenses (present, present perfect):

    Io credo + **che** + **venga.** (*I think he's coming.*)

    Crederò + **che** + **venga quando lo vedrò.** (*I'll believe he's coming when I see him.*)

    Credo + **che** + **siano andati.** (*I think they have gone.*)

- ✔ Imperative mood + **che** + subjunctive tenses (present, present perfect):

    Dimmi + **che** + **abbiano trovato il libro.** (*Tell me they found the book.*)

    Dimmi + **che** + **sia vero.** (*Tell me it's true.*)

- ✔ Any past tense + **che** + subjunctive tenses (imperfect, pluperfect):

    Credevo + **che** + **l'avessi.** (*I thought you had it.*)

    Credevo + **che** + **l'avessero mangiato.** (*I thought they had eaten it.*)

The clauses in this form must have different subjects. If not, you won't use the subjunctive but rather the infinitive, such as **Spero andare** (*I hope to go*) (*I hope I may go*).

One exception to having two subjects involves using the words **se** (*if*) and **magari** (*if only, don't I wish*). For example:

Magari fossi ricca. (*Don't I wish I were rich.*)

Se avessi il tempo libero, lo farei. (*If I had the free time, I'd do it.*)

The other exception to the two-clause rule involves indirect commands: **che sia contento** (*may you be happy*).

In general, you can rely on your English sequencing habits to guide you because they tend to coincide with the Italian. If you look at translations, however, you won't necessarily see the subjunctive at work in English. For example: **Volevo che avessero fatto il viaggio** (*I wished they had taken the trip*).

Sequencing takes practice. For it to become more natural, reading — especially children's stories and opera libretti — helps reinforce the verb progressions. Here's why:

✔ **Children's stories** often treat fantasy and opinion rather than fact. Cinderella may say, for example, **Magari avessi un vestito; potrei andare al ballo** (*I wish I had a dress; I could go to the ball*).

✔ **Opera libretti** deal with emotions and dreams and opinions rather than facts. For example, **Vorrei dir, ma non oso. Se venissi con voi?** (*I'd like to say, but don't dare. If I were to come with you?*)

If you compare, say, an editorial piece and a news report in a newspaper, you'll immediately see that opinion uses the subjunctive and factual reporting uses the indicative.

Fill in the following sentences, using the present perfect or pluperfect subjunctives according to verb sequencing rules. Here's an example.

Q. Credo che lui _____ (avere/mangiare) tutti i biscotti.

A. abbia mangiato

21. Il professore pensava che gli studenti non _____ (avere/studiare) abbastanza.

22. Le ragazze volevano che i genitori gli _____ (avere/dare) dei soldi.

23. Tu pensi che loro _____ (essere/partire)?

24. Il presidente voleva _____ (avere/cambiare) la legge.

25. I gatti insistevano che noi gli _____ (avere/dare) da mangiare.

26. È possibile che la nonna _____ (essere/perdersi)?

27. Io non lo avrei creduto se non lo _____ (avere/vedere).

28. Noi abbiamo paura che loro non _____ (avere/finire).

29. Volevo _____ (avere/visitare) i musei.

30. Voi sperate che quella squadra _____ (avere/vincere)?

Now translate the sentences you just completed into idiomatic English, following the example.

Q. Credo che lui abbia mangiato tutti i biscotti.

A. *I believe he ate all the cookies.*

31. _____

32. _____

33. _____

34. _____

35. _____

36. _____

37. _____

38. _____

39. _____

40. _____

And, finally, cover the sentences from Questions 21 through 30 and, working from your answers for Questions 31 through 40, put the English back into Italian.

41. _____

42. _____

43. _____

44. _____

45. _____

46. _____

47. _____

48. _____

49. _____

50. _____

Answer Key

1	abbiano capito
2	abbiano mangiato
3	sia stata
4	sia stato
5	siate arrivati
6	siano venuti
7	abbia avuto
8	abbia trovato
9	abbia fatto
10	sia andata
11	fossimo arrivati
12	avesse mandato
13	fosse finito
14	avessero guadagnato
15	avessero studiato
16	fosse piaciuto
17	avesse detto
18	aveste dato
19	fossimo stati
20	avessi scritto

21 avessero studiato

22 avessero dato

23 siano partiti

24 avere cambiato

25 avessimo dato

26 si sia perduta

27 avessi visto

28 avessero finito

29 avere visitato

30 abbia vinto

31 *The professor thought the students hadn't studied.*

32 *The girls wanted their parents to give them some money.*

33 *Do you think they've left?*

34 *The president wanted to change the law.*

35 *The cats insisted that we give them something to eat.*

36 *Is it possible that Grandma got lost?*

37 *I wouldn't have believed it if I hadn't seen it.*

38 *We were afraid they hadn't finished.*

39 *I wanted to have visited the museums.*

40 *You hope that team won?*

41 **Il professore pensava che gli studenti non avessero studiato.**

42 Le ragazze volevano che i genitori gli avessero dato dei soldi.

43 Tu pensi che loro siano partiti?

44 Il presidente voleva avere cambiato la legge.

45 I gatti insistevano che noi gli avessimo dato da mangiare.

46 È possibile che la nonna si sia perduta?

47 Io non lo avrei creduto se non lo avessi visto.

48 Noi abbiamo paura che loro non abbiano finito.

49 Volevo avere visitato i musei.

50 Voi sperate che quella squadra abbia vinto?

Part VI

The Part of Tens

For a list of ten common Italian idioms, visit www.dummies.com/extras/italiangrammar.

In this part . . .

✔ Build your confidence in Italian by being aware of some very common mistakes Italian learners make and figure out how to avoid making them yourself.

✔ Polish your Italian skills and sound more like a native speaker by adding practical expressions and phrases to your language arsenal.

Chapter 23

Ten Common Italian Grammar Mistakes (And How to Avoid Them)

In This Chapter

▶ Avoiding pronunciation pitfalls

▶ Keeping common grammatical mistakes in check

▶ Remembering the nuances of grammar and vocabulary

*P*icking up a new language, whether it's your second or fifth, forces you to take risks. You master a language by guessing, reasoning, and often taking quantum linguistic leaps. Sometimes, your risks pay off, and you're right. But you're also sure to make mistakes.

You usually make errors when you're trying to use a form, word, or expression that isn't playing by the rules. (Grammar rules are notoriously undependable.) For example, you've likely heard a child say, "Yesterday, we *buyed* it," rather than "Yesterday, we *bought* it." The child was following a logical progression and forming a past tense on the basis of other past tense forms, like *looked, baked,* or *collected.* But grammar isn't always logical. So someone corrects the child, and he moves on, learning from his mistake.

This chapter shows you ten common Italian grammar mistakes that are practically inevitable for the beginner. Being aware of these mistakes may help you avoid them as you move toward mastery of Italian.

Assuming Cognates Are What They Seem to Be

Cognates are words that are practically identical in two languages. Italian and English share a great many words, many of them having to do with food: **pizza** (*pizza*), **ravioli** (*ravioli*), **basilico** (*basil*), for example. You can usually guess the meanings of cognates but beware of *false cognates* or *false friends* — words that look the same in English and Italian but have different meanings; these words that can lead to terrible confusion and embarrassment.

Here are some false friends to watch out for:

- **Bimbo** in Italian refers to a *small male child* or *baby,* not a foolish person, as in English.

  For a time, a car sticker in Italy said **Bimbo a bordo** (*Baby on board*); a friend of mine got it for her husband's sports car because, thinking of the meaning of *bimbo* in English, she considered the sports car her husband's folly.

- At a hotel in Italy, you ask about a **camera** (*room*). If you want a photographic instrument (the English *camera*), you ask for a **macchina fotografica.**

- **Crudo** means *raw* or *uncooked,* not *crude.*

- A **libreria** is a *bookstore,* not a *library.*

- And a **parente** isn't a *parent* but rather a *relative.*

Confusing Conoscere and Sapere

Italian has two ways to say *to know:* **conoscere** (*to be acquainted with, to be familiar with*) and **sapere** (*to know [facts or information], to know how to*). You use **conoscere** to say you know a person, a place, or an object. For example:

> **Conosco Antonietta.** (*I know Antonietta.*)
>
> **Conosci Roma?** (*Do you know Rome?*) (In English, you're more likely to say *Are you familiar with Rome?*)
>
> **Non conosco quel libro.** (*I am not familiar with that book.*)

Sapere, meanwhile, refers to knowing how to do something, as in these examples:

> **Sai parlare italiano?** (*Do you know how to speak Italian?*)
>
> **Io non so guidare.** (*I don't know how to drive.*)

Confusing "di" and "da"

For some reason, people tend to confuse these two prepositions, perhaps because they sometimes share their meanings when translated into English. For example, in English, you say *I am from Chicago,* but in Italian, you say **Sono di** (*of*) **Chicago.** If you want to use the word *from* to indicate your place of origin, then you use the verb **vengo** (*I come*), as in **vengo da Chicago** (*I come from Chicago*).

Like all prepositions, **di** and **da** change meaning according to context, and they're idiosyncratic to the maximum extent possible. See Chapter 12 for details on prepositions.

Forgetting to Make Words Agree in Number and Gender

One of the things English speakers find most difficult is to make words agree in number (singular and plural) and gender (masculine and feminine) with adjectives (*good, bad, ugly*) and definite and indefinite articles (*the* and *a, an,* respectively). When a masculine singular noun, **un libro** (*a book*), for example, is modified by an adjective, the adjective must also be masculine and singular (**vecchio** [*old*]). Likewise, the indefinite article is masculine singular (**un**).

For example, the phrases **una gatta stupida** (*a stupid cat*) not only denigrates the cat's intelligence, it tells you that this particular **gatta** (*cat*) is a female. **Un gatto stupido,** meanwhile also isn't a terribly bright cat but is a male. **I gatti stupidi** (*the stupid cats* [masculine, plural]) tells you that several cats aren't smart.

Mixing Up "a" and "in"

People often confuse the Italian prepositions **a** and **in** because they both can mean *at, in, on,* and *to*.

Here are some general rules for when to use the preposition **a**.

- ✔ When you're talking about living *in* a city or *on* a small island, for example:

    Abito a Firenze. (*I live in Florence.*)

    Abito a Capri. (*I live on Capri.*)

- ✔ With some individual verbs, **a** means *in*: in Italian, you **partecipare a** (*participate in*). There is no general rule about which verbs use **a** to mean *in*; it is simply a matter of the Italian translating into a different preposition in English.

- ✔ When you're talking about going *to* a geographic destination, including a city or small island:

    Vado a Roma. (*I'm going to Rome.*)

    Andiamo a Capri. (*We're going to Capri.*)

- ✔ When you're talking about watching a program *on* television; in this case, **a** combines with the article **la** (*the*):

    C'è un bel programma alla televisione. (*There's a great program on TV.*)

- ✔ When referring to someone's or something's physical location (here, **a** means *at*):

    Francesca si trova a casa. (*Francesca is at home.*)

That seems straightforward enough, right? The confusion comes when you look at the uses of **in,** as listed here:

- ✔ **In** means *to* when you're talking about countries, continents, or large islands:

    Vado in Italia. (*I'm going to Italy.*)

Vado in Sicilia (*I'm going to Sicily*).

In also means *to* when used with *some* daily destinations, as in **Vanno in chiesa la domenica** (*They go to church Sundays*).

✔ If you add an adjective to a country, continent, or large island, **in** combines with the definite article (*the*), as in these examples:

Vado nell'Italia centrale. (*I'm going to central Italy.*)

Vado nella bella Sicilia. (*I'm going to beautiful Sicily.*)

Some country names are already modified, like the United States. To go *to* the United States, you say **Vado negli Stati Uniti.**

✔ **In** means *in* when you use it for many common destinations, such as the following:

Lavoro in giardino. (*I'm working in the garden.*)

Riccardo è in ufficio. (*Riccardo is in the office.*)

For more on prepositions and their idiosyncrasies, see Chapter 12.

Overusing Possessive Adjectives

You often omit the possessive adjective when talking about close family members, body parts, and clothing. **La mamma** translates as *my mom* but can also refer to someone else's mother: **Che ne pensi la mamma?** (*What does your mom think of it?*) In conversation, you may refer to **il babbo** (*my dad*). No need to say, for example, **la mia mamma** or **il mio babbo**. They're not incorrect; they just are unnecessary.

When talking about body parts and clothing, you use reflexive verbs, such as **mettersi**, *to put on* or **lavarsi**, *to wash oneself* (see Chapter 9). Because reflexive verbs refer to the subject of the sentence and indicate ownership, you don't need to show possession again with a possessive adjective. For example:

Mi lavo i denti. (*I'm brushing my teeth.*)

Carlo si mette la cravatta. (*Carlo is putting on his tie.*)

Pronouncing the Endings of Words Incorrectly

Often, two words differ by just one letter but are vastly distant in meaning. **Zanni** (i as in the English *ee* in *knee*), for example, means *zanies* or *clowns;* **zanne (e** as in the English *ay* in *hay*)**,** however, means *fangs* or *tusks.*

If you order **pesce** (**sce** as in the English *shay*) (*fish*) in a restaurant, but pronounce it **pesche** (**sche** as in the English *skay*, or with a hard *c*), you'll get peaches instead of fish, probably not the main course you were expecting.

See Chapter 2 for details on Italian pronunciation.

Repeating the Prepositions in Verbs That Already Include a Preposition

Some Italian verbs have built-in prepositions, so you don't need to add another. For example, **aspettare** means *to wait for.* If you say **Aspetto per Mario**, you're actually saying *I'm waiting for for Mario.* What you want to say is **Aspetto** (*I'm waiting for*) **Mario** (*Mario*). Here are some Italian verbs that already contain prepositions. (See Chapter 12 for the full discussion on prepositions.)

- ✔ **accendere** (*to turn on*)
- ✔ **approvare** (*to approve of*)
- ✔ **ascoltare** (*to listen to*)
- ✔ **aspettare** (*to wait for*)
- ✔ **cercare** (*to look for*)
- ✔ **chiedere** (*to ask for*)
- ✔ **conoscere** (*to be acquainted with*)
- ✔ **guardare** (*to look at*)
- ✔ **pagare** (*to pay for*)
- ✔ **spegnere** (*to turn off*)

Translating Idioms Word by Word

Idiomatic expressions add color to a language and make you sound competent and comfortable. All idioms are *culture bound;* that is, they reflect cultural values. They (may) make Italians think you know more than you do. Idioms change constantly and reflect what's going on in the world generally. Some of the older forms don't so much disappear as simply give way to more timely expressions of the same sentiments.

The problem with idioms comes when you try to translate them literally. If someone says to you **In bocca al lupo!** (Literally: *In the mouth of the wolf!*) but used it to mean *Good luck!*), knowing the meaning of **bocca** (*mouth*) and **lupo** (*wolf*) won't necessarily tell you what's being said. Also, the response to this good luck wish isn't *Thank you!* but **Crepi il lupo!** (*May the wolf croak!*) The idiom and its reply come from an old hunting reference. Note that the use of *croak* to mean *die* is an idiom in English.

In English, you say someone is *good as gold* or *ugly as sin.* In Italian, both these conditions reflect the value of food. Someone is **buono come il pane** (*good as bread*) or **brutto come la fame** (*ugly as hunger*). These expressions show the difference in what each culture values.

Using Subject Pronouns Unnecessarily

Every sentence in every language must have a subject. Whether you have to state that subject explicitly is what differentiates many languages and their constructions. In English, you must state the subject.

A verb can have many subjects, for example: *I go, you go, they go, we go*. In English, without the stated subject pronoun (*I, we, you, they*), you have no idea who's doing the going.

In Italian, the ending letter(s) of a verb tell you who the subject of the verb is. **Io parlo** and **parlo** both mean *I speak*. Adding the subject pronoun (**io**) isn't necessary; you use it only if you wish to be emphatic, as in **Pago io** (*I'm paying*), or to clarify the subject, such as **Lui canta** (*He is singing*).

For details on making sure definite and indefinite articles and adjectives agree with the subject in number and gender, see Chapters 3 and 5.

Chapter 24

Ten Italian Expressions You'll Use Every Day

In This Chapter

▶ Using colloquial Italian

▶ Sounding like a native

▶ Varying your daily speech

*J*ust as in English, Italian offers many ways to say the same thing. *Hello, Hi,* and *Good day* all convey the same idea, though they can be more or less formal. In this chapter, I list ten expressions that will help you sound more Italian and less monotonous. By the end of the chapter, you'll be more comfortable with everyday expressions — from greetings to goodbyes to simple (often emphatic) statements.

You can take your cue about whether to use these expressions from those around you. If someone greets you formally, **Buon giorno** (*Good day*), you reply in kind rather than say **Ciao** (*Hi*), for example.

Salve

Salve is a direct descendent of spoken Latin. It's a modified form of the Latin greeting and salutation and an alternative to **Ciao, come va?** (*Hi, how are things going?*) You use **salve** informally, making you sound at ease, more like the English *hi* as opposed to *hello.* Occasionally, you hear it used in the English, as an expression: **Salve regina** (*God save the queen*).

Un Abbraccio (ne)

To end a note to a friend or even a phone call, you can send **un abbraccio** (*a hug*), or **un abbraccione** (*a big hug*). This phrase usually precedes **ciao.** At the end of a letter, for example, you may sign off: **un abbraccione a tutti** (*a big hug to all of you*). To end a phone call, you simply say: **abbracci!** (*hugs*). In English, you may use *xoxo* at the end of a letter or note to indicate *hugs and kisses.* The difference in Italian is that you actually say (out loud) **abbracci.**

Figurati or Non C'è Di Che

To say *you're welcome* but not sound overly formal or stuffy, you can use either **figurati** or **non c'è di che** instead of **prego.** Each of these phrases comes close to the English *it's nothing, really.*

Ecco

Ecco is an all-purpose word with many meanings. In its basic form, it means *okay* or *right.* By adding pronouns (**eccotelo** [*here you are*], for example), it can indicate that you're giving something to someone. **Ecco** is used to indicate, show, announce, or to give something to someone or as a substitute for **c'è** (*here is, there is*) or **ci sono** (*here are, there are*) in a physical or immediate sense: **Ecco Gianni!** (*Here's Johnny!*) or **Ecco i libri** (*Here are the books*).

Allora

Allora is another word with multiple meanings. It's often used as a filler, or for opening conversations, such as **Allora . . .** (*Well then . . .*). It also means simply *then* and can be used in a mildly emphatic sense: **Allora, siamo d'accordo** (*Then we're agreed*).

Buon Appetito and Altrettanto

Manners count! Before beginning to eat, you say to your companions **Buon appetito!** (*Good appetite!* Although in English the French *bon appetit* is frequently used.) Should someone else at the table say it first, the standard reply is **Altrettanto!** (*And the same to you!*) **Altrettanto** can also be used sarcastically, to mean, roughly, *Right back at ya!*

Fallo Pure

When a friend is dithering about deciding whether to do something, saying **Fallo pure!** is close to the English *Just do it already!* Needless to say, you should use this expression only with friends and family, not in a formal situation.

Non Vedo L'ora

Simply put **Non vedo l'ora!** means *I can't wait!* It can be used in a multitude of situations to demonstrate enthusiasm. As with other idioms, a change in your tone of voice can lend a sarcastic meaning to this phrase. For example, you have a dentist's appointment and say to a friend **Non vedo l'ora!**

Ti Parlo Da Amica/Amico

Giving advice? Even if it's unsolicited, you can make your motives clear by saying **Ti parlo da amica/amico** (*I'm telling you this as your friend* [feminine/masculine]). A common variation is **Ti parlo da mamma!** (*I'm speaking to you as a mother!*)

La Solita Menata

La solita menata (literally, *the usual thrashing;* in this context, it means *the usual* or the equivalent of the English *beating of a dead horse*) is a variation on the French **plus ça change** (*nothing changes*). If, for example, a public figure is caught out doing something illegal, you may comment on this by saying **la solita menata**. It has become something of a commonplace expression in the last few years and can reflect a distrust of authority, disgust, or a lack of optimism generally. A variation of this expression is **il solito tran tran** (*same old, same old*).

Index

About the Author

Beth Bartolini-Salimbeni teaches languages and literatures (Italian, Spanish, Latin, and English) and history at the high-school and university levels.

Beth grew up in a household that valued languages, and her parents, Art and Ellie Gard, made it possible for her to travel, study, and work abroad. She has studied and carried out research in Italy, Spain, England, and Argentina (where she was a Fulbright Fellow). She holds a bachelor's degree in Spanish literature and history and a master's degree in comparative literature. Beth has founded and directed summer programs for high-school students, university undergraduate and graduate students, and adults in Latin America and Italy since the 1970s.

Dedication

In memory of my parents, Art and Ellie Gard, who told me I could. . . .

And for my sister, Midge Roof, who made so much possible.

Author's Acknowledgments

Thanks to my literary agent, Grace Freedson, for recommending me to work on *Italian Grammar For Dummies,* and to Michael Lewis, my acquisitions editor, for working closely with me to shape this book. Profound thanks also to my project editor, Tracy Brown Hamilton, for taking such good and thorough care with this manuscript and for shepherding the whole book through production. My thanks also to the copy editor, Jennette ElNaggar, who saved me from typos and pedantry. Special thanks to the technical reviewer, Milenny Then, for her expertise and keen attention to detail. And, finally, **grazie infinite** to my students — high school, college, and adult — and to my colleagues, in particular Antonietta Di Pietro, Frank Nuessel, and Beppe Cavatorta, who have taught me so much.

Publisher's Acknowledgments

Acquisitions Editor: Michael Lewis

Project Editor: Tracy Brown Hamilton

Copy Editor: Jennette ElNaggar

Technical Editor: Milenny Then

Art Coordinator: Alicia B. South

Project Coordinator: Patrick Redmond

Cover Photos: ©iStockphoto.com/Sadora